The Christian Self-Formation
Anthropology of Becoming

Krzysztof Stanibula

CONTENTS

A tribute in loving memory of my dear parents Janina & Czesław Stanibuła

ACKNOWLEDGMENTS

I am grateful to all whose help and kindness contributed to this publication. In a special way, I thank my professors for their many relevant suggestions on the literature to be consulted. Furthermore, I am grateful to the Auschwitz Museum's archivists as well Library Services at the John Paul II Catholic University of Lublin and Harvard University. Finally, I am also thankful to my family for their guidance in my life.

MOM'S PREFACE

In the context of *the self-formation and the anthropology of becoming,* I am privileged to place my mother Janina's life journey in the preface to this book. Her lifetime was certainly a time of anthropology without God. Through the insertion of her precious diary fragments, which she entrusted to me on her 86th birthday, I hope to commemorate her formative love in my life. My mother writes:

"*I have experienced much trauma in my childhood.*[1] *I clearly remember in 1939, when Nazi Germany attacked Poland, my homeland. I was nine years old and excited about beginning the fourth-grade school year. On September 1st, my dreams and wishes vanished. On that day, I packed all my books in my carefully decorated homemade school bag. I had not yet expected the worse. My dad was drafted into the Polish Army and had to report to his army unit in Lvov, to respond to the Nazi Germany aggression. When he was leaving, I cried so much. He tried to explain to me about his duty to our country, but it was impossible for me to understand. That was the worst time in my life. I clung to him so tight. I did not want let him go. I remember instinctively clinging to his leg for some time while he tried to leave and at the same time comfort me. Finally, he ordered me to go back to my mom, for he had to catch his military transport. Mom found me around 500 meters away from home before she could calm me down. I was determined to pray to God with my rosary, hoping my dad would come back home healthy and sound.*

"*Not long afterward Germans tanks set up positions in the hills of Zamość province, near the town of Rachanie, about four miles from Wożuczyn, where I was born. Everyone was in great desperation and wanted to evacuate as quickly as possible. They hurriedly packed household essentials like food, bedding, clothing, and belongings, taking them to the nearby orchards with hopes that they would be protected there. It was a time of despair. Then, the enemy's artillery began their bombardment. I was the eldest at nine, my brother Henry was seven, and my sister Mary was five in our family. Each of us had to carry our own luggage based on what we could lift: a warm sweater plus food and drinks. Suddenly, early in the morning around 9 a.m., we heard the sounds of sirens, and the bombardment of Wożuczyn's civilian population began. A terrible bomb exploded in our yard. We were the first hit in the village. The whole community panicked. People ran, looking for anywhere they could hide. Some ran to the church, others to their basements, and my family ran to the nearby Palace Park. There was a basement of a ruined building at the park that we used for shelter to hide while the artillery shells exploded over our heads. My mom had to carry Mary. I was holding Henry by the hand while I clung to mom's dress. Henry, in his traumatized state, tried to run into the explosion's crater and developed*

---

[1] J. Stanibuła. **Life** *is a* ***Journey.***

the heart condition he struggled with for the rest of his life. Without a dad's presence, the fear was unbearable.

"While the Polish army was defending their position a few miles near Wożuczyn and taking a heavy German attack, our whole village suffered the front-line attack. The aggressors did not care whether they were attacking the regular Polish army or civilians in the village. My family stayed in that military fire zone for about twenty-four hours. After their military front passed toward Poland's eastern borders, there remained only repression, which destroyed the eastern part of nearby Rachanie. Fields of wheat and potatoes that were ready for harvesting were burned. Once the attack ended, we were not left in peace. Soldiers set up in the villages and created labor camps. Anyone with two rooms was required to give one to the aggressors for their quarters. In our house, occupiers' forces assigned two soldiers. One was relatively nice because he said he left his children, who were the same ages, back home in Reich. The other was stern and unkind. They had their daily exercises and their own place to eat, and they stayed overnight in our home."

On August 22, 1939, in Obersalzberg, the democratically elected Chancellor of Germany instructed the High Command of the Wehrmacht as follows: "Our first priority is the destruction of Poland, our most important objective, to destroy the resources for life in Poland (…). Mercy and compassion have to be removed from your minds. Therefore, I have ordered the SD to kill without mercy, men, women and children of Polish origin."[2]

This part of his plan was implemented by way of an agreement with Soviets on September 17, 1939, also known as the Ribbentrop-Molotov pact. The dual attacks by German Nazi and Soviet forces were not accidental but mutually orchestrated aspects of the infamous pact. The Easter Frontiers of Poland were brutalized as well. In September 1939, both aggressors signed the Treaty on Borders and Friendship, in which they sanctioned the "downfall of the former Polish state" and made agreements about the fourth partition of Poland. In this document, they confirmed that "both sides will not tolerate in their territories any Polish opposition (…) and inform each other of appropriate measures undertaken for this purpose."[3]

Three leading historians, Anna Cienciala, Natalia S. Lebedeva, and Wojciech Materski, using 122 source documents, detailed the Soviet killings in a book titled, *Katyń A Crime without Punishment.* During the Soviet occupation of eastern Poland in the period of 1939–41, Communists terrorized the largest ethnic group, approximately 5,274,000 ethnic Poles. For instance, with the assistance of known collaborators, the Red Army deported about 1 million Poles to Soviet camps in Siberia, confiscating their properties. Soviets also killed thousands of Polish officers in Katyń, Piatichatki, Miednoje, and other places in brutal massacres. Places all over Russia, which

---

[2] Jan Moor-Jankowski (2013). "Poland's Holocaust: Non-Jewish Poles during World War II." *Polish American Congress.* Retrieved 4 April 2014.

[3] www.currenteventspoland.com/analysis/German_Soviets_Genocide.html

still have not been reached, stand "the most heinous yet least known of the Stalinist crimes" in spring of 1940.[4] The main Commissariat for Internal Affairs (NKWD) officer responsible for the Katyń Massacre was Leonid Reichmann, also called "Eichmann of the East," who died without any court trail in 1990.[5] The number of more innocent Polish victims of the NKVD (e.g., prisoners of war) is unknown to his day because graves continue to be discovered all over Russia. Largely, the Katyń Massacre remains a mystery due to widespread Soviet's cover-ups.

"It was not long before the German's army relocated its bases on an agreement with the Soviets. Significant territories of Zamojszczyzna were settled, where continued another tragedy. The Germans settlers behaved ruthlessly toward Poles working for them on farms. My family's life was very hard."

The final number of "people displaced (by the middle of March 1941) from the territories annexed to Reich in the General Government amounts to about 460,000 people, including 420,000 Poles. Additionally, by the autumn of 1944, over 670,000 Poles were transported from Reichau, Wartheland to Reich for labor."[6] One mass deportation of Polish citizens called, *A-B action*, lasted from November 28, 1942 to March 1943 and was followed by a pacification-deportation action from June 23 to July 15, 1943. "Of key importance, was Himmler's edict No 17c issued on 12 of November 1942, which initiated German action in the Zamość Region. The whole resettlement enterprise was given to F. W. Kruger, a higher ranked SS and Police leader. The SS-man responsible for its direct implementation became Odilo Globocnik—the commander of the SS in the Lublin district."

During the following days, at Globocnik's order, the Special Task Force was created, consisting of 500 soldiers from the 25th Regiment of the Police in Lublin. The 25th Regiment commanded Schutzpolizei Captain Wilhelm Meurin." [7] In total, about 110,000 people were displaced. "According to German plans, 696 villages were to be emptied, and about 140,000 of their inhabitants were to be displaced and replaced with 60,000 German settlers. In the end, during the resettlement action in the Zamość region, 293 villages were emptied, and about 110,000 Poles were displaced (including 30,000 children)." [8] "Zamość was to have only 25,000 inhabitants—members of the SS and their families, and it was called

---

[4] Katyń: *A Crime without Punishment*. Red. Anna M. Cienciala, N. Lebedeva, W. Materski. Trans. M. Swartz, A. Cienciala and Maia A. Kipp. Yale University Press. New Haven: 2007 p. 2.

[5] *Ibid* p. 404.

[6] Agnieszka Jaczyńska. *Sonderlaboratorium SS*. The Zamość Region "The First Settlement Area in the General Government." Instytut Pamieci Narodowej: Lublin 2012 p. 27.

[7] Ibid. A. Jaczynska. *Sonderlaboratorium SS* p. 73.

[8] Ibid. A. Jaczynska. *Sonderlaboratorium SS* p. 94, 301.

Himmlerstadt."[9] In the area of today's Rachanie commune, resettlements included Rachanie, Grodysławice, Józefówka, Wożuczyn, Kozia Wola, Siemnice, Werechanie, Falków, and Michalów. This displacement action "in the Zamość region was met with strong counteraction from the Polish underground resistance of the Home Army, AK, and Polish Farmers' Battalions (B Ch) in the years 1942–1943. These events are sometimes referred to as "the Zamoyski Uprising."[10]

"The SS-man began to rap at the doors. At that moment, I realized even though I was a child, that this misfortune was befalling us. When the soldiers rushed into our dwelling, they gave us only several minutes to take some essential things and immediately pushed us out of the house, disregarding the weeping from my siblings, Henry and Mary and the requests of our mother. Mom took only bundles with bedding because it was already very cold. One of the settlers known as Smidt, counted ten houses including our own and yelled at us, 'Alles meine!' meaning, 'Everything is mine!'

"So we had to evacuate on short notice with only a few items to an unknown location. Someone referred us to a rental house several miles away in the village of Michalów, which was also occupied by the aggressors. When Michalów became filled with displaced people, we had to move to another town. My mom had to work hard from sunrise to sunset because the occupiers charged high rent. By this time, I turned ten, and with my sister, I had to do housework, wash dishes and cook for settlers. My younger brother worked all day, sharpening tools. I always carried my rosary and often prayed for my father at night, so nobody could disturb my prayer for his safe return.

"One day, God heard my prayers and my father Stanislaw, came back to us. He was unable to reach his broken-up Polish army unit. He returned to us healthy, and I firmly believed that it happened by God's grace. From this point on, I felt more secure. Before the invasion, he worked in the Sugar Factory as a machinery operator. My father returned to the work there, but it was now under new German ownership. On an extremely hectic day, during the sugar making process, machinery caught his clothes, lifted him high and struck him back to the floor. He lost consciousness and ended up in hospital. Doctors during unconsciousness kept him in the hospital for several days. Our family experienced terrible terror, Nazi Germanization, great despair, extra work for us children, and no chance for any school. But prayers saved my dad again, and he regained consciousness, reaching full recovery. This gave us a chance to become a little bit stronger although we were still starving and any peace was still far away."

SS-men were stationed in the nearby grammar School in Rachanie, where they tortured local patriots and civilians under Schreiner's security police.[11] The worse Nazis were the SS troops. They had Ukrainian

---

[9] Ibid. A. Jaczynska. *Sonderlaboratorium SS* p. 75.

[10] "Zamojszczyzna—Sonderlaboratorium SS." Red. Cz. Madajczyka, t. II, Warszawa 1977 p. 190.

[11] Zygmunt Mańkowski, quoting F. Bartłomowicz's "Grzmot," writes that SS-men "in Rachanie had on their consciences around 100 shot civilians." Besides Leon

collaborators like Antoniuk and others. Antoniuk belonged to the local *Kriminalpolizei* (kripo). After cruel interrogations, the head of the school in Rachanie, Bronisław, Kulikowski, was sent to a German Nazi concentration camp in 1940. Lucjusz Lewczyński, the former Rachanie mayor, was arrested with others on January 19, 1943 by the gendarmes of *Schutzpolizai* and was murdered during their interrogation. Only one surviving witness, a schoolteacher from Pawłówka, Mieczysław Szczygła, was able to escape imprisonment in the school attic and survive the war. His story is told in Dr. J. Peter's book, *Tomaszowskie za okupacji*, based on Ewelina Vonau's account.[12]

"SS-men were so scary looking that every one of us could not even look at them. Anybody could be imprisoned in the school building, beaten and tortured on a hot stove. Often the SS-men rounded up Poles on the streets for the German Nazi concentration camps." Polish prisoners in Auschwitz were executed from early 1940 onward. It was in the Konzentrationelager Auschwitz German death camp where my father's brother-in-law, Leon Kosiorski, perished.[13] Leon Kosiorski born on April 12, 1907 in Rachanie with his name visible in appendix. He was taken from his farm with Bronislaw Kulikowski and Jan and Felix Kaczorowski. They were arrested with assistance from SS collaborators with the local *Schutzpolizai*, Wasyl Hłynskie, Aleksandr Buszyniani, and others.[14] Leon was reduced to the number 16084. The *Zugangliste* and *Sterbebücher* reveal some information about the fate of Leon in Auschwitz.[15] However, his agony went largely undocumented. In the second half of 1942, German Nazis established

---

Kosiorski and B. Kulikowski, the gestapo arrested Felix and John Kaczorowski in 1940. They were given numbers 16081, 16083 and sent to the Konzentrationelager Auschwitz. Z. Mańkowski, *Franciszek Bartłomowicz's "Grzmot" dowódca Batalionów Chłopskich w Obwodzie Tomaszów Lubelski:* Annales Universitatis Mariae Curie-Skłodowska. Section K, *Politologia* 6, (251–262) Lublin: 1999 p. 260.

[12] J. Peter, A. Homziak. *Tomaszowskie za okupacji.* Tomaszowskie Towarzystwo Regionalne.Tomaszow Lub.: 1991 p. 537–543.

[13] The information originates from the "Auschwitz Sterbebücher" ("Death Books").

[14] J. Peter, A. Homziak. *Tomaszowskie za okupacji.* Tomaszowskie Towarzystwo Regionalne.Tomaszow Lub.: 1991 p. 436.

[15] Death certificates can be found at pages on houston.indymedia.org

According to Indymedia, "In 1989, the Soviets released much of the German documentation, death certificates, (…) that they had found at Auschwitz, in January 1945. The Germans had simply left this documentation when they evacuated. The Soviets came across it and conveniently 'lost' in their archives for some 45 years. In 1989, Gorbachev presented it to the Red Cross who then 'lost it' in archives in Arolsen, Germany. The death certificates themselves, were official German documents, issued by Auschwitz camp doctors, upon the death of an inmate. Each death certificate consists of the deceased person's full name, profession and religion, date and place of birth, pre-Auschwitz residence, parents' names, time of death, cause of death and a camp physician's signature. (…) There is a little documentation from the year 1941, none from the year 1944, nor from January 1945 (when Auschwitz was evacuated). The death certificates record the names of 68,864 Polish citizens, who died at Auschwitz, of whom about 30,000 were listed as Jews."

the Auschwitz Birkenau II concentration camp for more than twenty nationalities including Polish citizens and people of Mosaic faith—just three kilometers away from Auschwitz.[16]

"Then, just three months later, on September 7, 1941 occupiers murdered my husband's brother-in-law. In late 1942, they started transporting Jews from all over Europe for extermination. At the same time, scheduled roundups continued, however, this is more difficult for me even to describe. SS-men would make victims lie face down on the ground and shoot them in the head. In the same way, they murdered both my former Polish and Jewish classmates with whom I had been very close while attending school.

"One time, the Gestapo SS went to the house of my Polish classmate, seized their father, and shot him along with the whole family including five children, for hiding Jews. My classmate's family perished because they broke the German's criminal law for hiding Jews, which punished not only the one who was hiding but also his entire Polish family. Despite the imposed death penalty, many Christians hid Jews. My family was so pauperized by the war brutality that we were lucky to survive. The automatic risk of the death penalty was imposed on any Pole and his entire family who helped Jews. Often, it required the secret cooperation of as many as twenty people to save one Jew. Nowhere else were the occupiers so brutal. Nevertheless, God miraculously saved us from death. I remember how we cried and grieved their loss. Let no generation ever experience that kind of violence."

Another blow to Poles at the borders of Tomaszow region came from pro-Germany Nazi-Bandera faction nationalists (The Organization of Ukrainian Nationalists, OUN-B was established in 1942) and the extremist militants (UPA). They carried out cruel terror against Polish civilians, burning their villages to the ground and exterminating women, children, and elderly ethnic Poles in Eastern Lesser Poland under German control. Many Ukrainian militants who volunteered in SS Gallizen carried out bloody pacifications, removing native Poles to "de-Polonize" the Polish territories they wrongly claimed as theirs. Where it was possible, the Polish Home Army (AK) responded with resistance to the cruelty of both German Nazi and Ukrainian extremists. [17] As weakly armed as they were, the Polish underground was successful in making extremists less oppressive toward innocent Polish peasants. Ukrainian nationalists (UPA), under the protection of Nazi Germany, committed horrifying massacres on defenseless Polish elderly, women, and children: "Polish researchers cautiously estimate the

---

[16] www.myheritage.com/research/record-10460-28463/leon-kosiorski-in-auschwitz-death-certificates

[17] Germans deported around 200,000 Polish children for Germanization. "Once word spread through the country about the pitiful plight of the children—and there were approximately 30,000 of them expelled from the Zamość area—the Polish people responded admirably. As the trains loaded with children moved westward across Poland, Polish women waited for hours at railroad stations in the hope of helping them." Richard Lucas. *The Forgotten Holocaust: The Poles under German Occupation 1939–1944*. 3rd edition. Hyppocrene Books: New York 2012 p. 5–9.

number of Polish victims of the Volhynian massacres, which started during the winter of 1942/43 and ended in mid-1945, at approximately 100,000."[18] Earlier, Polish men had been taken to the Soviet gulags. UPA genocide against Polish minorities took place in nearby neighbor areas of Volhynia, Eastern Galicia, parts of Polesia, and in the local Lublin region.

"German losses on the East front resulted in eased repressions and allowed us to attend school again. We only had limited exposure to mathematics and were not taught any history or any other subjects. Three classes with one teacher were still far from any regular school activities. The school was often interrupted by prolonged breaks. That occurrence had happened in 1943."

According to parish records, before the Nazis were defeated by the Allied Forces, Rachanie residents suffered home evictions on July 11, 1943. *Schutzpolizai* carried out several public executions behind a school field on September 28, December 14, 1944, and January 14, 17, and 23, 1945.[19] Families of murdered civilians were given permissions from the German settler, Landart to bury recovered remains after paying a fee, without the presence of a priest, at the local cemetery. E. Kaptur, the teacher and brother of Leon from the nearby Werechanie village, wrote to J. Peter: "I have seen in my life various pictures that breathe terror. However, you cannot describe the view of dozens of carts with coffins and people crying about digging school gardens in search of relatives.[20] A massive retinue with nearly a hundred coffins brought crowds of citizens to the cemetery." *"Many Varsovians relocated to villages including ours because the Nazi Germany destroyed Warsaw."* Eighty five to ninety two percent of Warsaw's buildings were deliberately burned and demolished. More than 40 percent of the country's cultural heritage, including paintings, sculptures and books, were reported destroyed or stolen.[21] The material losses alone, caused by the Third Reich, were estimated by the Polish parliament at $850 billion. No reparations were paid in any form from any of the aggressors. Many, due to their own incomplete interpretation of the Polish history, do not know or don't want to know the enormous war destruction and the loss of almost 20 percent of the Polish citizens.[22] *"For my luck, a talented seamstress with the diploma was hosted in my neighborhood. All of us wanted to learn her skills, but she had only one room to teach this profession, and she chose me. From the very beginning, I loved it very much, and after a year, she invited me to go with her to help staff re-open a Warsaw factory so I could*

---

[18] zbrodniawolynska.pl/ftp/zbrodnia_wolynska/Volhynian_Massacres-Basic_Information.pdf p. 9.

[19] rachanie.tnb.pl/news.php?readmore=36

[20] J. Peter, A. Homziak. *Tomaszowskie za okupacji*. Tomaszowskie Towarzystwo Regionalne. Tomaszow Lub.: 1991 p. 543.

[21] www.reuters.com/article/us-poland-germany-reparations/germany-owes-poland-over-850-billion-in-ww2-reparations-senior-lawmaker-idUSKCN1S215R

[22] Richard Lucas. *The Forgotten Holocaust: The Poles under German Occupation 1939–1944*. 3rd edition. Hyppocrene Books: New York 2012 p. 10–15.

work there, however, my parents refused to let me go. Instead, they bought me a sewing machine, which then I started teaching five girls at our home for several years. While this was a positive thing, trauma of russification, continued in my life. When the Soviets arrived as our 'liberators,' we had no peace or safety. Young women went hiding because of their soldiers." The Soviet aggressors continued arrests and made *the Konzentrationslager in Lublin,* the prison facility on the skirts of Majdanek. This became the prison for many who opposed communism. Only a few came back alive.[23] A number of other towns of Tomaszów that came under

---

[23] After the Soviet Army captured the KL Lublin German concentration and extermination camp, it, it became the NKVD-retained, ready-made facility in Majdanek. Poland was handed over to Josef Stalin at the Potsdam Conference in 1945. This time, Majdanek continued to be the prison for soldiers of the Armia Krajowa (AK, the Home Army resistance), loyal to the Polish Government-in-Exile and National Armed Forces, BCh, NSZ, which were opposed to both German and Soviet occupation.

More than sixty thousand Home Army veterans were sent to the Soviet gulag between 1948 and 1956. In another concentration camp in Świętochłowice, one of the commandants was Salomon Morel, who killed one-third of the prisoners. When Polish people wanted to make him respond to his crimes, Israel did not allow for his extradition. Poles, throughout the war, did not create military units to collaborate with Nazis. One example is a war hero general Emil Fieldorf "Nil." He was the highest officer of AK anti-Nazi resistance who organized a successful attack on Frank Kutchera, a cruel SS-man responsible for the death of thousands in Warsaw.

Communists often engaged collaborators, who terribly persecuted and killed thousands of Polish people after World War II. Colonel Helena Wolińska-Brus, who was involved in a Stalinist show trial, fled to Great Britain and never paid for her judicial crimes and sentencing General Emil Fieldorf "Nil" to death. Communist Colonel Józef Różański, originally Goldberg, became deputy prosecutor of many patriots. Another prosecutor, General Benjamin Wajsblech, was the main accuser of Fieldorf "Nil." Similarly, Włodzimierz Brus, born Beniamin Zylberberg retired and never stood for an honest trail. The presiding judge, Gurowska vel (under the changed name Górowska) was never tried and died peacefully in 1998, like Stalinist lawyer Emil Merz, court murderer and officer of the Ministry of Public Security did.

Out of thirty-four sentences of capital punishment imposed in the first instance, Merz kept fourteen. In the investigation of the murder of General Fieldorf, initiated in 1992 by the Main Commission for the Investigation of Crimes against the Polish Nation, Merz was one of the main suspects. Because of his death, he did not suffer any consequences. Gustaw Auscaler (Department III of the Criminal Chamber of the Supreme Court) acted in a secret mode, approved the death penalty of many Poles, and left with his family for Israel in 1968 under Szmulem name.

Kazimierz Łaski, born Hendel Cygler was the head of the notorious Security department IV, and also the deputy prosecutor of the General Prosecutor's Office Division in the socialist Poland. The Supreme Court judge, Paulina Kern, died in 1980 without any punishment in Israel. Plenty of prosecutors and judges hunted Polish fighters of anti-Nazi and anticommunist resistance like Paulina Kern,

Russian control experienced acts of violence. They beat teachers, shot the owner of the nearby Czartowczyk, Józef Gałczyński, imprisoned village leaders, and murdered any surviving soldiers of the September campaign in 1939 or the Polish underground soldiers, "AK." A welcome committee made up of Jewish collaborators and communists, including brothers Edward and Adam Humer, served in notorious Public Security Office (SB) in Tomaszow. Adam Humer became the first deputy of Aleksander Żebrun, the head of the Poviat Public Security Office. After the war, his sister Olga Żebrun became a deputy to the Sejm and a member of the Central Party Control Committee. Aleksander Żebrun was a prewar criminal who prepared a welcome gate decorated with spruce and red flags for Russian Army.

'My mom has often reminded me her intense grief of losing her close friends and neighbors, saying, 'How could I have not had post-traumatic stress disorders, after all, my childhood trauma?' "Such were the years of my youth. It was a sad time filled with fear and a lack of safety. After World War II, Czesław Misztal, our well-known parish organist, helped us rebuild our social life. He gladly accepted us all to the choir to sing songs and Christmas carols. Such religious opportunities gave me great joy. Afterward, we would often socialize or dance. Outside of choir activities, everything was otherwise unfortunate. We would often sing in neighboring parishes. It was in that way that I met Czesław, a brother of the future doctor Franciszek Stanibula, who also was in the underground resistance movement.[24]

Maksymilian Litynski (Lifszyc, Chief Military Prosecutor), Marian Frenkiel, Colonel Józef Swiatlo (Isaak Fleischfarb, Deputy Director, department X), and Stefan Michnik (a former Stalinist military judge, born as Schechter).
Above data is disclosed by historians in their numerous publications. Polish population at the Central Office. *MSW addresses archive no. 1/6526 SUSW Warsaw 1984.*

Captain Witold Pilecki had been given a show trial in 1948 and secretly executed. He was the one who reported German's everyday atrocities as early as 1941 in Auschwitz. It is known that over 20,000 Poles died in communist prisons including those executed "in the majesty of the law" such as Witold Pilecki. Witold Pilecki, the hero soldier in the Polish Army and of the Polish resistance, who entered and escaped from the Auschwitz concentration camp. He provided the world's first record of the Holocaust. These reports informed the Allies about the Holocaust but the first publication of Witold's Report took place in 2000, 55 years after the war. Soviets hided his and many others burial places which still have not been found. archive.org/details/WITOLDREPORT/page/n15

[24] Cf. D. Paczkowski. Gazeta Iławska. *Difficult origins and hospital stories chilling blood in veins. The History of the iławski hospital.* Vol. II Cf. D. Paczkowski. *Gazeta Iławska. Trudne początki i historie szpitalne mrożące krew w żyłach. Historia iławskiego szpitala.* Cz. II – Iława 2016.04.23

1494/1941

Sr.

lo.September 41

Auschwitz, den 19

er Landwirt Leon Kosiorski,römisch-katholisch

wohnhaft Rachanie,Kreis Tomaszow

7.September 1941 um Uhr Minuten

Auschwitz,Kasernenstraße verstorben.

er 12.April 1907

Rachanie,Kreis Tomaszow

(Standesamt Nr.)

Vater: Mikolaj Kosiorski wohnhaft in Rachanie

Kreis Tomaszow

Mutter: Maria Kosiorski geborene Lapinski zuletzt

wohnhaft in Rachanie,Kreis Tomaszow

er mit Stefania Kosiorski

Verstorbene war nicht verheiratet

geborene Stangula

des Arztes Doktor Heschl

Eingetragen auf mündliche schriftliche Anzeige

in Auschwitz vom 7.September 1941

Die Übereinstimmung mit dem
Erstbuch wird beglaubigt.

Auschwitz, den lo.9. 19 41

Der Standesbeamte
In Vertretung

Der Standesbeamte
In Vertretung
Quakernack

Todesursache: Darmkatarrh bei Rippenfellentzündung

Eheschliessung de Verstorbenen an in

(Standesamt Nr.)

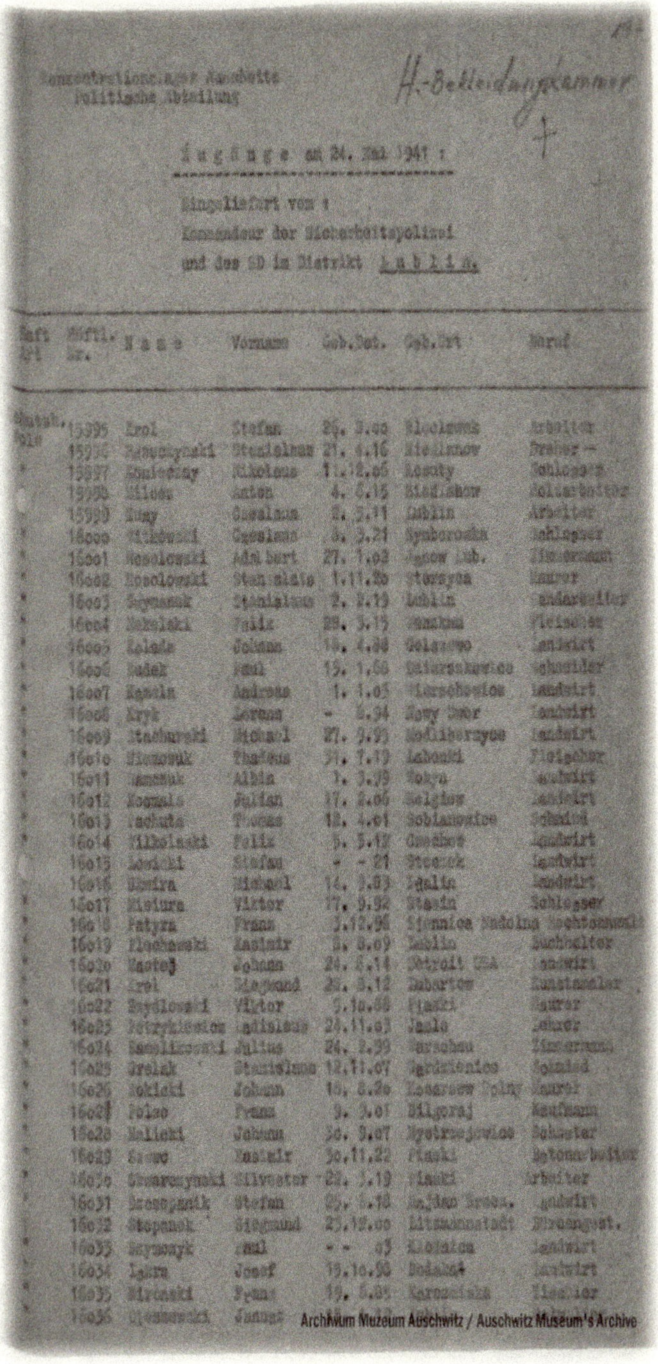

Archivum Muzeum Auschwitz / Auschwitz Museum's Archive

198

Haft Art	Häftl. Nr.	N a m e	Vorname	Geb.Dat.	Geb.-Ort	Beruf
Polnisch.P.	16037	Golian	Stanislaus	11. 3.98	Bychawka	Berufsunteroff.
"	16038	Szczesniak	Ladislaus	21.10.99	Sacharaoszyn	Senator
"	16039	Prodaresuk	Wasil	21. 7.21	(Russland)	Landarbeiter
"	16040	Klimiuk	Stanislaus	22. 6.21	Danco	Landwirt
"	16041	Samoluk	Adam	? ? 16	(Russland)	Landwirt
"	16042	Kwiatkowski	Siegmund	15. 3.96	Bihale	Lehrer
Deutsch.Jude	16043	Kac	Josel,Isr.	1. 5.94	Lublin	Arbeiter
Polnisch.P.	16044	Krason	Josef	17.12.19	Sobiszka Wola	Landarbeiter
"	16045	Suchlicki	Matheus	22. 7.93	Krzeszowo	Landwirt
"	16046	Chaps	Stanislaus	23. 4.03	Dubów	Landwirt
"	16047	Matysek	Marian	12. 2.14	Pinski	Bücker
"	16048	Kosak	Rhoden	31.16.11	Pinski	Stellmacher
"	16049	Dankowski	Adam	14.10.00	Donsk	Bürozugestellt.
"	16050	Chojnacki	Anton	16. 6.90	Kojonice	Organist
"	16051	Wojciechowski	Viktor	12. 6.03	Kursk	Arzt
"	16052	Kolniuk	Peter	22. 6.13	Annopol	Schlosser
"	16053	Kusma	Jakob	24. 7.05	Pieskie	Priester
"	16054	Stanko	Felix	14. 5.04	Samoec	Sägewerksleiter
"	16055	Kinelman	Felix	1. ?.96	Warschau	Schneider
"	16056	Kaszewski	Johann	24.10.97	Irkuck	Arzt
"	16057	Luta	Eduard	23. 7.88	Opole Lub.	Landbau
"	16058	Pszefiniuk	Eduard	12.11.96	Koszadki	Landarbeiter
"	16059	Matuszek	Paul	29.12.90	Ostry	Senator n.D.
"	16060	Junski	Eduard	25. 1.06	Dublin	Zimmermann
"	16061	Dobrowolski	Stanislaus	16. 3.19	Lublin	Landwirt
"	16062	Dombrowski	Ladislaus	17. 6.14	Ichartor	Landwirt
"	16063	Slabbe	Johann	10.12.10	Wygnanka	Arbeiter
"	16064	Muszynski	Anton	28. 9.16	Korenpol	Bahn-Ingenieur
"	16065	Szczesniowicz	Richard	5. 7.18	Korostyn	Schlosser
"	16066	Kondracki	Marian	6. 9.09	Sarncki	Kaufmann
"	16067	Kasiejuk	Stanislaus	16.11.97	Biala Podl.	Bauhändler
"	16068	Sagan-Borowicz	Heinrich	6. 1.00	Warschau	Senator
"	16069	Parys	Stanislaus	29. 3.17	Krasnien	Bauer
"	16070	Soun	Ignatz	1. 3.18	Russland	Landarbeiter
"	16071	Supa	Vaclaus	2.10.14	Biala Podl.	Kraftfahrer
"	16072	Radisjewski	Vaclaus	26. 9.02	Choroszcz	Schuster
"	16073	Drozdziel	Vaclaus	24. 8.13	Kamoec	Rodzmkur
"	16074	Piros	Josef	24. 6.22	Drandocia	Tischler
"	16075	Zoladek	Johann	? ? 14	Karol-Wies	Landwirt
"	16076	Adamczyk	Marian	6.10.02	Irena	Zimmermann
"	16077	Adamczewski	Boleslaus	16.11.95	Ingsezow	Friseur
Deutsch.Jude	16078	Bystelpine	Aron,Jakob	22.12.09	Lublin	Arbeiter
Polnisch.P.	16079	Kaniavozuk	Ladislaus	16. 8.13	Ruiba Izsaha	Landwirt
Polnisch.D.	16080	Jagdhold	Erich	15.10.99	Alt Auto	Oberförster al
Deutsch.P.	16081	Kaczorowski	Felix	29.10.97	Machanie	Müller
"	16082	Grzesiuk	Eduard	25. 9.96	Kotlica	Tischler
"	16083	Kaczorowski	Johann	24.11.99	Machanie	Müller
"	16084	Kosiorowski	Leo	14. 4.07	Machanie	Landwirt
"	16085	Supyra	Kazimir	12. 3.16	Kiew	Bauer
"	16086	Olszewski	Stanislaus	8. 9.04	Radzyn Lub.	Maurer
"	16087	Niessior	Leo	20. 7.04	Studzienki	Landwirt
"	16088	Walczak	Alexander	16. 7.92	Wola Calaçowska	Landwirt

"Despite governmental persecution of the Catholic faith in January 1950, we got married in the Church. We tried to rebuild our lives and started our family. Then, we were raising a family of five children. I continued to work as a seamstress while Czesław rebuilt our house." About 518,000 farmers were arrested by communists because they were against collectivization.

"He also worked part-time, distributing seed potatoes for regional farmers while trying to establish his own brick company. It was again a very challenging time, with high taxes on any private ownership. After the war, Poland's socialist puppet pro-Russian government imposed on us all sorts of repressions, including crop quotas on almost everything we produced.

"Injustice and censorship continued in many forms by the post-war socialists and related libertine establishments. My family suffered terrible injuries from all occupiers. My husband Czesław was heavily wounded by occupiers, and Dr. Peter miraculously saved his life. My husband's brother-in-law Leon perished when he just became thirty-four year old.[25] Germans tried to punish and dehumanize my family even harder when they sent a letter from Auschwitz that they wanted a fee for his ashes. After my future husband's sister and Widow Stephanie made a payment, occupiers sent ashes in the wooden box. My family had felt terrible grief and pain, unsure whether these ashes were truly Leon's remains. In light of another anniversary of the World War II, I would like to remind everyone about the responsibility for preserving the historical truth and defending historical justice. Today, different groups of interest present Nazis as not having anything to do with German's ideology."

"Fifty years after World War II, Poles were under the 'iron curtain' and were not allowed to express their freedom until the Solidarity protests with Polish flags on streets. Still, some foreign groups of interests continue to prevail falsified narration and media publications regarding occupied Poland. Polish martyrology and deportations were not even allowed to be mentioned under the Russian censorship. My family resisted dehumanized sinful foreign ideologies for which Poles paid the heaviest price. In the face of the corrupt ideologies and perpetrated defamation of Poles, Solidarity must remind the world of who the victims and oppressors were. My plea after years of the terrible atrocities perpetrated on Poles is that our younger generation remembers always to love their homeland and form their patriotic character. "

"Today, young people have a choice of educating themselves; attending different schools, wearing fashionable clothes, enjoy computers, cars, cell phones, or any conveniences. Many of them forget about growing their lives according to God's loving design. Anyone who wishes to be wise must learn much and not destroy it while taking advantage of the educational opportunity. He or she ought to evolve one's given humanity to another level. Young people need to realize that life is precious and short. "

"Each one of us has received one life, and that given life by God ought to manifest the greatest values. The one who is smart ought to give his/ herself formed life

---

[25] **Kosiorski, Leon** (prisoner number **16084**) born 1907-04-12, place of birth: Rachanie, religion: Catholic, profession: farmer. **Fate:** 1. 1941-05-24 Auschwitz, arrived to camp, 2. murdered 7-9-1941 in Kl Auschwitz. **Sources:** 1. Memorial Book Lublin 2. Zugangliste 3. Sterbebücher.

meaning. But the other, who dwells on nihilism, continues to destroy it in the most pitiable way." –Janina Stanibula

INTRODUCTION

Christian formation is, undoubtedly, one of the most important dimensions of self-development. Integral formation covers the whole life of a man who is both the subject and object of this evolution. Because moral self-formation involves all dimensions of human life, its foundation is a fundamental concept of humanity. Human development, which is based on knowledge of *who we are* and *who we ought to be,* helps us find desired answers to the big questions. Only when one understands who he is as a human being and what the ultimate purpose of his life journey is can he achieve the mature goals of his existence. Moral self-formation encompasses becoming in all spheres and dimensions of human life. Understood this way, self-formation becomes a path to mature personality development.

Moral self-formation cannot exist without appropriate anthropological assumptions about and reliance on postmodern knowledge about man. In the modern world, there is a constant confrontation between ideological and philosophical currents, which impart different visions of man. Unfortunately, in the postmodern world, the integral image of man is sometimes replaced by forms of reduction. With partial truths about man, it is much easier to manipulate human beings using various techniques of social engineering designed to subjugate them. This kind of anthropotechnology stands in clear contrast to the integral anthropology of the individual. These anthropotechnological programs and educational methods often interrupt or counteract balanced and mature process of personality development.

In this anthropological search, it is entirely reasonable to prove that Christian self-formation is a meaningful path to mature personality development. Integrally applied formation, including the moral self-formation of human values, can protect a person from today's fashionable libertinism, which reduces him to something he is not. It must be emphasized that each person is responsible for his own ongoing development and behavior, which is sanctified by the needs of larger society. Therefore, the most important role of someone who has been neglected by family and educational systems is moral self-formation.

Presently, the issue of self-formation, including moral formation toward mature personality development, has become an interest in various fields of knowledge including pedagogy and psychology. However, these schools of thought focus more on issues of formation or the characteristics of a mature personality. In this book, I want to demonstrate that sophisticated character development is obtainable by lifelong self-formation—the fundamental process of becoming. I will present a self-formation based on the personalistic teaching model of Harvard professor Gordon Willard Allport (1897–1967), one of the founding figures of personality psychology. Allport believes that even after the worst atrocities of the twentieth century, man has the capability to overcome modern anthropological reductionism. With frequent references to the teachings of the Church, Allport points out that people need stable, well-planned self-formation in terms of their moral character. The aim of this process is the "new man," who is distinguished by a mature personality and the capability to live in harmony with the world and himself.

Allport's work provides the primary source material for this publication. Auxiliary sources, essential for anthropological considerations, are drawn from the *magisterium* of the Catholic Church. Aware of the richness of magisterial teachings, I have chosen the documents relevant to Christian formation. I will include numerous studies focused on Allport's scientific achievements as well the Church's wisdom. Among other anthropotheological studies on which this research is built are the works of A. Derdziuk, K. Jeżyna, S. Mojek, J. Nagórny, and M. Pokrywka. The very insightful thoughts of Cz. Walesa, W. Prężyny, and Z. Płużek will substantially supplement my discussion on the subject in the field of personal maturity. The psychological studies of L. Kohlberg, R. Kegan, and J. Piaget are likewise useful. Interdisciplinary studies will also be considered to present human self-formation from analytical and synthetic approaches. Therefore, this study will organize and synthesize documents in such a way that it might be possible to show the essence of self-formation and its role of developing individual maturity.

My research methodology is demonstrated in the four-chapter structure of this book. It is necessary to begin by looking at the social circumstances in the United States during the first half of the twentieth century, which affected Allport's self-formation, family, and social maturation. The profound faith, creativity, and business ethic of Allport's established personalistic school is the starting point for our discussion of moral formation. Allport's accomplishments, as well as the environmental conditions under which he worked, will help us understand America's major cultural trends during the first half of the twentieth century. To more deeply understand Allport's attitude and thoughts, one needs to examine the self-formation and evolvement he received at his family home. Only in that mature context will it be possible to determine the basis of his growth.

The remainder of the book will present essential aspects of Christian self-formation. First, I will explain the terms "self-formation," "upbringing," and "education." Then, I will show the great social necessity for such development, paying close attention to the communal formation of conscience. Further steps will uncover the stages of human formation from infancy to old age. In this way, we will be able to view formation first and then self-formation as a lifelong process. After this inquiry, I will focus on formation in terms of becoming "fully" human. It will be necessary to emphasize that Christian formation should be Christocentric because it is Jesus Christ who fully reveals man to himself. Internal formation that leads man toward living the highest capability of humanity takes place at both the natural and supernatural levels. That is to say that it combines human effort with the grace of a loving God. Because the self is a product of learning and experience, integral human development demands active participation in various communities of formation, especially family, school, and church. One must emphasize the priority of parents in education. A great portion of modern culture undermines parental authority. Good parents do not merely communicate physical life but also attend to their children's psychological and physical development and growth. This task presupposes unconditional love and acceptance from the very start.

Another critical environment is school, where formation ought to be continued on another level. The mission of the school is to support family formation. In addition to intellectual education, in what way does school affect further development in terms of imparting moral standards and teaching respect for others? Schools should provide formation as an integral way to activate responsible participation in society and, among other things, in patriotism. The rest of this work focuses on a discussion of the educative role of communities of faith.

The Church not only supports the integral self-formation that occurs within the family (the "domestic Church") but also dispenses God's abundant grace. Our human life has been very much defragmented due to the dichotomy of values that deconstructs classic patterns of morality. Deconstruction models of morality pose difficulties to basic education and integral human formation. The consequence of this dichotomy is a departure from ethics and the deformation of universal laws and religious behaviors. These destructive phenomena reduce man, anthropologically speaking, making him helplessness in the face of evil, which is also the effect of materialistic educational systems.

Thus, an anthropological analysis of the issues related to self-formation is profoundly justified. Of course, the problem of moral self-formation is not new. Interest in perfecting man can be found in Aristotle as well as in the inspired authors of the sacred Scripture. The New Testament authors and church fathers were very much alert to possibility of man's natural spirit (i.e., the "old man" referred to by the apostle Paul) being replaced by the Holy Spirit, forming "the new man" in Christ. On this topic, we will look to Origen, Tertullian, and John Chrysostom, among others. There is "formative space" to fill in and reinforce with Allport's personal psychology and divine wisdom, and these might serve as a *via media* between

Rome and the Protestants.[26] Analyzing the integrating vision of the Church Fathers is necessary to rediscover the meaning of Christian formation again. As Andrew Derdziuk rightly points out, the problem of formation represents a threefold range of pedagogical interactions on the human person through education, teaching, and learning, as well as moral formation.[27]

Problems of moral deformity in postmodernity repeatedly call for change. Civilized life and cultural transformation can happen changing fragmented man's narcissistic thinking. Moral sensibility is a vital part of his intelligence, and he might be able to determine what educates, what develops, and what destroys him. Therefore, formation in the moral sphere is an essential element of the personalism postulated by Allport. A need for a stable, well-planned formation of conscience, to form a new man with a morally mature personality, capable of living in harmony with the world and oneself is necessary.[28] Self-formation in no way relates to the world of things or to the animal world; rather, it exists only in the sphere of evolved humans for their well-being. Being a human person means having conscious existence, freedom, and responsible action for one's present and future. "Efforts of course, always refer to the future. In fact, a whole range of mental states requires consideration of future events. Aspirations go hand in hand with interests, dispositions, expectations, planning, problem solving and intentions."[29] Today's world creates a particularly difficult situation to form a mature conscience operating on common sense and natural law and with an accurate assessment of integral life; good and evil are often wrongly equated with good and bad feelings only. The community of faith has the duty of helping individuals through the purification of reason and moral self-formation to meet the demands of the contemporary society and living justly.[30]

Postmodernity does not care much about forming the mature conscience required for living in harmony with others who desire integral living—that is to say, those who prefer the common good over personal preference. Therefore, self-formation constitutes evolved moral and mature decisions that are often difficult to make. Christian anthropology has, since its origin, sought truth in the larger context of our relationship with God.

---

[26] Cf. DF p. 16. Cf. A. Flannery. *Vatican Council II: The Conciliar and Post Conciliar Documents*, "Decreeon." Dublin: LEV1981 p. 719.

[27] A. Derdziuk. *Formacja moralna a formacja sumienia* IN: *Formacja moralna, formacja sumienia*. Red. J. Nagórny, T. Zadykowicz. Lublin: Wydaw. KUL 2006 p. 13–19.

[28] "In the depths of his conscience man discovers the right, which itself does not impose, but which ought to be obeyed and that voice calls him to do good and avoid evil." (KDK p. 16).

[29] Cf. G. W. Allport. *Osobowość i religia*. Transl. H. Bartoszewicz, A. Bartkowicz, I. Wyrzykowska. Warszawa: Pax 1988 p. 45.

[30] DCE p. 28a.

People of faith have always wanted to discover a deeper reference to their Creator and surrounding environments. Thus, they tend to seek meaningful ways of life that allow them to achieve happiness and harmony with others.

Allport was one of them. A moralist and psychologist, he found that man, even after the bloodiest atrocities of the twentieth century, has the moral strength to overcome the disastrous results of anthropological reductionism, or theologically speaking, of sin. Accurate decisions based on the common good are the responsibility of mature individuals. Allport rightly argues that human evolution has no connection with the world of things or animals but with *people* who are co-Creators with the God of peace and harmony. [31] Such an anthropology promotes healthy decisions for the common good and creates the expression of a mature individual's responsibility. When decisions result from the privatization of responsibility, we can see relationships full of immaturity.[32] Another author, J. Nagórny, believes that internal "formation is one of the most important dimensions of human responsibility for their personal development. Unfortunately, this aspect is neglected by many."[33] Nagórny notes that human responsibility needs to be addressed for the advancement of human development and evolution. The principles, morals, and virtues play a major role in individual formation.

A person is both subject and object of integral formation in Christian self-realization. The term "person" has a specific meaning in philosophy and

---

[31] "Normal men everywhere reject, in principle and by preference, the path of war and destruction. They want to live in peace and friendship with their neighbors; they prefer to love and be loved rather than to hate and be hated. Cruelty is not a favored human trait. Even the top Nazi officials who were tried at Nürnberg pretended that they knew nothing about the inhuman practices in the concentration camps. They shrank from admitting their part because they too wished to be thought of as human beings. While wars rage, yet our desire is for peace, and while animosity prevails, the weight of mankind's approval is on the side of affiliation. So long as there is this sense of moral dilemma there is hope that it may somehow be resolved and that hate-free values may be brought to prevail." Allport. *The Nature of Prejudice* p. 16.

[32] "Why does this privatism exist in America to such a high degree? Summarizing the answers, we find that leading reasons are offered. The United States enjoys relative security from invasion—at least the students so believe (...) economic security and personal freedom felt by American youth as compared with youth of most other nations. A strong pressure toward success (...) defined in terms of the rich and full personal life that we have neither time nor energy left for good citizenship. (...) The prolonged adolescence of American youth as compared with youth in many other countries encourages irresponsibility and disinterest in civic matters through the college years. Older American adults should manifest less privatism than younger. The discouragement tempts American youth to escape into a private world." G. W. Allport and Gillespie J. *Youth's Outlook on the Future: A Cross-National Study.* Garden City: Doubleday 1955 p. 17–18.

[33] J. Nagórny. *Wprowadzenie* IN: *Formacja moralna – formacja sumienia.* Red. J. Nagórny, T. Zadykowicz. Lublin: Wydawnictwo KUL 2006 p. 9.

theology, which have a holistic view of man. The thoughts of Thomas Aquinas fascinated Allport, who was no stranger to the base nature of human consciousness, which indicates two levels of human activity resulting from the conscious and unconscious processes occurring within.[34] Therefore, learned principles, morals, and virtues play an important role in the self-formation of one's life. At the level where one is both the subject and object of internal formation, Allport treats the human person as "ineffable mystery." The mystery of subjectivity requires guidance.

Principles are necessary traits, because without these traits, imperfect rules often mislead. A conscious man with a developed personality can prevent the destructive actions of his future. He who can retain higher feelings is able to connect with the world as well as with the Creator by means of healthy motivation. In confronting his sinfulness, however, man often feels lost. Manifestations of this condition are often the result of misconceptions and rambling thoughts.

Self-formation is an ongoing task; maturity comes after a long process of self-education. Therefore, if a common, ordinary man desires to maintain full internal autonomy and really wants to save his identity, he must build a healthy and mature personality motivated by the love of God. Absent the disposition to act according to goodness and truth, says Allport, and man is unable to choose and take responsibility on another level of obligation. That claim is confirmed by the Kantian dictum: "Principles without traits are impotent, and traits without Principles are blind."[35] It is necessary to shape such traits and attitudes to find the right course of life, free from the sin of hatred and unhealthy competition.[36] Currently, it is necessary to form attitudes that point to a meaningful way of life. The more one is internally free, the more he can become integrally mature. The more noble motivation man chooses, the more beautiful becomes his personality, which manifests itself in his mature actions that exhibit less prejudice, a higher tolerance for frustration, and a higher control of risk.[37] With a developed value system, one is more capable of finding a way out of a difficult situation.

At the same time, the manifestation of universal Christian values raises objections in the materialist, secularized world.[38] In achieving his

---

[34] Cf. Cz. S. Bartnik. *Personalizm teologiczny według Kardynała Karola Wojtyły.* ZN KUL 1979 no. 1–3 p. 52–53.

[35] J. P. Sterba. *Ethics: The big questions.* Malden: Blackwell Publishing 1998 p. 12.

[36] Cf. Benedict XVI. OŚDP. "Wolność religijna drogą do pokoju." (01.01.2011). OsRomPol 32: 2011 no. 1 p. 10, Benedykt XVI teaches that Christians must get rid of hatred and prejudice.

[37] Z. Płużek. *Psychologia pastoralna.* Kraków: Instytut Księży Misjonarzy 1991 p. 55.

[38] Taking care of human self-formation always bears fruit in a well-integrated life. Previous life, under the influence of totalitarianism, gave rise to an unconscious tendency, hiding under it as an external mask, and in consequence, man was enslaved

objectives, man needs ethics and continuous internal formation that allow him to not only make his life more meaningful in the external form but above all, internally richer. Certainly, openness to metaphysics and the wisdom of the humanities—combined with personal internal formation—is valuable for every educator, but the ministers of the Sacraments and catechists are especially vital. Good recognition of others and one's own personality forms the basis for overall success and has an effective educational impact.

Through theological anthropology, an attempt has been made to answer the question of whether a purely secularist upbringing constitues a sufficiently mature way of life without internal self-formation. Allport's positive approach to religious formation as a personalist psychologist, humanist, and moralist broke previous barriers. It is important to acknowledge that it is difficult to find many comprehensive publications and reasonable models expounding on the self-formation process in terms of it leading to maturity within the family.[39] I claim that the process of formation demands Christian traditions that introduce necessary humanistic personalism. Through connections among persons, such personalism fosters integral teaching and learning.

The Second Vatican Council stressed a personalist "ethos" that is altruistic in its range, whereby one is capable not only of becoming a gift for others but also (and more importantly) being joyful about doing so.[40] In a broader sense, being integrally self-formed requires freedom as well as being responsible for others and having an active good will. As God's creatures, humans experience *metanoia* and transition through the necessary tasks associated with personal maturing. Since ancient times, philosophers and intellectuals have taken interest in the evolution of the "new man" who has great skills and engagement with achieving personal transformation. They searched growth patterns for signs of evolution and transformation. They wondered, for example, why vices such as pride did not (and do not) foster human development toward new potential, whereas the virtue of love in action, despite suffering and deprivation, leads to anthropological becoming.[41]

Without appropriate concentration on self-inspiration and sacrificial love, one lacks the strength to become more sophisticated in human expression. Poetry, reflection, imagination, and the use of metaphors and

---

by hypocrisy. This does not promote authentic fraternal relations and can lead to exaggerated concentration on oneself. We grow in affective maturity when our hearts adhere to God. Cf. Benedict XVI. *Przemówienie podczas spotkania z duchowieństwem w archikatedrze św. Jana.* OSRomPol 25: 2006 no 6–7 p.15.

[39] K. Majdański. *Zadania rodziny chrześcijańskiej: tworzenie wspólnoty osób i służba życiu.* AK 76: 1984 T. 102 z. 449 p. 5–20.

[40] LdR p. 14.

[41] Cf. D. M. Lang and D. R. Dudley. *The Companion to Classical Oriental and African Literature.* T 4. New York: Penguin Books 1969 p. 127.

fairy tales are valuable, formative, and educational tools; they help us see life more deeply and thereby "extend" our personality, as it were. The fruits of self-reflection can be found in beautiful biblical metaphors, too, that contribute to raising awareness of wholesome integration. Frequent neglect of self-formation in our postmodern age leads to a materialistic deformation of life, where egoism, individualism, and the "culture of death" prevail. Torrents of misleading information—focusing attention on human cognitive methods aimed at acquiring only specific knowledge without forming character—obviously do not prepare man for the mature attitudes of a well-integrated life. Educators today focus excessively on personality processes relating only to the ability to absorb knowledge, neglecting holistic formation.[42] Contrast this with Pope John Paul II's teachings: that the subject of integral formation is the whole man, called to seek God and to love him "with all his heart, with all his might" (cf. Dt. 6:5), and his neighbor as himself (cf. Lev. 19:18; Mt. 22:37–39). Loving God and neighbor is a powerful vehicle of maturation and fidelity.[43]

Meanwhile, pedagogical education focuses on techniques for measuring learning outcomes. [44] In analyzing self-education, Allport postulates a method of critical dialogue, which, he argues, is morally right because it respects personality and humanity. By using Locke's thinking, he reveals a human subject who is susceptible to external formation—an unused blackboard (*tabula rasa*) in ethical acting. Then, drawing on Leibniz, he points to the source of human acts as freedom and responsibility in inner formation. [45] Allport refers to the dignity and subjectivity of a person as opposed to the neo-liberal psychologists of his time who reduced man to unconscious motives alone. Often, such reductionism indicates human manipulation. Awareness of the spiritual and moral needs of the interior life helps one discover deeper decks of his humanity and uniqueness, which in turn positively acknowledges other people.[46]

In some irrational environments, critics of self-formation see old-fashioned standards as restricting human freedom. I disagree with that reductionist way of thinking in regard to the human person, because it is destructive anthropology. In environments deeply concerned with human development, integral self-formation is a kind of scientific intelligence that

---

[42] Cf. K. Olbrycht. *"Dylematy współczesnego wychowania. Znak"* 43: 1991 no 9 (436) p. 40. Excluding formation as an additional task and setting specialized goals within a curriculum to achieve only one kind of success concerns many teachers.

[43] VC p. 71.

[44] Ibid s. 40.

[45] Empiryzm understood what we know now, especially from experience and observation. Since the seventeenth century, the British Experience, as defined by Hobbes and Locke as a *tabula rasa*, comes from the sensory experience.

[46] Cf. G. W. Allport. *Becoming.* New Haven: Yale University Press 1983 p. 23.

can distinguish destructive urges and mere pleasure-seeking from inner growth. Simply put, intellectually mature behavior protects one from inflicting harm on oneself and others.[47]

This publication attempts to answer the following anthropological questions: What is the potential of human self-formation, and how can it help to solve conflict? What evolving path is available to reach maturity in personal development? I will include different perspectives of personal, intellectual, and emotional formation in dialogue with Allport's personal psychology. Among different perspectives, the analytic method serves an important role in the critical dialogue because it will show conditions by which we can shape our own personality. Hence, among many common traits of human motivation and personality, we might discover the appropriate path of true self-formation. Formation based on a higher intelligence rather than intellectual or emotional intelligence, and based on reflection often derived from divine revelation, together with faith, enables individuals in their own humanity so they co-Create with the God of Truth and Goodness. Citing John Paul II, J. Nagórny states that the role of Christian self-formation is to engage in building the kingdom of God: the kingdom of truth, life, justice, love, and peace in the families and communities in which we live.[48]

In the modern world, appropriate tools and exercises that help one enter the path of Christian life involve the formation of the moral self to create a deeper internal life. The path to maturity, as proposed by Allport from his Presbyterian faith, does not differ from the Catholic view in its intention, because the man with no ethical formation is more likely to do what is easier over what is harder, wiser and more valuable (viz., the acquisition of values with high goals of life), which is desired good.

To further explore Allport's thoughts on personal development, it is worth presenting his primary thesis, life's maturation at each developmental stage. Analysis of his stages of childhood, adolescence, and adulthood can help us discover the validity of purposeful self-formation within self-work, philanthropy and charitable activities. Allport is considered to be one of the most prominent experts in human personality, as evidenced by the fact that he is the most-cited author in authoritative publications on the subject. As an educator, he shows interest in the integral education of the "post-war man"

---

[47] "Especially encouraging is the fact that in recent years men in large numbers have become convinced that scientific intelligence may help us solve the conflict. Theology has always viewed the clash between man's destructive nature and his ideals as a matter of original sin resisting the redemptive process. Valid and expressive as this diagnosis may be, there has been added recently the conviction that man can and should employ his intelligence to assist in his redemption. Men are saying, 'Let us make an objective study of conflict in culture and industry, between people of different color and race; let us see out the roots of prejudice and find concrete means for implementing men's affiliative values.'" Cf. Allport. *The Nature of Prejudice* p. XVI.

[48] Cf. Nagórny. *Wprowadzenie* IN: *Formacja moralna: Formacja sumienia* p. 12.

who is deeply ravaged by exposure to erroneous and fatal (indeed atheistic) anthropological theories. Allport took the road less traveled, concerning himself with what man can become in the light of a proper anthropology with a view to avoid yet another world war.

As C. Rogers posits, a man learns and matures by a healthy set of references: specific ideas, designs, his intimate experiences of the knowledge of others, and corresponding actions in the real world. [49] Among other authors, Allport confirms that the expectations of a child or adult are transmitted and formed in large part by experiences, thoughts, comparative studies, and deeds.[50] I submit that a person who was deformed by stereotypes and often targeted by negative feelings and desires has great difficulty in living harmoniously. It is difficult to expect, from a deformed individual, any mature morality or mature personality. A multitude of experimental research confirms that this is corroborated by the educational institutions and teachings of the Church.[51] To form a human being who strives to exist in peace and maturity requires self-participation and personal commitment. A moral formation trims social factors that determine a man's participation in pro-social behavior. As Paul VI eloquently writes, "We should start a new ideological education, education for peace. Yes, peace is born inside the human heart (…). Our job is to remind people that they are brothers. It is also our mission to encourage people to love one another and to educate them in love of peace." Similarly, in his Message for the Celebration of the Day of Peace (New Year's Day, 1972), he declared: "If you desire peace, work for justice."[52]

It is important to avoid the deformations and stereotypes derived from afflicted educators. We must therefore exclude "anti-value" views and attitudes such as extreme nationalism. Students at all levels should be instructed in social responsibility—and patriotism, too—but they should be inspired by noble personalities who exemplify prudence and balance. Christian formation must then take into account attitudes of an interpersonal dialogue between relevant needs, avoiding the determination of ready-made solutions. We have been encouraged to fight ignorance and build personal philosophy and theology in the acceptance of meaningful life worthy of human values. Hence, self-formation transforms individuals at the same time

---

[49] Cf. C. Rogers. *Toward a Science of the Person.* JHP 3: 1963 no. 1 p. 83.

[50] Cf. G. W. Allport. *Personality and Social Encounter.* Boston: Beacon Press 1960 p. 327.

[51] Cf. C. Conaway. "A psychological effect of stereotypes: Countering stereotypes changing the rules." *Q1 Regional Review* 2005 p. 41. C. Steele. "Thin Ice: Stereotype Threat and Black College Students." *Atlantic Monthly* 1999.

[52] Paweł VI. OŚDP. *Samowychowanie do pokoju poprzez pojednanie* IN: Paweł VI, Jan Paweł II. *Orędzia papieskie na Światowy Dzień Pokoju* p. 45. Paul VI. *Message of Pope Paul VI. Libreria Editrice Vaticana.* Dec 8, 1971, for the celebration of the day of peace.

allows for collaboration, healthy moral evaluation, and personal growth.[53] In the same spirit, John Paul II says that formators and educators should know, from natural law, the normative rules enabling them to accompany others on the path of self-development.[54] In this way, the concept of "virtue" leads to proper Christian self-formation and human evolution. In this regard, Allport and people of faith agree on the need to build an integral source of well-founded formation.[55]

The fruits of Allport's scientific work culminated in twelve books, many-times edited, centered on personality integration and the psychology of religious values, which together with the human tradition emphasize the psychological and anthropological peace resolution common to all people. Allport was interested in building a culture of harmony that John Paul II defined as "the civilization of life." Positive psychology nurtures the individual becoming that Allport expresses in *The Individual and Religion.*

Allport also studied the social, interpersonal and cross-cultural interactions. As an anthropologist, he predicted the suppression of the white population of Africa. As a psychologist of becoming, he combined his deeply humanist Presbyterian faith with his knowledge of human nature. His thought developed under the influence of Thomistic philosophy, and he advanced the personalistic system of inquiry against theories of man that marginalize and fragment human beings. He still was criticized for his lack of a comprehensive and integral assessment of the human being. His "personology" opens the way for the psychology of virtues, which is essential to Christian self-formation. In this regard, Allport sought different professionals and leading organizations in building world peace through a matrix of integral personalities. He received many distinctions and scientific awards, including the American Psychological Association Gold Medal for work in the field of personality psychology.

Using provocative language, Allport tried to position his reflection at the deep ethical level to aspire to self-formation of moral action and participate in building a harmonious and peaceful human coexistence. Like Maria Braun-Gałkowska, he was a precursor to issues of education and formation, striving to resolve the tension between who the human person is and who that person should become through integration. In critical dialogue, human development is a continuous process of acquiring universal values and skills. Its basic embeddedness should be seriously considered by many institutions including schools, universities, workplaces, and churches, which are the essential structures of an evolved man. These structures of higher learning ought to combine all human experiences, from family values to

---

[53] Cf. Allport. *Personality and Social Encounter* p. 344.
[54] Cf. VC p. 66.
[55] Cf. Ch L p. 60, PDV p. 42, and p. VC 65, in which John Paul II calls for integral formation including human, spiritual, and intellectual formation.

ethical reasoning, in various organizations toward a culture of harmonious development.[56]

Therefore, the richness of faith, life, motivated creativity, and the work of Gordon Willard Allport are the starting points for my reflections on maturity and the essence of self-formation. His work and preserved speeches, as well as the environmental conditions in which he worked, make it possible to understand the mainstream culture of the first half of the twentieth century. The examined socio-cultural hypothesis is the contextual study of the first chapter, determining anthropology of moral self. The anthropology of becoming is also the starting point for further reflections on Allport's pioneering theory of "evolving" or personal "becoming" grounded in personalism, social ethics, and human experiences. According K. Jeżyna, the essence of self-formation is participation in truth and love, which shapes the fundamental vision of man seen always in relation to God.[57] Integral formation involves both the spiritual and the material and requires in-depth assessment vis-à-vis the family, the basic structure of the People of God. Moral formation, involving as it does the tasks of education and formation, exercises its moral and normative rights within the contemporary community.[58] So, within its mission, the human formation of youngsters is naturally assigned to the family. And this core neuralgic structure becomes a societal mission.[59] The Christian family is the "domestic Church,"[60] which "Sacramentalizes" family life locally and universally.[61]

Chapter II presents the essence of the human becoming as a continual process. Man, as the subject and goal of this process in Allport's realistic personality theory, creates a mature attitude capable of meeting the lifelong commitment. Later, I will define the purpose of self-formation as an important dimension of the moral development within the personality, the relationship between faith and mature motivation, and the external and internal qualities people acquire at various stages of personal growth. At the end of the first part of this section, I will present a hypothesis that the

---

[56] Cf. M. Braun-Gałkowska. *Środowiso wychowawcze: dom, szoła, grupa rówieśnicza, parafia* IN: *Katecheza w szkole.* Red J. Krucina. Wrocław: Kuria Metropolitalna Wrocławika 1992 p. 57.

[57] Cf. K. Jeżyna. *Moralne przesłanie nowej ewangelizacji. Wezwanie do odnowy Kościoła i świata.* Lublin: Wydawnictwo KUL 2002 p. 329.

[58] Cf. I. Mroczkowski. *Odpowiedzialność świeckich za odnowę Kościoła w Polsce* IN: *Ewangelizacja w tajemnicy i misji Kościoła. Program duszpasterski na rok 1994/1995.* Katowice: Wydział Duszpasterstwa Kurii Metropolitalnej 1994 p. 281.

[59] S. Dziekoński. *Formacja chrześcijańska dziecka w rodzinie w nauczaniu Kościoła od Leona XIII do Jana Pawła II.* Warszawa: Wydawnictwo Uniwersytetu K; S. Wyszyńskiego 2006 p. 66.

[60] Ibid p. 182–196. Cf. p. LG p. 11.

[61] Ibid p. 444–544.

acquisition of moral qualities attests to stronger person's values and leads to the successful self-formation of a child in healthy environment.

Second Chapter also presents the core values of humanity from which the continuous process of formation takes root. Man, as the subject who has a purpose, builds a mature attitude that makes him capable of facing life's challenges. In a later section, I define self-formation as a specific purpose and necessary moral dimension of personality development. There, we will find a platform for integral formation of the individual. Analyzing internal and external personality traits allows us to emphasize the virtues that a person acquires at various stages of personal growth. We will then evaluate the hypothesis that one's personal becoming is partly the result of environmental influences and self-formation in a broader context. We will consider the essential tasks, roles, and objectives others have on lifelong self-formation. Included are the gift of life and the fruit of love at the early *stage of incorporating needs* to highlight how relationships form partnerships. Heteronomy of youth leads to the *interpersonal stage* as the basis for practical formation described by proven adage, "What shell soaked in his youth, this smacks of old age."

The next section provides an analysis of the educational process, with an emphasis on the formation of references within mature personality.[62] We will look at the education process through the prism of developmental stages as interpreted by Kegan, Piaget, and other theorists including the contributions of the long cultural tradition of the Church. Because the community of believers shape models for the family and school environments, it is important to recall here Vatican II's Declaration on Christian Education, *Gravissimum Educationis,* the apostolic exhortations, *Familiaris Consortio* and *Catechesi Tradendae.* These documents underline that responsible parents, schools, and Sacramental life complemented by catechesis provide grounds for good social formation, for they generally shape the mature social personality of the individual.[63] Detailed analysis of different stages of human development will show the process of moral personality growth respectively conditioned by externalized or internalized

---

[62] The educational process of self-formation contains educational action but is also influenced by circumstances and educational incentives that favor the integral development of individual. Cf. A. Gurycka. *Struktura i dynamika procesu wychowawczego. Analiza psychologiczna.* Warszawa: PWN 1979 p. 33.

[63] The task of education springs from the most original vocation of spouses to participate in God's creative activity by begetting in love. Parents, because they gave life to children, in the highest degree, are required to raise their offspring and therefore must be considered as being the first teachers of their children (FC 36 p. 67).

attitudes.[64] Allport's intrinsic–extrinsic scale tools will aid the diagnosis of maturity and well-internalized conduct.[65]

Chapter III, as listed in the theological-personalist perspective, will attempt to answer the question of how to achieve the objectives of moral self-formation supported by healthy motivation and interaction. The second part of the chapter takes on dignified interactions with pupils. When asked what formation will raise man's capability of self-control, the answer lies in the process of acquiring a sustainable conscience and meaningful choices made in accordance with his directives. Pastoral and Sacramental interaction within the Church, says John Paul II, "insists on the same demeanor and ethical actions that allow working together in mutual respect."[66]

The Church, among many influential groups shaping mature development, calls for a new evangelization in the *Letter to the Youth of the World*. Based on available studies, the Christian community brings the issue of self-formation to higher education, whereas elementary influence takes place in the family. Christian faith has always been a great influence on the family in the self-formation of its members in that it calls them to take the exemplary road rather than "owning" anyone. So, the *domestic church* as a socializing agency also propagates a basic community of personality formation. A family's religiosity is always been strengthened under the influence of Christian culture within the Church.[67]

The third chapter will include a biogenic analysis of the process of individual development. The first paragraph specifies the biogenic traits which allow favorable moral formation. On the one hand, there are heritability factors associated with the socialization process; on the other hand, moral socialization through Christian culture forms wisdom, good will, imagination, and perception—in a word, the responsible maturity needed to properly shape the family, peer groups, schools, and the mass media.[68] The next section considers the "whole man not only with his natural attributes, but also supernatural and eternal." Not to be overlooked, therefore, are the

---

[64] Allport's intrinsic/extrinsic valuation fits well with the Christian way of life and internal cleansing leading to personal integration. In this process, man's external conduct, actions, and morals comply with his desire to implement what he believes and professes. Cf. A. Cencini, A. Manenti. *Psychologia a formacja. Strutura i dynamika.* Kraków: Wydawnictwo WAM 2002 p. 315.

[65] G. W. Allport. *The Nature of Prejudice.* Reading: Perseus Publishing 1979 p. 14–15.

[66] K. Wojtyła. *Rodzina jako communio personarum.* AK 66: 1974 T. 83 p. 353.

[67] Jan Paweł II. Konstytucja Apostolska Ojca Świętego. *O uniwersytetach katolickich Ex corde Ecclesiae.* OsRomPol 11: 1990 no 10–II p. 8. A Catholic School teacher, especially, should express his Catholic identity by setting forth the character of his catholic mission.

[68] M. Dziewiecki. *Cielesność, płciowość, seksualność.* Kielce: Wydawnictwo "Jedność" 2000 p. 2–25.

supernatural factors in human formation, above all the grace of God, but also liturgical formation, which focuses on the person of Christ in our midst.

In Chapter IV, I discuss mature emotional and intellectual formation within the influence of religion (cognitive, volitivity, and emotional dimensions). Next, I try to verify the hypothesis contained in the question: can a mature personality be formed without the help of a healthy environment and sound religious principles? I am convinced: ethical principles are essential to the acquisition of healthy personality characteristics. I subsequently present the justified characteristics of mature behavior as distinguished by Allport. Therefore, mature personality is someone who knows his physicality. He has balanced emotionally and at the same time expresses his greater capacity in loving and responsibility.

Analyzed self-formation presents an internal road map for acquiring values in the process of becoming mature. I will highlight the cross-disciplinary analysis of emotional responsibility, which is an integral activity in the process of everyday maturation. I then discuss formation in terms of intellectual maturity. Analysis of social learning leads to understanding its significant impact on the process of the intellectual education of youth. Socially self-gained knowledge speeds up the process of accepting rules and eliminates reactions to traditional learning. In the third paragraph, I portray internal self-formation as a free, mature desire to develop in the context of social ethics. Achieved through social learning, self-discipline is a positive reaction to the negative phenomena such as ignorance. It is a result of the dynamism of self-evolving through educational personalization.[69]

The last section highlights the integrative role of mature religion. Well-interiorized religious faith inspires children, adolescents, and adults to extend their personalities in the directions of interpersonal relationships with others and thus improves the level of humanity in general. I will then point out aspects of mature and immature emotionality. The emotionally stable man is free of erratic behavior, which enables him to establish and maintain warm interpersonal relationships. An important criterion of such maturity is the coupling of emotional and intellectual functioning. The conclusion will develop the substantive argument that the religious and spiritual dimension is the chief milieu for personal becoming. Let us hope that self-formation will better integrate people with the task of eliminating prejudice.[70]

---

[69] EG p. 150.

[70] "Language labels play an important part in category formation, and often lead to emotional attitudes even before the idea-system itself is formed. We have suggested that three roughly chronological stages can be distinguished in the formation of prejudiced attitudes: pre-generalization, total rejection, differentiation. It is not until adolescence that the child is able to handle ethnic categories in a culturally approved way, and only then that his prejudices can be said to be fashioned in the adult form." Allport. *The Nature of Prejudice* p. 312.

Christian self-formation results from searching out the Creator in man's life. In Christ, man gains knowledge of God and can overcome the prejudices accumulated by sin.[71] The case of moral self-formation in postmodern times is particularly important and timely. At the same time, it is important that the interdisciplinary anthropological study of becoming involves everyone who is concerned with human progress. Multifaceted scientific interaction is necessary to form an integrated personality free of hostile traits.[72] There are new models for self-formation, which highlight on immature human behavior that increases societal disorder and pathologies. Through the prism of scientific analysis, we will see the foundations of ethical self-formation in forming a moral man.

The aim of this study is the application of self-formation to the life of a student. A Christian personality is linked with the person of Christ, for Christ and the Christian life are one in the new self: "The old self, of sin and the world, is contrasted with the new self in Christ" (Col. 3:9–10). This synthesized summary will show the accurate role of moral self-formation in shaping personal growth through healthy, mature motivation that decodes many signs of religious immaturity of modern man.[73]

This study's methodology is based on an analysis of natural law principles in reference to the achievements of the empirical sciences, including psychology and the anthropology of becoming. The personology method is mutually correlated to self-formation in an anthropological context.[74] It is therefore possible to defend the necessity of self-growth "for all intellectually rational people."[75] The objective is nothing more than finding truth for the betterment of society.[76] The reference to self-formation articulates the co-forming cultures of school, family, and community. Pope Benedict XVI emphasizes that Christian initiation comprises, primarily, the discovery of the origins of human beings by adoption through the grace of baptism.[77] "Input" into the mystery of baptism is a life-giving, which forms hope and disposes us to the virtue of charity, or love. Christian Sacramental and aretological formation allows us to experience the love of God and thus tends to change us for the better, says Benedict, which makes things happen

---

[71] A. Derdziuk. *Teologia moralna w służbie wiary Kościoła.* Lublin: Wyd KUL 2010 p. 101.
[72] The principles of Christian education should be duly completed with new achievements of healthy psychology and pedagogy. Cf. DFK p.11.
[73] KDK p. 4, KDK p. 21.
[74] Cf. D. Tracey. *The Foundations of Practical Theology* IN: *Practical Theology.* Red. D. S. Browning. San Francisco: Harper & Row Publishers 1983 p. 62.
[75] Ibid p. 67.
[76] Ibid p. 68
[77] SS p. 2.

and is a life-changing experience.[78] My assumption is that moral self-formation should be like post-baptismal catechesis, which incorporates every loving person into the community of faith. I find methodological help in the auxiliary sciences, especially Allport's personal psychology or "personology." An essential task therefore exists in synthesizing the post-Vatican II attention to the personalist dimension of theological and moral studies, which will be highlighted for people undertaking self-formation. My intention is to recognize and apply a sufficient measure not only of universal principles but also of the achievements of the secular sciences—especially personalistic psychology and the anthropology of becoming—in order to lead the faithful to a cleaner and more mature life of faith. An appropriate method of growth also involves drawing conclusions. It consists in discovering the truth about man arising from man's uniqueness and the responsibility for his potential future grounded in the values of supreme Truth. As R. Gula says, the role in the self-formation of moral instinct strengthens the virtue that cultivates a life of a disciple of Christ.[79]

In response to negative trends in postmodernity, self-formation needs to be well-rooted in family life. Aristotle's *Nicomachean Ethics* stresses that the basic function of the family—the elementary social unit comprising procreation and the formative upbringing of offspring—gives children necessary ethical socialization. As Aristotle eloquently said, normative discipline and morality is less a science than an art; hence, moral people are not those who only talk but never do any good.[80] So, a correct methodology of becoming involves finding self-formative clues (who a man is and who he should be) in our contemporary times. Present research defines the well-integrated person and how interpersonal relationships can lead to better formation. In this study, much attention will be paid to the self as the primary subject of moral formation. This study draws on American literature relative to utilitarian, humanistic, social, and loyalty ethics of the individual in the context of personal growth. So, the search centers on an integral, realistic theory of man that interrelates human growth.

It should be noted that Allport's anthropology of becoming has been translated into many languages, but it is difficult to find new formative approaches to it these days. So far, there has been no analysis of the scientific achievements showing maturity as the element of personal Christian journey. The literature cited herein comes from Allport himself and from formative materials available at Harvard and at libraries elsewhere. This analysis will be

---

[78] KDK p. 62. Cf. J. Majka. *Metodologia nauk teologicznych*. Wrocław: Wrocławska Księgarnia Archidiecezjalna 1981 p. 284–312.

[79] R. Gula. *Making Disciples: A Handbook of Christian Moral Formation*. IN: "Theological Studies" 60: 1999 no. 2 p. 394.

[80] Aristotle. *Nicomachean Ethics*. Trans. T. Irwin. Indianapolis: Hacett 1999 p. 22. "For no one has the least prospect of becoming good from failing to do them." (T. II 3. 1105 b)

focused also on the comparative-synthetic studies of sources, through the prism of contemporary theories of learning and becoming. The method in the context of self-actualization and personality formation is therefore multifaceted.[81] Consequently, through the adoption of these methodological assumptions, I will discuss self-formation and the anthropology of becoming in four complementary chapters. In addition, my ecumenical dialogue will be conducted from an anthropological theology perspective, as well as auxiliary sciences. This multifaceted approach will shed light on the question of what constitutes the essence of human self-formation, inspired by my research on mature personality development.

---

[81] "*Personality* is so complex a thing that every legitimate method must be employed in its study." G. W. Allport. *Personality: A Psychological Interpretation*. New York: H. Holt and Company 1937 p. 370. In the taken-their formation of mature personality, there is a need to apply anthropology, pedagogy, moral theology, and many other disciplines.

CHAPTER 1

The life and work of G. W. Allport

G. W. Allport's lifetime encompassed two world wars, both of which were marked by the highest levels of human cruelty and social injustice. He is considered to be one of the most cherished personalists whose research led to new discoveries in human development. The experience of war and the rivalry between deadly sociopolitical systems precipitated a military arms race during his lifetime, and the boom in military technology, associated with sociocultural change, led to the urbanization and industrialization of the United States. Internal growth, however, lagged behind technological progress. Human development did not come easily amid progressive depersonalization, secularization, and conflicts. [82] Rapid change and technological revolution outpaced human integration, and consequently, post-war social sciences centered on the need to heal and better integration of human life. Allport saw an urgent need for research in the field of personology, which he knew, in its method of peaceful resolution, could deepen knowledge of the human person. Research on family formation at Harvard University confirmed his belief in the necessity of future personality tests that could integrate man.

Allport's home environment had enormous influence on the formation of his character, freedom, and ability to choose healthy development that expressed patriotism, volunteerism, and a work ethic. Allport focused on reducing the causes of human depravity such as social injustice, prejudice, and discrimination. He reached a healthy outlook on life, mature personality, and resolutions to become a "transparent" person. So, his life and work come from seeking a deeper quality of life made possible only by means of responsible behavior in attaining a well-integrated mature personality.

A. Sociocultural factors of the USA in the early twentieth century

---

[82] "The present century, in spite of its unexampled inventiveness, has been the bloodiest century on record concerning international, civil and criminal violence. Secularization (…) led humanity to forget the Commandments of Moses, the ethics of Confucius, the self-discipline, and the vision of Christian Brotherhood. (…) Many, perhaps most inhabitants of the earth would recognize 'Love thy neighbor as thyself' as a worthy imperative." Allport, *Personality and Social Encounter,* p. 347.

Socio-cultural conditions in the United States in the first half of the twentieth century resulted from an inadequate human vision obsessed with a notion of "freedom" that absolutizes personal liberty and corrodes human morality. Often, leaders of society moving away from the Decalogue fostered discrimination and a vision of man without God,[83] a vision that also diminished knowledge of *man*. Material prosperity fostered a reductionism with limited trust in natural law and little reference to the transcendent or to God. The early twentieth century was a time a great self-confidence in creating a fairer society by means of democratization, religious freedom, and liberalization of the law: to be an American meant to live a "free" life fueled by maximized profits. The vision of an arbitrary and individualistic life without God concerned the popes: in fact, Leo XIII condemned it in his Apostolic Letter, *Testem benevolentiae*.[84]

The noticeable decline of Christian morality in the early twentieth century gave rise to individual abuse of freedom on the part of many Americans. Libertinism contributed to more egoistic relationships unencumbered by the moral demands of religion. Authoritarianism cultivated by one religious group against another, often grounded in totalistic truth-claims, was not conducive to a common language of dialogue and social tolerance. Uncertainty, at times born of financial insecurity, accompanied skepticism about higher moral values. Material pursuit and increasing demand for comfort forced children at an early age to work very hard both in urban and rural areas. Differences in religion between parents made it more difficult to resolve tensions in poor families. Ethnic, linguistic, and religious differences also put barriers between teachers and students. At the same time, immigrants were coming to the United States in greater numbers than ever before due to pending industrialization. World War I brought America leadership, substantial influence in the world, and a significant demographic increase. Larger cities and industrial districts expanded their workload because of greater numbers of people arriving from different countries and cultures. The ravages of war and impoverishment in Europe intensified labor immigration to the United States as people sought a better life.

Shortly after the war, a new wave of white nationalism arose, targeting immigrants (particularly from southern Europe) and black people. Racism against people of color took different forms, such as the activities of the Ku Klux Klan in Indiana and the South. S. Gaines claims that extremism

---

[83] Cf. J Ellis. *The Life of James Cardinal Gibbons*. Westminster: Christian Classics 1987 p. 147–148.
[84] Cf. Ch. Curran. *Catholic Moral Theology in the United States: A History*. Washington DC: Georgetown University Press 2008 p. 35.

coincided with immigration and the processes of urbanization and industrialization in rapidly growing cities like Chicago.[85] S. Gaines also notes that those antisocial reservoirs of hatred prompted scientific research and independent, detailed study of these problems. Nevertheless, contemporary psychology did not have a positive influence on human behavior and pathology. Thus, the social sciences operating by current anthropological knowledge have not met the tasks of overcoming prejudice and the deformation of human attitudes[86]

Since the beginning of the twentieth century, there was a notable wave of discrimination. This was promoted by successive governments of the United States that favored northern European immigrants over people from southern and eastern Europe. The Immigration Act of 1924 reviled the latter as lower-rank immigrants. Unjust civil law deprived certain classes of their fundamental personal and moral rights. The sociocultural study of F. Pincus shows that a new kind of discrimination became evident in the less-industrialized districts that were inhabited mostly by immigrants and the poor. [87] The same author's research statistics show that prejudice and discrimination are still a serious problem. The first strong wave of prejudice appealed to alleged biological racial differences among different communities. Certain groups were rejected for their way of life, which was different from that of other communities.[88]

Perhaps it is a clash of values that cannot be imposed by others. In the early twentieth century, despite the introduction of a variety of educational programs, the problem of inequality and injustice had not been remedied. Unfair wages and promotions based on racial and economic discrimination were commonplace. Allport and other progressive thinkers aimed to counter the forces of prejudice, inequality, bigotry, and authoritarianism.[89] Allport traced the roots of inequality and resolved it in his life by a self-formative approach and strong criticism of his discriminative

---

[85] "The plea of immigration was reached in the decade preceding the World War when in the years (…) 1913 and 1914, more than a million immigrants landed each year." p. 207. R. Garis. *Immigration Restriction: A Study of the Opposition to and Regulation of Immigration into the United States.* New York: Macmillan 1927.

[86] Cf. S. Gaines. "Two social psychologies of prejudice," Gordon W. Allport, W.E.B. Du Bois, and the legacy of Booker T. Washington. JBP 20:1994 no. 1 p. 21.

[87] Cf. Ibid p. 192.

[88] Cf. Ibid p. 1.

[89] "My plea, therefore, is that we avoid authoritarianism, that we (…) come to evaluate our science rather by its success in enhancing—above the levels achieved by common sense—our powers of predicting, understanding, and controlling human action. As an aid to progress, I have tried especially to strengthen the case for research on complex patterns of human mental organization, frames of reference, the subject's point of view, and the act of understanding." p. 28. G. Allport. *The Psychologist's Frame of Reference.* PsB: 37: 1940 no. 1 p. 28.

group affiliation. His anthropological approach suggests a positive way of addressing issues of injustice and inequality.

Now, it is well-known that social discontent seen in prejudice results from authoritarian behavior, injustice, and human rights and dignity violations. For this reason, the social, anthropological, and theological sciences have cooperatively striven to protect humanity against this negative antisocial phenomenon that leads to dysfunction and even war. Noticeable is a dependent pattern: when principles and ethics have little impact on everyday life, the reductionist sociocultural phenomenon deepens prejudices.[90]

In the first half of the twentieth century, on the grounds of unjust civil law, churches and local communities were unable to resolve the problems of segregation and discrimination. Despite the progress of the sciences, many non-profit civic and church organizations could not cope with extreme forms of prejudice, social injustice, and exploitation of the poor. Particularly egregious was authoritarianism among different faith communities. Many religious leaders (according to the social sciences) claimed exclusive possession of the truth about God and man—an attitude that did not dispose them favorably to accepting criticism or embarking on the path of ecumenism and religious tolerance.[91] Prejudices, ill will, and immaturity can blind a seemingly religious person to the evils of racial segregation, discrimination, and the denial of natural rights to others. The self-formative anthropology of becoming, consistent with God's truth relative to humility, justice, and mercy, can repair this by instilling respect for others and a desire to help them overcome feelings of rejection and discouragement.

In smaller sociocultural environments, we see segregation in neighborhoods and schools both culturally and racially as well as between sexes. These are based more on years of human deformation than on the law. Acts of discrimination that went "unnoticed" in previous years became unacceptable because of proper upbringing and integral self-formation. Overcoming social inequalities under the influence of healthy feminist movements expanded the place of women in society. The 19th Amendment to the U.S. Constitution gave women the right to vote for the first time, effectively placing them on legal parity with men.[92]

---

[90] "Prejudice is ultimately a problem of personality formation and development; no two cases of discrimination are precisely the same. No individual would mirror his group's attitude unless he had a personal need, or personal habit, that leads him to do so." Allport. *The Nature of Prejudice* p. 41.

[91] Cf. Allport. *The Individual and His Religion* p. 65.

[92] L. Banaszak. *Why Movements Succeed or Fail: Opportunity, Culture, and the Struggle for Woman Suffrage*. Princeton: Princeton University Press 1996 p. 5–6.

Sociocultural transformation, with regard to ethics in American society, was furthered by radio communications. Reginald Fessenden's radio transmission on Christmas Eve of 1906 was the world's first wireless broadcast and a "breakthrough" for good winning over evil. Americans first heard objective truth through the media news in 1920. Subsequent years brought more broadcasting development, allowing regular radio entertainment and cultural transmission. However, with new abilities in communication from great distances, the educated man would initiate faster progress and the integrative development of civilization and culture. Mass radio access was an informational aspect of improved family life, noticeably leading to better co-education. National media access contributed to the popularization of proper cultural life in the ballroom dance, new Charleston, and jazz music. Similarly, cinematography during the so-called "Golden Age of Hollywood" often presented good characters prevailing over bad ones.

Nevertheless, governmental financial incompetence resulted in the American stock market crash of 1929, and economic collapse and massive unemployment led to the Great Depression of the 1930s. The difficult period of economic downturn favored prohibition and glorification of criminal personalities and debauched celebrities. In the early years of the 1940s, the financial situation considerably improved due to the development of the fashion industry. So much did American fashion trends improve that the "fashion center" of the world moved from Paris to New York. Quick development continued but not for long, as world peace gave way to the next, even more brutal world war. The Japanese attack on the American naval base at Pearl Harbor on December 7, 1941, provoked America's entry into the Second World War on the side of the allied nations against the Axis powers Germany, Italy, and Japan. Naturally, radio was used for war propaganda to promote successes in the battlefield. And the media then did not hesitate to broadcast violent images of enemy's brutality.[93]

The brutality of the world wars is perceived as a primitive form of social and personal destabilization. Americans dropped the first atomic bomb on the cities of Hiroshima and Nagasaki to force the Japanese to surrender and bring an end to World War II. Mass-destruction technology caused the loss of about 90,000 inhabitants of Hiroshima, and three days later, 50–70 thousand inhabitants of Nagasaki. Any war brings great social and personal

---

[93] "The present century, in spite of its unexampled inventiveness, has been the bloodiest century on record regarding international, civil and criminal violence. Secularization (...), led humanity to forget the Commandments of Moses, the ethics of Confucius, the self-discipline, and the vision of Christian Brotherhood (...). Many, perhaps most inhabitants of the earth would recognize 'Love thy neighbor as thyself' as a worthy imperative." Allport. *Personality and Social Encounter* p. 347.

devastation to humanity and always involves high degrees of prejudice bias.[94] The twentieth century was the bloodiest in human history. From the perspective of anthropological theology, it was the evilest century thus far: the age of the death culture, in which 180 million were killed, owing to the influence of extreme and irrational visions of man. Materialistic ideologies, including anti-Christian anthropologies, greatly expanded prejudice.[95]

The aftermath of human devastation became the hotbed of social conflict in the 1950s. Unjust laws codified segregation of the American population in the southern states, restricting people of color and other "lesser" citizens to designated places in public transportation, restaurants, and schools.[96] Serious social conflicts arose with regard to race and sex.

Modernization and inventions in the early twentieth century paved the way for technological progress while reducing respect for human rights.[97] In the 1960s, Americans could witness, via television, the brutality of war in Indochina. Bigger TV audiences meant bigger profits for media conglomerates, which transmitted violent images against human dignity including war crimes against innocent civilians. It is interesting that the development of visual techniques was not sufficiently utilized in bringing relief to people in their plight. In response to glaring social injustice, many social activists and movements emerged, pressing government for social change in an egalitarian direction.[98]

Postmodern liberalization in the twentieth century affected much the epistemic development of the core unit of society: the family. Postmodernists privilege private judgment in determining truth or falsehood. Absolute individual freedom is often directed against the well-being of families and is unmotivated by concern for its core structure but rather by financial profit.[99] Thus, the traditional role of father and mother in bringing up children became restricted by government policies. Radical individualism triggered dependence on advertised fashion trends and liberal media. Life fragmentation disallowed the valuable implementation of mature principles

---

[94] "While there may be such things as 'just wars,' in the sense that threats to one's values are genuine and must be resisted, yet war always entails some degree of prejudice." Cf. Allport. *The Nature of Prejudice* p. 27.

[95] Cf. I. C. Pogonowski. *Poland: An Illustrated History*. NY: Hippocrene Books 2000 p. 215.

[96] "United States Supreme Court ruled, in May 1954, that segregation in the nation's public schools is unconstitutional. Its directive of May 1955 ordered that desegregation should be instituted 'with all deliberate speed.'" Allport. *The Nature of Prejudice* p. 21.

[97] Allport. *The Individual and His Religion* p. 70.

[98] Cf. F. Pincus. *Race and Ethnic Conflict: Contending Views on Prejudice, Discrimination, and Ethnoviolence* p. 2.

[99] Cf. Allport. *The Individual and His Religion* p. 70.

in the family and by the family. Personal convenience and the ideology of the autonomous self, in opposition to the will of the Creator and the natural law, fueled the pathology of killing unborn children. The same ideology, despite the growth of the US economy, also caused harm to the military industry through the liberalization of social and political life after the victories of the two world wars.[100]

Liberal state legislation, in the form of democratic constitutions, laws, and manifestos, exclude reference to God, the Decalogue, or any other moral principles. The Church has criticized social experimentation by which the rich become richer by means of repeated injustices against the poor.[101] Egoistic materialism rejects any form of equitable distribution of wealth that God bestowed upon humanity. The Magisterium of the Church makes it clear that evil does not cease to be evil just because it is a social activity willed by a democratic majority. Failure to apply important ethical values opens the door to destructive behavior, leading to human indifference. By promoting the concept of human indifference, majority officials elected atheistic solutions, opposing obligation to the moral life of the community. Philosopher Jacques Maritain foresaw the results of excessive liberalization of ethical standards and principles. He warned against the agony of the materialistic world resulting from the expansion of atheism, with its reductionist view of the human person. As a result, the "reduced" person departs from the ethical standards in community life.

Today, the influence of lobbyists on human beings is more intense than ever. The battle for basic human rights is now the exclusive domain of the electoral vote, where American federalism in core questions of right and wrong remains silent.[102] And fundamental questions of right and wrong may not be resolved in voter opinions only. Even in the 1950s, many Americans were unaware of the immoral hazard of destructive prejudice. Established prejudice stems from injustice and severe problems in the life of the individual and society. Widespread contention about a human person and human values creates a multitude of opinions based on many stereotypes. Such unfair stereotypes passed in circles of friends, and workplaces segregated American society even more. General attitudes about the marginalized were often authorized in the circles of power, educational

---

[100] Cf. Ibid p. 70.

[101] Cf. Paul VI states: "If today's technical civilization is not regulated by any plan, the inequalities of the peoples as regards the growth of material goods will inevitably not only diminish but rather increase: and therefore the progress of the richer nations will be faster." p. 8.

[102] Cf. A. Hendrickson. "The Survival of Moral Federalism." *Public Interest* 2: 2002 no. 148 p. 96.

institutions, media, and even some churches. Conservative and liberal attitudes presented radically different stances on social inequality.[103]

In the face of social injustice, many ethnic groups became helpless and alienated for want of proper ethical norms and patterns of behavior. At the same time, lack of social justice led liberalized culture to abuse of human freedom. Consequently, the heart of such liberalism allowed Americans every possible free will choice. Because liberal democracy tends to individualize lifestyle, the arbitrariness of conscience has been ruled out to be reactive in pursuit of personal rights, often at the expense of the public good. Increasing liberalization weakened the process of true unification among peoples, hurting the core values of family and social ties. The unjust law—mainly expressed in free elections, the right to free media, excessive sexual freedom, and religious freedom—was restricted only to participants in the legislative process who enjoyed protection from the state interfering with their privacy and was preparing the ground for the legalization of abortion. This "absolutizing" of individual freedom generated the collapse of Western civilization. The experience of the twentieth century promoting absolute freedom brought new forms of human enslavement in the breaking of interpersonal norms. Change of residence associated with the migration of people in search of better living conditions contributed to the development of the nuclear community. That dislocation and search of better living intensified a peculiar division among ethnic and religious groups. Jews, like other ethnic groups, isolated themselves in clubs and associations but created gender divisions within their groups. Thus, they were more inclined to segregate from other.[104] Many social life organizations have such a generic nature that they did not grasp diversity. The diversity of social life included women who wanted to be independent from the influence of men's clusters. However, children's playgrounds fostered neighborly relationships and emerging friendships. For example, working class Irish-American women organized in Rosary sodalities or altar server groups.[105]

Authentic religious life also constituted an integrative force among new American suburban neighborhoods. Churches were built not only for worship but also for socialization, which provided more reasons for attendance at church services and affiliation within the church.[106]

Churches through the religious services promoted higher culture. This could be a pioneering element of socialization assimilating new

---

[103] Cf. F. Pincus. *Race and Ethnic Conflict: Contending Views on Prejudice, Discrimination, and Ethnoviolence* p. 6.
[104] Cf. M. Clapton. *Social Change and Urban Growth in England and the USA*. New York: Berg 2003 p. 143.
[105] Cf. Ibid p. 151.
[106] Cf. Ibid p. 152.

immigrants especially of Italian origin, northern Europe and then coming from Eastern and Jewish heritage. During the 1950s and '60s new cities saw similar patterns of growth. With the increase of neighborhood friendship taking various forms of cooperation and association, many were inspired to campaign for better communication. In contrast, large corporations virtually failed to make appropriate transitions in social aspects of enculturation. However, one could expect that the peaceful way of neighbor life in non-urban settlements would not require any special invasions, revolutions or forms of intervention for better American alliance. Neighborhood watch organizers prevented destructive patterns of violence. Neighborly cooperation enabled a spirit of volunteerism, philanthropy and participation in social activities. All these factors had a rather positive influence on the families of the settlements. One can easily argue that healthy living of the smallest social organism cultivated a civilization of ethical standards to establish poor neighbors in truth and peace.[107] Common-sense solutions recognized for centuries were unfortunately rejected by contemporary liberal leading thinkers. Heavily secularized leaders of that period denied objective truth, and did not promote long-established patterns, thereby undermining the validity of normative understanding of truth as truth (i.e., the compliance and adequation of the mind with reality).[108] The effect of such utopian system is the rejection of normative truths and further outbreak of social injustice, combined with the "culture of death." Therefore, some areas of social life gradually lost ground on unquestioned moral keys, at the same time putting the individual from the standpoint of multiple choices, subjecting him to disintegration.

B. The social environments of G. W. Allport

Gordon Willard Allport was born on 11 November 1897 in Montezuma, Indiana. He was the youngest of four sons (his brothers being Harold, Floyd, and Fayette) of the Scottish country doctor John Edward (b. 1862) and Nellie Edith (Wise). Another biographer of Allport, D. Winter, describes Allport's father as a Presbyterian.[109] John Edward won medical training after combining a general medical practice with a range of businesses including the supervision of hospitals.[110] He turned his home into a makeshift hospital with patients and nurses residing there. Allport's mother Nellie (b.

---

[107] "Today we are faced with the preeminent fact that, if civilization is to survive we must cultivate the science of human relationship—the ability of all peoples, of all kinds, to live together and work together, in the same world, at peace." G. W. Allport. *Personality and Social Encounter: Scientific models and human morals.* Boston: Beacon Press 1960 p. 66.

[108] Cf. M. J. Adler. *The Time of Our Lives.* New York: Fordham U. Press 1996 p. 134.

[109] Cf. D. G. Winter. *Allport's life and Allport's psychology.* JP 65: 1997 no. 3 p. 723.

[110] Cf. A. Kazdin. *Encyclopedia of Psychology.* Oxford: University Press 2000 p. 223.

1862) had a powerful influence on the decent education of her children, she herself being reared in Methodism. Pursuing a teaching job brought up her children in high moral standards with her great emotional attachment.[111]

The Allport home fostered the "Protestant ethic" of hard work, honesty, and piety. Nellie's association with the Women's Christian Temperance Union (WCTU) influenced her commitment to teach children the values of service, morality, and respect for women. [112] Family sanctification centered on charity, as taught by Nellie. Gordon Allport had *savoir-vivre* and lived a deep faith rooted in Scotch family tradition. From an early age, his family built strong family ties with neighbors. The attitude of cooperation among family members formed important, above average virtues. And growing up in Cleveland's house of hard work ethics with a commitment to the gospel bore good fruits.[113]

Older brother Floyd studied at Harvard and fascinated the younger one in social science. Encouraged by his brother, Gordon arrived at school in 1915, shortly before the beginning of the academic year. To the family's great astonishment, he passed the entrance exams successfully, albeit with considerable difficulty. Floyd had a bold personality, which taught Gordon to be more scientifically independent. So outside of two books in social psychology, Floyd did not influence Gordon's publications. Yet, the emotional influence of mother and older siblings was visible in his life. Instilled in his childhood with trust in God and a desire to serve God's will, Gordon the collegian was well-equipped to structure and assimilate that integral knowledge. In one sense, he was quiet but quite interested in science, all the while admiring the personality of his older brothers. In another sense, his brothers showed him their "professional integrity" and much criticism, which enlarged his personality and gave him a wide range of experiences. He applied himself punctually to each subject of study. His development was also shaped by the principles of the Scottish tradition, which promoted the habit of letting nothing go to waste.[114]

---

[111] Cf. His father, a physician and entrepreneur, combined his general medical practice with a variety of business endeavors (e.g., founding a cooperative drug company, building and renting apartments, and the construction and supervision of hospitals). His mother, who had been a schoolteacher, was a devout Methodist. The Allport home was remembered as a "peaceful but sheltered place with kindness exhibited on every hand." Cf. Woźniak. *Floyd Henry Allport and the Social Psychology* p. 5.

[112] Cf. B. F. Skinner. *G. W. Allport*. IN: *A History of Psychology in Autobiography*. Red E. Boring & G. Lindsey. New York: Appleton-Century-Crofts 1967[5] p. 4.

[113] Cf. L. A. Hjelle. *Personality Theories: Basic Assumptions, Research and Applications*. New York: McGraw-Hill Boo Company 1992 p. 172 (coauthor D. J. Ziegler).

[114] N. Sheehy. *Fifty Key Thinkers in Psychology*. London: Routledge 2004 p. 3.

Allport was not very attached to money. He subscribed to a kind of Aristotelian ethic of moderation by which his pursuit of success and prosperity was guided by the Golden Rule and optimum balance for personal happiness. Allport applied this principle in his study of mature personality. He entrusted material gains and tax returns to the care of his secretary, Eleanor Sprague. Deeming waste a great evil, he was tormented by an inability to harvest blueberries in abundance on his Maine property. For this purpose, he agreed with his neighboring farmers that they would sell and collect crops for him. Although the costs always exceeded the value of sold berries, his friend, Professor Stouffer, jokingly called him "the blueberries king." Humor and strict Presbyterian ethics shaped his attitude of hard work. In this atmosphere of ethical principles, Allport lived according to moral codes. In part, his development can be explained by the influence of duty and devoted trust in science in his life, which was a result of his confidence in reason and ethical obligation.[115]

From an early age, he perfected his ethical responsibility for others, never pretending to be someone he was not.[116] He never saw himself as being better than anyone else. Even in high school, he supported himself, editing the school newspaper (he was editor-in-chief). His first major success occurred when he graduated from Glenville High School as salutatorian. Academic excellence earned him a scholarship to Harvard University, where he studied economics, social ethics, and psychology.[117]

The values he acquired in the culture of his Protestant home were much different from those he experienced at university. His main difficulties emerged in confrontation with libertine students.[118] Despite hardships, he was able to graduate with a bachelor's degree in economics and philosophy. But the significant influence professors Hugo Münsterberg, Edwin Holt, Leonard Troland, Walter Dearborn, Ernest Southard, and Herbert Langfield inspired him to purse the field of humanistic psychology.[119] Gordon's interest

---

Allport's early sense of duty was rooted in the "I should" structure of his family's values, which underpinned his normative ethics of duty. Kant's theory of duty was more of axiological or teleological in terms of ethics rather than of value theory. The concept of Kant's duty seems to be axiologically "blind" because it is insufficiently morally internalized. (P. Blosser. *Scheler's Critique of Kant's Ethics*. Athens, OH: Ohio University Press 1995 p. 125.)

[116] "The Allport family required its members to develop independence, responsibility, integrity, and sensitivity to the needs of others." Cf. G. A. Kimble. *Portraits of Pioneers in Psychology*. Washington: American Psychological Association. Washington 1998³ (Coauthor Michael C. Wertheimer) p. 123.

[117] Cf. D. Katz. *Portraits of Pioneers in Psychology*. Washington: *American Psychological Association* 1998 p. 125–128 (Coauthors B. T. Johnson, D. R. Nichols).

[118] Cf. R. I. Evans. *Gordon Allport: The Man and His Ideas*. New York: Dutton 1970 p. 15.

[119] "My first teacher was Hugo Münsterberg at Harvard. He was such a bad teacher, in the traditional sense, that he intrigued me, and I decided to go into psychology to

was human psychology relative to anthropology and social ethics. He was the first to offer a course on personality growth. He even used his knowledge in many charitable organizations, namely scouts and troubled teens in the Boston area, as well as aiding immigrants and foreign students in Phillips Brooke House.[120] Cooperating with the Peace Corps as a volunteer, Allport taught English and sociology at Robert College in Istanbul and in Greece, where he gained proficiency in Modern Greek. Of special impact on Allport's life was his meeting with Sigmund Freud, who changed his attitude toward psychoanalysis.[121]

---

find out what he was talking about. Since then I have never known what a good teacher or bad teacher really was because his influence was so great. He lectured with a heavy German accent and his text was often not too clear. I had some behavioristically inclined teachers, such as E. B. Holt and H. S. Langfield, who almost persuaded me while I was a student. But after receiving the Ph.D., I went to Germany where I encountered the Gestalt movement. It hadn't been known in this country at all before then." Evans. *Gordon Allport: The Man and His Ideas* p. 18.

[120] Cf. T. F. Pettigrew. "Gordon Willard Allport: A tribute." JSI.55:1999 no 3 p. 416–417.

[121] "*Gordon Willard Allport: A tribute.*" JSI.55:1999 no. 3 p. 416–417. "Not long after I finished college, I found myself in Vienna where Freud was not as renowned as he became later. At any rate, I wrote him a note announcing that I was in Vienna, and that he no doubt would be glad to know it. He was very courteous and sent me a hand-written note inviting me to his office at a stated time. So I went to the famous Burggasser office which was papered in red burlap and decorated with pictures of dreams.

"At exactly the appointed time, Freud opened the door of his inner office, invited me in smilingly, sat down, and said nothing. It suddenly occurred to me that it was up to me to have a reason for calling on him, but actually, I didn't have any. I was just curious. I fished around in my mind and came up with an event which occurred on the tramcar on the way to his office that I thought would interest him. There had been a little boy about four years old who apparently had already developed a dirt phobia. His mother was a Hausfrau, well starched and very prim, and the little boy would say he didn't want to sit there; it was dirty. He didn't want that man to sit next to him; he was dirty.

"And so it went throughout the whole trip. I thought this might interest Freud since the phobia seemed to be set so early in this case. He listened till I finished; then he fixed his very therapeutic eyes on me and said, 'And was that little boy you?' It honestly was not, but I felt guilty. At any rate, I managed to change the conversation. In thinking over the experience, it impressed me that Freud's tendency was to see pathological trends, and since most of the people who came to see him were patients, it was natural that he'd thin I was a patient and break down my defenses to get on with the business. He mistook my motives in this case.

"Had he said to himself that I was a brassy American youth imposing on his real nature and time, he would have been fairly correct. But to ascribe my motivation to unconscious motives as he did, in this case, was wrong. As I thought about the

Having completed his charity work, Allport returned to Harvard in 1921 to earn a master's degree in psychology. Only a year later, he wrote his doctoral dissertation, *An Experimental Study of the Traits of Personality: With Special Reference to the Problem of Social Diagnosis*. Herbert Langfield was its promoter, and William McDougall and James Ford were its reviewers.[122] His dissertation research highlights his dual interest in personology and social ethics, as he mentions in *Person in Psychology*: "Professor Ford offered me lectures on social ethics at Harvard at the beginning of 1924."[123] His social life in various university activities was priceless. Further research helped him get the Sheldon Traveling Scholarship, which enabled him to continue studying in Germany (1922–23)[124] as well at Cambridge University (1923–24).[125] After returning to Harvard, he taught social ethics from 1924 to 1926 and established Harvard's Department of Social Ethics.[126]

His courses on social ethics were occasionally preceded by morning discourse and ethical rhetoric in the Memorial Hall Chapel.[127] Allport's reference to social ethics was due, in part, to his research on the relationship

---

experience in subsequent years, it occurred to me that there might be a place for another type of theory to account for personality and motivation." Evans, *Gordon Allport* p. 3–5.

[122] Cf. J. S. Bowman. *The Cambridge Dictionary of American Biography*. Cambridge: University Press 1995 p. 13.

[123] "Prof. Ford offered me an instructorship in the social ethics at Harvard to begin in the fall of 1924." G. W. Allport. *The Person in Psychology*. Boston: Beacon Press 1968 p. 440.

[124] "One of my German teachers, Eduard Spranger, was the source for the Study of Values test that I devised in the American vein. The test was American, but the idea that there are six fundamental types of values or evaluations that man may hold or make was a German. These are perhaps my most influential teachers, but I have found a great deal of congeniality among my colleagues such as Rogers, Gardner Murphy, Kurt Lewin, and Professor Henoy Murray. I always felt they were supporting whatever line of development on my thinking too. I would call them first cousins of my thinking." Evans R. *Gordon Allport: The Man and His Ideas*. 1970 p. 18

[125] "In 1924, Gordon became a Harvard instructor in social ethics under Richard Clare Cabot. Two years later, he temporarily severed his connection with Harvard to accept an assistant professorship in psychology at Dartmouth. Yet even during his brief four years at Hanover, he returned repeatedly to Harvard to teach in summer school." T. F. Pettigrew, *Gordon Willard Allport: A tribute*. JSI 55: 1999 no. 3 p. 419.

[126] "My earliest years of teaching were in the Department of Social Ethics at Harvard University. This in part explains my interests in applying psychological principles and methods." Allport *Personality and Social Encounter* p. 271.

[127] "Gordon occasionally spoke briefly at morning chapel in Memorial Church. But a corrective note for the record is in order here. He was an Episcopalian who gave several famous lectures at divinity schools and conducted research on the relationship between religious beliefs and intergroup prejudice." *Ibid* p. 422.

between religion and intergroup bias.[128] Commenting on a Swedish student relations, Allport showed his faith, despite Harvard's secularism. Later, that Swedish scholar even wrote to Allport's student, Thomas Pettigrew, to confirm his account. Allport sought an authentic expression of faith that integrated the whole person. For this reason, his lectures at Harvard Divinity School often made reference to the philosophy and theology of Thomas Aquinas. Such thoughtful direction integrally led his students to the classical triad of truth, goodness, and beauty. Deep patriotism also directed him toward the democratization of social life and a clear commitment to the moral elements in public life.[129] In his life as a teacher, he strongly opposed prejudice, segregation, and racially discriminative legislation. He supported the equality of all citizens (civil rights, civil justice).[130] His views on social justice reinforced his high moral authority based on honesty and authenticity.

On June 30, 1925, Allport married Ada Lufkin Gould, a specialist in clinical social work. They had one child, Robert Bradley (b. June 29, 1927), who became a pediatrician.[131] In 1925, probably as the first American personologist, he taught a course entitled, "Personality: Its psychological and social aspects."[132] For four years, he taught introductory courses on social psychology and personality at Dartmouth College (1926_1930) but devoted the rest of his life to teaching at Harvard. First, in the years 1930–1936, he worked as an instructor and then as a lecturer.[133]

Allport's philanthropic nature found encouragement in his favorite professor Dr. Richard Cabot. Allport describes Cabot as a man of action,

---

[128] "Concurrently, social scientists and educators are increasing their attention to reducing intergroup prejudice as a method of reducing the potential for intergroup conflict. In the United States, such programs as Teaching Tolerance, Days of Dialogue, Study Circles, and related programs have been deemed 'promising practices' by the 1997-98 Presidential Advisory Commission on Race, charged with promoting interracial understanding through a national conversation about race. These developments underscore the need to promote better articulation between theory and practice in preventing and resolving intergroup conflict." A. Wittig & S. Grant-Thompson, *The utility of Allport's conditions of intergroup contact for predicting perceptions of improved racial attitudes and beliefs.* JSI 54: 1998 no. 4 p. 795–812.

[129] "A democracy believes that the maximum development possible in each individual is for the best interests of all." G. W. Allport. *The Nature of Democratic Morale.* IN: *Civilian Morale.* Red. G. Watson. Boston: Houghton Mifflin Company 1942 p. 8.

[130] Cf. Allport. *Morale: American style* p. 13.

[131] Cf. N. Sheehy. *Fifty Key Thinkers in Psychology.* London: Routledge 2004 p. 3–4.

[132] "In 1924 and 1925 he taught what is thought to be the first course on personality offered in an American college." Evans. *Gordon Allport: The Man and His Ideas* p. 17.

[133] Cf. G. W. Allport. *Studies in expressive movement.* New York: Macmillan 1933 p. 13. (Co-author P. E. Vernon).

"fascinated by both theory and charitable activities in such a way that spoke to my value system. He just believed in the integrity of each person."[134] Like Cabot, Allport very much liked involvement in philanthropic activities, having a deep belief in the dignity of every human life. His courageous examples of charity and help with achieving universal integrity, backed by hard work, provided unique learning experiences for many of Allport's students. Many European scientists of different nationalities are grateful to Allport, primarily for saving their lives, for he alone helped them leave Nazi Germany. Despite a deep recession in America, he found employment for many immigrants.[135] At the same time, with Cabot's support, Allport completed his manual, *Personality: A Psychological Interpretation*. After the death of his teacher and mentor, he assumed the position of director of the famed Cambridge-Somerville Youth Study program.[136]

From 1938 to 1966, Allport delivered thirty-three meditations at Harvard's Appleton Chapel, which were published posthumously in 1978. The simplicity of his messages and the meekness of his demeanor disabused not a few students of the stereotypes they had of their Harvard educators. (Allport's work as chairman of the Committee on Higher Degrees might have fostered the preconception.) As Thomas Pettigrew said, the image of Allport being distant could not have been more wrong.[137]

Allport's teaching method was formal but not cold. A teacher with high expectations, he did not try to force perfection; rather, he patiently waited for the best results from his students. Repeatedly he edited his own work he wrote, he taught his students correct spelling, noting in the margin mistakes to be corrected or paragraphs to be realigned. Allport believed in the uniqueness of each person while trying to work very patiently with every doctoral student. In the years 1936–1942, he became an assistant professor, and in 1942 assumed the chair of the Social Sciences Department and was involved in its development until his death in 1967. Much of his life's interest was the integral aspect of personal development in a web of social relationships.[138] As described by Allport's pupil, H. Craik, in the last years of his life. He became an icon for many scientifically developed disciplines of man in ethics, social psychology, and personology, for which he received

[134] He followed a theory and practice of philanthropy that appeals directly to my own sense of value. He believed, as "I" do, in the integrity of each human life. Hasło. B. F. Sinner. *G. W. Allport*. IN: *A History of Psychology in Autobiography*. Red E. Boring & G. Lindsey. New York: Appleton-Century-Crofts 1967[5] p. 11.

[135] Cf. T. F. Pettigrew. *Gordon Willard Allport: A Tribute*. JSI 55:1999 no. 3 p. 425–427.

[136] "The study was action research; it instituted a program of long-continued treatment of pre-delinquent children." Allport. *Personality and Social Encounter* p. 273.

[137] Cf. Pettigrew. *Gordon Willard Allport* p. 427.

[138] Cf. H. Craik. *50 years of personality psychology*. New York: Plenum Press 1993 p. 4.

numerous honors and awards.[139] One of those prestigious awards was the presidency of the American Psychological Association (APA).[140] Another honorary award was the APA's Gold Medal.

Allport founded and headed the Society for the Psychological Study of Social Issues (SPSSI) and the Eastern Psychological Association. Enjoying prestige, he was elected director of the National Committee, the National Commission of UNESCO, Prospect Union Association, the National Opinion Research Center, the Social Science Research, and the National Research Councils. He became an honorary member of the British Psychological Society, as well as the Deutsche Gesellschaft für Psychologie. He was, however, skeptical of Gestalt theory and therefore not fully committed. In 1965, for the first time in fifty years, Allport moved his lectures from Emerson Hall to the new fifteen-story William James Hall, shortly before his planned retirement. He was already well known as a co-author of two widely used tests including "Research reactions A–S," which allowed scientists to study whether a subject was dominant or submissive. Overall, he contributed widely to the professional study of religion. Investigation in self-realization inspired Allport to ask important questions about the roles of philosophy and religion, where rational response helped him find some deeper truths about religious faith.

In the scientific environment, he received excellent opinion as a teacher, professor, and researcher of the subject of personality knowing what to do to fit in different social situations.[141] Despite his outstanding intellectual capabilities and reasons of recognition, he always remained humble. His teaching activities at the university were unique and multifaceted. More than

---

[139] "At the time of his death, in 1967, he was a preeminent figure in the human science; his work encompassed social psychology and the social ethics as well as personality inquiry." Cf. Ibid p. 131.

[140] One last point about this classic work requires mention. Gordon addressed the problem of prejudice primarily in terms of his own in-group: white, Protestant, American males. The examples of prejudice cited throughout involve anti-Black, anti-Jewish, anti-Catholic, and anti-female sentiments. He was clearly lecturing to "his own kind." It is safe, easy, and politically expedient to attack the prejudices of out-groups who hold negative views of one's own in-group. It is quite a different matter to attack the prejudices of one's own in-group toward others. Pettigrew. *Gordon Willard Allport* p. 425.

[141] "In relating to graduate students, Gordon was typically formal yet supportive. Rather than demanding excellence, he simply expected it from his students. And toward that end, he gave unstintingly of his time in carefully editing everything we wrote—even years after we had received our doctorates. Indeed, he taught us how to write, though his old students still remember his single word, 'Recast.' When scribbled in the margin, it meant the entire paragraph required a complete reworking." Pettigrew. *Gordon Willard Allport: A tribute* p. 426.

300 doctoral students found him in his eighteen years of research to be the best teacher who earned great respect at the Department of Social Relations. One of his doctoral students, playfully expressing his admiration, said that Allport knew all the principles of life, without having studied them.[142]

Allport undoubtedly was regarded as universally gifted. He was a psychologist, anthropologist, philosopher, personalist, and a Protestant man of great personality and responsibility for others. He saw that one's self-realization is a lifelong process, therefore contributing to becoming a self-formed genuine and sincere man. Personality research had a profound influence on his Thomistic vision of man. As a psychologist and anthropologist, he made a significant contributions to the Neo-thomistic thoughts; he saw the human person as having both logical drives and drives for perfection, depending on how much one can exercise his or her freedom.[143]

To show Allport's charisma and integrity, it is fitting to recall the testimonial gathering at which fifty-five of his former students, laudatory and grateful, gave Allport two bound volumes containing published articles from each of them, all representing Allport's influence. The dedication reads: "From his students—in appreciation of his respect for their individuality."[144] Allport's social environment included many well-known and well-formed psychologists: John and Jean Arsenian, Alfred Baldwin, Raymond Bauer, Jerome Bruner, Hadley Cantril, George Coelho, Leonard Doob, John Harding, Robert Knapp, Sheldon Korchin, Bernard Kramer, Bernard Kutner, Lewis Long, Gardner Lindzey, Donald McGranahan, Betty Mawardi, Henry Odbert, Thomas Pettigrew, Leo Postman, Henry Riecken, Fillmore Sanford, Brewster Smith, Renato Tagiuri, Philip Vernon, Lauren Wispe, et al. The impact of this unique, outstanding scientific and social environment allowed Allport to research a variety of scientific inquiries about the integral man. Allport's wife Ada was also inspirational. She led a youth social rehabilitation center, counseling and leading experimental delinquency studies in the Cambridge-Somerville Youth Study program.[145]

---

[142] Cf. Ibid p. 421.

[143] Allport. Osobowość i religia p. 13.

[144] "In 1963, fifty-five of Gordon's PhDs and close friends surprised him with a testimonial gathering in Washington, DC. We gave him two bound volumes containing a published article from each old student that best represented his influence on us. Inside was the dedication: 'From his students—in appreciation of his respect for their individuality.' The occasion deeply moved Allport. What I recall best from the evening was a revelation about Gordon that I had not known. One by one, we rose during the night to express our appreciation for his support throughout our careers. We were especially grateful for his patient help on our dissertations." Pettigrew. Gordon Willard Allport: A tribute p. 430.

[145] The experiment failed on the following terms: (1) educators put middle-class values and patterns onto poor social children who were rebelling; (2) teachers

In cooperation with Ada's program, Allport noted that the treatment and prevention of criminal behavior is often very difficult, if even possible. However, he postulated that the development of pro-social behavior among troubled youth should be based on empathy to help youth better understand themselves and find the right path.[146] He stressed that pro-social, preventive behavior is born of friendship with others and a positive attitude on the educator's part, whereby formative virtues make possible a happy life. Only solitary participation in a meaningful common interest teaches self-control and self-determination and places the young person in a broader social perspective as well as in the economy of self-salvation.

After losing a battle with lung cancer, Allport died in Cambridge, Massachusetts, on October 9, 1967.[147] For many generations, his authority has been recognized: he was the author of thirteen books and 228 scientific articles.[148] He received honorary doctorates and numerous awards and made significant humanistic achievements that built a better world—a world free of prejudice and hatred. His corpus of work is still being discovered; it can be found in scientific journals and social circles, reaching a high circulation of about half a million editions to date.

C. G.W. Allport's thoughts and ideas

Allport's main trends of scientific activity resulted from his humanistic interests in philosophy, anthropology, psychology, [149] and personality.[150] Respectively, his research can be divided into several branches

---

developed profound dependence by not giving adequate freedom to youth, and (3) teachers failed to provide follow-up support after the end of the program.

[146] "This affiliative relationship, of course, should be established early in life before bad habits and an antisocial outlook becomes too firmly rooted. A youngster, even in a dismal home and given to defensive and rebellious conduct, may conceivably be steered away from a criminal career and toward useful citizenship, if a devoted individual outside his own family gives him consistent emotional support, friendship, and appropriate guidance." G. W. Allport. *An Experiment in the Prevention of Delinquency: The Cambridge-Somerville Youth Study*. New York: Columbia University Press 1951 (co-authors E. Powers and H. Witmer) p. 6.

[147] Cf. K. Alan. *Encyclopedia of Psychology*. Oxford: Univ. Press 2000 p. 120–122.

[148] Cf. A. Sheehy. *Biographical Dictionary of Psychology*. New York: Routledge 2002 (A. J. Chapman, W. A. Conooy) p. 9–11.

[149] "One of the first psychologists to study personality, Allport researched human attitudes, prejudices, and religious beliefs. His theory of personality, which rejected both Freudian psychology and behaviorism, emphasized the uniqueness of the individual and the need to treat problems in terms of present conditions as opposed to childhood experiences." R. Evans. *Gordon Allport: The Man and His Ideas*. New York: Dutton 1971 p. 21–22.

[150] Cf. R. Evans. *Gordon Allport: The Man and His Ideas* p. 15–21.

of knowledge: philosophical personalist, psychological, humanistic, anthropological, and lexical. Allport's achievements were significantly influenced by his family, especially his eldest brother, Floyd Henry, who was called "the father of experimental social psychology." Floyd was a critic of Gordon's views, perhaps, strangely enough, out of brotherly love.[151]

One of Floyd's criticisms concerned the issue of prejudice. Floyd maintained that supposedly ethnic conflict contributes to in-group prejudice. Prejudices, according to Floyd, arise from conflict between and among different groups. Gordon disagreed, maintaining that conflicts have nothing to do with negative prejudice. Prejudice is preconceived; it does not arise from reason or actual experience but hostile dislike of a person or group on the basis of race, sex, religion, or personal traits. Allport's *The Nature of Prejudice* (1954) is one of the most frequently cited books in humanistic psychology. Allport highlighted that a lack of virtues and values contribute to discrimination and prejudice.

Long-life exercised values help one overcome unhealthy behaviors. Therefore, better personality integration is possible where learned values contribute to the life of the healthy man. He emphasized the role of cultural influences on value education. Allport notes that family values positively impact society, are desirable, and are necessary in the integration of the individual into society. Consequently, in his educational and pedagogical approach, he often discussed deforming aspects of the person in spreading rumors, prejudices, and immaturely lived religion.

Allport's work in the field of personality psychology deepened mainstream humanistic philosophy. The thesis of his philosophy of life refers to the world of moral principles and basic values. In harmony with the moral life, the individual creates the meaning of his existence. Allport's meaningful approach to life inspires the person to be what he can become. He recognizes the human potential for self-realization that exists in every human. The human need to overcome weaknesses is the internal driving force for full development. In some ways, Allport recognizes that intuition is a guiding tool for self-development. He points out that the man with an impoverished interior life, who lives only to satisfy instinct, is the subject of slow development and has disproportional psychophysical unity. The man who lives in the past, especially, does not reach full development.[152] Allport uses philosophical existentialism and is often referred to in existentialist thoughts, emphasizing the levels of maturity responsible for human desire, duty, and a sensible lifestyle.

Like Victor Frankl, Allport appreciates the motives of duty and the meaning of life as the most central in the hierarchy of human desires necessary to be fulfilled and true to oneself. In extreme life conditions of existence, essential needs of loving become real, as opposed to human

---

[151] D. Katz. *Floyd H. Allport (1890–1978)*. *American Psychologist* 34:1979 no. 4 p. 351.

[152] Cf. Allport. *Osobowość i religia* p. 211.

desires. Man is always searching for the meaning of his suffering. During suffering, he focuses on what he should do to survive in abusive abnormal conditions. Allport says that three to five years of concentration camp depravity and deformation is enough to break the morale and healthy desire of the imprisoned.[153] Finding the healthy cause of existence becomes a central motive of man because without that understanding, he cannot live well with others. Allport's concept of personhood is based on Cartesian philosophy and the assumption that a person is a unitary substance in the rational nature.[154] Therefore, the decisive motive of retaining his humanity becomes the survival element of concentration camp suffering. One usually seeks reasonable answers to the question of why brutality occurs.

The human being was originally created in a loving relationship with God, his fellow humans, and nature. The moral system of a human being is consistently linked to the natural law of loving where the past and future match in accordance with the professed values of good and truth. Any person who wishes to participate in the lives of others needs understanding and loving, because without truly loving his own subjectivity, man cannot understand another human being. Allport's concept of a person is formulated on the Aristotelian ontological personal potency of loving. Man exists for a perfect purpose and manner, but each is also an individual. Therefore, the personality of a person is internally and dynamically organized with that of others.[155]

To avoid extremism, Allport opposed disparities, being always in favor of a positive outlook on man and his potentials. As a humanist, he praised dialogue and never monologue, always giving a reasonable part of any argument to his opponent. Hence, most of Allport's discourse is polemical. This is mainly in relation to Freudian psychoanalysis, which he admits were only partially right: "I know in my bones that my opponents are partly right." Allport opposed all forms of extreme controversy. His criticism was precisely directed at the misleading and irrational beliefs that were fashionable at his time.[156] Always at the center of his interests remained a man capable of transformation through healthy motivations and intentions. He balanced philosophies of pleasant, good, and meaningful life with its permanent interests in rich socio-religious and co-educational implications.[157]

---

[153] Cf. G. W. Allport. *A Secondary Principle of Learning*. PsRev 53: 1946 no. 6 p. 347.

[154] *"Persona est substantia individua racionalis nature."* Cf. Allport. *Osobowość i Religia* p. 42.

[155] "The person is something and does something, combining being with action. Thus, the individual always faces futures, is 'in advance of himself,' and travels toward a port of destination." Cf. Allport. *Personality* p. 219.

[156] G. W. Allport. *The person in psychology: Selected essays by Gordon W. Allport*. Boston: Beacon Press 1968 p. 405–406.

[157] He is the "country's foremost authority on problems of morale. His most recent contribution to the *Quarterly* is an analysis of the effects of newspaper headlines on

Allport saw human interaction as a social meeting of those who educate and those who are being educated for the in-group's co-formation.[158] Parents, teachers, and students always experience better teaching and learning in groups interactions. In his teaching methods, he looked for what was working well and could work even better. Based on his teaching approach, we can assume that his maturation took place in four stages of engagement: son, student, teacher, and parent. Therefore, his mature development was shaped by commitment, which is essential to self-formation.

Allport's concept of personhood stems from the logical diagnosis of positive traits. Positive stimulation allows a student to become an integrated person. The theme of self-fulfillment dominates his psychological creativity and throws significant light on the theory and practice of self-formation. The man, understood in psychoanalytic terms, is operated by defense mechanisms and conflict situations. This is a man who has lost his intentionality in life. In opposition, the work of Allport shows positive mechanisms, interest in the intentionality of the person, and personality development that becomes a critical issue in the self-formation process. He felt to alleviate controversies in the study of the human person. Allport discovered anti-personalistic and reduction decks of a person. Also, noticed reductionism visible in the world that rejects natural faith. Allport, who was opposed to psychoanalysis, understood the deformative impact of reductionist techniques and saw Freud's theory as being too narrow and lacking scientific data.[159] Freud believed that personality formation comes from the early unconscious, instinctual patterns, and the human development of unconscious actions (i.e., *unconscious operating*).[160] Psychoanalysis of Allport's time reduced a person to his low impulses and immature behavior. But a whole person's valuation cannot be interpreted only as wishful fantasies, or "unfulfilled wish-full phantasy."[161]

Allport's critical and fuller approach to psychoanalysis also reveals Freud's bias against Christian morality and Christian formation. Freud's anti-Christian thinking included many methodological errors resulting from a lack of a true cognitive theory that carefully explained the complex issues of religion and faith. Mostly, it shed a reductive and negative light on the phenomenon of faith. Freud's well-publicized study on neurosis, affecting many followers focused only on the typology of the archetypes of the mentally ill, unsuitable for reliable and common-sense assessments of religion

circulation and morale." Allport. *Restoring morale in occupied territory. Public Opinion Quarterly* 7: 1943 no. 4 p. 606.

[158] Cf. Allport. *The Nature of Prejudice*. Cambridge: Perseus Boos 1979 p. 427.

[159] Cf. J. Feist. *Theories of Personality*. Chicago: Holt and Winston 1990 p. 567.

[160] G. Lindsey. *G. W. Allport*. IN: *A History of Psychology in Autobiography*. Red. C. A. Murchison. Worchester: Mass 1966[5] p. 213.

[161] S. Freud. *Moses and Monotheism*. Transl. J. Jones. New York: Vintage Boos 1967 p. 110.

and human aspirations. Freud's concept, in Allport's opinion, is well-suited only to the neurotic personality, which seeks to satisfy its infantile urges.[162]

Allport, using many lexical terms, describes a person as a meaning-seeking entity. He concludes that a mature, healthy personality has the proper balance between individualization and socialization and between autonomy and heteronomy. The psychoanalytic interpretation of nature led Allport to distance himself from Freud's theory and develop an integrated approach in his personology research. He never strayed from qualitative methodology in assessing the weight of evidence—the value of human life and conscience.[163]

Allport believed that parents influence their children before any education plays a major role in the learning process; they do not only give their children food and water but also core values, affective support, and approval. Their moral conduct does not include adverse control because it is ineffective in the long process of education. Allport, given the tragic experience of war, posits that social education has an influence on a mature personality formation through the development of the human attitude, "I should." Thus, the self-formation of an upright conscience becomes a path of socialization, elevating moral standards and the common good. Shaping healthy life attitudes, according to Allport's ethics of duty, offer educational institutions in the inevitable question: Are they able to teach people to make wise decisions given the pluralism of the individual?[164]

In search of patterns of maturity, Allport's *Personality: A Psychological Interpretation* remains an important analysis of mature personality self-formation. The author emphasizes that human maturity is associated with unique, whole psychophysical development. In *Pattern and Growth in Personality,* he notes that what causes self-formation is the inner desire for maturity. Thus, the desire to implement self-realization leads to an appropriate model of inner harmony, which is consistent with the fulfillment of its vocation.

Often, Allport emphasizes that personalistic teaching helps shape the moral person. Therefore, his first positive personology actualizes and extends humanity toward his religious nature. Spirituality includes personal development, the causative agent of avoiding mistakes, and the internal

---

[162] "However, I don't believe that this concept Freud's applies at all to normal personality development. We are obviously not finished developing by the age of five, and many people show entirely contrary tend." Evans. *Gordon Allport* p. 5.

[163] Allport uses the idiographic method to describe and explain life events and individual facts. The nomothetic method used in anthropology allows for the discovery of general, universal norms, and laws.

[164] Cf. S. Maddi. *Personality Theories: A Comparative Analysis.* California: Pacific Grove: Brooks/Cle Publishing Company 1989 p. 127–129. The free choices of a man, as a result of the duty ethic, are more mature because they do not bear elements of coercion.

forces in the process of becoming a man. Based on his religious outlook and affiliation with human spirituality, Allport promotes a balanced view of human nature. His work on philosophical personalism, *Becoming: Basic Consideration for a Psychology of Personality* (which was translated into many languages), presents the aspects of religion that develop an integral personality. Allport's rational thought was formed under the influence of his brother, Floyd. However, his concept of becoming required a personalistic view of man—a person who is open to deeper contact with the world and other ethical systems.

Another of Allport's significant contributions is his trait theory of personality. Allport holds that certain traits might be learned and shared by all.[165] For example, in children, a commonly desired feature is moral behavior based on the primacy of honesty.[166] Moreover, personality traits can be dominant (e.g., the authoritarian personality) or have central characteristics (e.g., self-confidence, sociability, openness) or secondary (i.e., less important for description). Allport describes both the nature of and methods for measuring inherent human traits such as intelligence, mobility, and temperament, as well as traits acquired by continuous self-formation (e.g., internal or external experienced moral conditions such as extroversion/introversion, insight, ascendance/submission, and sociability).[167] He also identifies levels of self-formed personality in the activities of the same person, such as factors of neuroticism (coping in stressful experiences: fear and sadness, often developed in situations of sin), extroversion (evidenced by the intensity of experience), openness (which determines one's readiness to adopt new ideas of higher moral values), agreeableness (an appropriate moral attitude in social relations, such as trust, humility, and devotion), and conscientiousness (the level of professional activity, defining responsibilities, goals in life, prudence, and laziness).[168]

In his pedagogy, Allport is concerned about training personal characteristics whereby a student develops realistic attitudes, described by great spontaneity, focused on solving general and ethical problems without paying undue attention to oneself. In educational institutions, the school must pay attention to a robust class curriculum. School activities need to have the right tools to engage students in responsible objectives like learning study methods, ethical rationale, and a fundamental philosophy of life.[169] Always pursuing higher goals for the wellbeing of a community is a required social

---

[165] Cf. G. W. Allport. *The Nature of Personality: Selected Papers*. Reading: MA 1950 p. 40.

[166] Cf. Ibid p. 24.

[167] Cf. R. H. Woźniak. *Allport and the Social Psychology*. London: Routledge/Thoemmes Press 1994 p. 6.

[168] Cf. G. Matthews. *Personality Traits*. Cambridge England: Cambridge University Press. 2003 p. 59–61. (Co-authors: K. Deary and M. Whiteman).

[169] "I would never remove from the child a certain sense of responsibility." R. I. Evans. *Gordon Allport: The Man and His Ideas* p. 17.

value.[170] Allport notes that a good parent, a good neighbor, or a patriotic citizen is not good simply because his goals are accepted by the public. They must be always pro-social, because the progressive realization of the higher purpose of becoming a better man and fostering a better society is desirable in terms of values.

The educational approach is therefore determined by the personalistic interaction described as scientific achievements—not so much as anti-scientific measures. Education ought to include necessary elements of pro-social and patriotic formation. A significant portion of Allport's work is related to the dimension of meaningful participation of the individual in society. For instance, one's patriotism contributes to national morality, which collaborates with that of others and yields social solidarity.[171] Therefore, any participation in the common good of society must teach self-control and self-determination.[172]

It seems that the adoption of a patriotic attitude is necessary for interpersonal dialogue in a broader perspective. Lack of interpersonal or communal relationships often underlay problems of social injustice, stereotypes, rumors, and media propaganda. To seek better solutions in human progress, the media must become a source of mass communication. With Leo Postman, Allport coauthored *The Psychology of Rumor* (1947), which discusses how stories are distorted and in some cases are relative to racial and religious prejudice. Allport addresses these problems in *The Nature of Prejudice*.[173] A whole chapter of this publication is devoted to the nature of inter-ethnical issues that contrasted with the views of some pseudo-religious groups that were opposed to dialogue and the promotion of peace.[174] He engaged himself in South African cultural studies, focusing on white supremacy.

---

[170] G.W. Allport. *Scientific models and human morals*. PSRev 54: 1947 no. 4 p. 189.

[171] Allport writes in the first chapter: "It seems that only in times of national peril do we take an interest in a sound and invincible democratic morale in America. (…) Morale, like health and sanity, has to do with a background condition in living (…) to form a faith in the sacredness of the human person. The really important support for our national morale resides in remote corners of our personalities, and are not easily accessible to analysis." G. W. Allport. *Nature of Democratic Morale*. IN: *Civilian Morale* p. 3–4.

[172] Cf. Allport. *Personality and Social Encounter* p. 188.

[173] "Perhaps the briefest of all definitions of prejudice is: thinking ill of others without sufficient warrant." Allport. *The Nature of Prejudice* p. 6.

[174] Allport. *The Nature of Prejudice* p. 420–422. Allport suggests the critical distinction between the "institutionalized religious outlook and an interiorized one." These groups, which have more-ethical internalized worldviews, live more deeply in faith and are more tolerant and less biased.

An important message of *The Nature of Prejudice* relates to human social injustice based on discrimination against access to human rights and the right to dignity. [175] As a pioneer of social ethics in the fight against social prejudice and hate groups, Allport developed a scale for measuring intolerance, ranging from 1 to 5. At level 1, majority bias against ethnic minorities takes the form of stereotypes, hate speech, and insensitive jokes. At level 2, bias is expressed as contempt for minorities, albeit with no intention of causing harm except isolation. At level 3, it denies personal rights, refuses kind treatment, blocks opportunities for advancement, and willfully inflicts harm. Level 4 involves acts of physical violence, vandalism, lynching, and programs against the minority population. The fifth and most extreme stage is outright extermination or "ethnic cleansing" of minority groups.[176] Allport also identifies monstrous forms of slavery.[177] He points out that hatred, jealousy, fear, and threats are dangerous phenomena that magnify prejudices and personal immaturity.[178] Of course, to show the bias of deformed behavior, the study refers to Allport's own demographic: white, male, American Protestants. He concludes that is harder to spot and oppose immoral behavior and prejudices of one's own ethnic group against others. Therefore, in self-formation, it is necessary to understand the nature of prejudice.

Allport included issues of religion in *Waiting for the Lord: 33 Meditations on God and Man* (1978) and *The Individual and His Religion: A Psychological Interpretation* (1950). He warns against the glorification of science and technology in the absence of ethics and morality. Four centuries ago, Allport noted that Rabelais spoke of the disintegration of the integral man resulting from science without conscience, which "spells the ruin of the soul."[179] In 1960, Allport published *Personality and Social Encounter*, which conveys the educational influence of environment, showing the network of references divided into *extrinsic* and *intrinsic* motives.[180] The degree of mature self-formation results from the corresponding externalization and

---

[175] Cf. Allport. *The Nature of Prejudice* p. 52.

[176] Concerning the genocide of the Polish minority population by the Ukrainian Insurgent Army (UPA) under German occupation, see: I. Katchanowski. "Terrorists or National Heroes? Politics of OUN and UPA in Ukraine." Davis Center for Russian and Eurasian Studies, Harvard University p. 7.

[177] G. Allport finds that a family connection to one group does not necessarily breed prejudice toward other groups. Discrimination is mainly motivated by seeking better treatment of one's own group. To understand this, we need to look more closely at impact features of the group. "The familiar is preferred. What is alien is regarded as somehow inferior, less 'good,' but there is not necessarily hostility against it." Allport. *The Nature of Prejudice* p. 42.

[178] Cf. E. M. Ligon. *Their Future Is Now: The Growth and Development of Christian Personality*. New York: The Macmillan Company 1939 p. 16.

[179] Cf. Allport. *Personality and Social Encounter* p. 276.

[180] Cf. Ibid p. 263–266.

internalization of rules, social norms, and faith. A man involved in social life correctly actualizes, observes, plans, and analyses own life. Thus, a person attending to his knowledge shapes the world and adapts to it accordingly.

In the center of the Allport's work remains the person, and from its higher context, it provides a basic understanding of the personality. Therefore, personality is a dynamic organization of those psychophysical systems that determine an individual's unique adaptation to the environment.[181] He later slightly modified his personality interpretation in another publication, *Pattern, and Growth in Personality*. Personality is a dynamic organization within the individual comprised of psychophysical systems that determine his character, behavior, and thoughts.[182] We may claim that personality is what a man *is*. Personality, because of its unique unity, means the whole group of characteristics a person creates. The personalistic precursor of positive psychology in the United States notes that "somewhere in the cracks of the nomothetic laws, psychology lost the human person as we know it in their daily life"—that is, a person capable of developing his positive features.[183]

The Christian formation of the person, considering his potential, in part with the release of Allport's claims, is the answer to the problems of the stagnant reductionist interpretation of man with all its impulsive urges theory. As a witness of totalitarian regimes (both Communism and National Socialism), he figured out man's capacity for both destruction and self-reformation. In his humanistic anthropology, he sought to protect man against selfish, antisocial, and inhuman behavior. Deformative behaviors tied to aggression, low self-esteem, and selfishness lead to self-destruction and militate against man's role as co-Creator with and under God. Godless anthropology has no place for *homo cognans, homo Dei*, as evidenced by the twentieth-century literature portraying both religion and morality as "the opium of the people."[184]

Allport's humanistic anthropology reveals the ethical aspect of life, which gives man the affective capability of human compassion and much warmer attitudes. Using the knowledge of positive human transformation, where a person has a great capability to love, he rediscovered the essence of humanity that allows for a better future than that which he experienced,

---

[181] "Personality is the dynamic organization within the individual of those psycho-physical systems that determine his unique adjustment to his environment. This definition is narrowed to adapt to the educational environment. Personality is the integration of those systems of habits that represent an individual's characteristic adjustments to his environment." Cf. Allport. *Personality: A Psychological Interpretation* p. 45–48.

[182] Cf. Allport. *Pattern and Growth in Personality* p. 28.

[183] Allport. *Personality* p. 558.

[184] Cf. Allport. *The Individual and His Religion* p. 112.

creating a space to conquer all social evil. By engaging anthropological analysis and looking for answers to the question, "Who is man?" Allport found *the integral man*. To understand this concept of the integral man, we need to keep in mind what man can become in the future. Drawing from the philosophy of J. Locke and Leibniz, Allport provides us with complementary answers. Locke, who gave modern expression to the ancient epistemological theory of *tabula rasa*, posits that individuals are born without mental content (that is to say, the mind begins as a "blank slate"), and therefore all knowledge comes from experience or schooling. One experiences his environment with all of the senses, acquiring interpersonal conditions and skills.[185]

In the human mind, these conditions are like footprints of external inspiration. According to Leibniz, man is a source of meaningful acts and deeds which, for Allport, meant a sense of personal freedom and responsibility.[186] All of these forces positively impact the individual in his activity, and man is intentionally pushed and pulled by their energy. Somehow, integral development is rooted in St. Thomas Aquinas's theory of intentions.[187] Thus, Allport's ethical anthropology flows from the theory of intentions and the meaning of life. Anthropology like this is an exact science where ανθρωπος (i.e., anthropos) manifests himself. Through his personality, one conditions his proper manners and social interactions. At the same time, one motivates oneself to maintain peace and stability.[188]

Allport formulates the personalistic concept of the person built into a system of sociocultural interactions ("a system within a matrix of sociocultural systems.")[189] Hence, his Christian personality is expressed in personal relationships with others. A loving relationship with God (who in Christian theology is tri-personal *and* perfectly one) is the path toward meaningful existence. He emphasizes that human personality is a dynamic complex of attributes in the process of a self-realization.[190] Therefore, a mature personality needs to be formed on the path of deeper Christian life

---

[185] Cf. Allport. *Osobowość i Religia* p. 14–17.

[186] Cf. Allport. *Becoming* p. 7–18.

[187] Allport's anthropological thoughts, in many ways, depend on the moral theology of Thomas Aquinas regarding both the doctrine of intention and the prejudice phenomena. The theory of intention refers to believers and has the great support of analytical rational. Thomas Aquinas persuaded him that valid reasoning needs faith and vice versa. Human faith is a major factor in the life of the human person: faith shapes awareness and responsibility to the best of man's moral conduct. To put it in more dignified terms, let's use Thomas Aquinas' definition that prejudice is "thinking ill of others without sufficient warrant." Cf. R. Evans. *G. W. Allport: The Man and His Ideas* p. 59.

[188] Cf. N. Rapport. *Social and Cultural Anthropology: The Key Concepts*. London: Routledge 2000 p. 7.

[189] Allport. *Pattern and Growth* p. 194.

[190] Cf. Allport. *Personality* p. 28.

through the conversion, enlightenment, and divine–human union, which guarantees a continuous process of personal growth.[191]

Growth begins, in other words, with the expansion of one's personality and insight. The social process of growth takes place through the acquisition of the valuable traits of others to be more loving and striving toward God's love. Then, we may talk about becoming. If Christian anthropology is a branch of study that discovers a perfect man, this knowledge of self-giving is confirmed on the path full of hardship and important goals. Therefore, proper inspiration, coming from a positive image of God as a model of participation, can yield desired fulfillment.[192]

With a vision of optimism, Allport forms the concept of a man who sees a much broader perspective of becoming more fully human. His anthropology improves the reductionist view of man developed in the past century.[193] So, Allport, in his anthropological research, processes the adoption of stronger determination with which a person can perform moral good. The fundamental importance of Allport's anthropological thought comes with strong, healthy motivation. Developing responsible decisions in the direction of affirmative action among personal frustration and distractions is a priority for him. Understandably, that is why Allport collaborated with researcher Henry A. Murray in creating the Department of Social Relations to discover lost human roots and traits.[194] Their interdisciplinary work prepared the foundation for Harvard's Anthropology Department. Allport noticed that current terminology of the human person is too-individualistic. The individualistic ethic, does not orient people toward the triad of truth, goodness, and beauty.

Allport observes that, in educational work with troubled children, adolescent decision-making involves tension between what empowers the young and what enslaves them.[195] If a young man follows the reductive

---

[191] Allport identifies approximately 4,000 personal characteristics that define the maturity of the individual.

[192] Cf. Allport. *Civilian Morale* p. 4. "Morale has to do with individual attitude in a group endeavor. Two of its essential features are predominantly personal and private in character, and the third is predominantly social."

[193] Allport reasons that the possibility of human self-formation is based on values, which stands in contrast to psychoanalytic theory that lacks an integrative vision of meaningful life events.

[194] "During the Second World War (...), the sociologist T. Parsons, the social psychologist G. Allport, and the psychoanalyst H. Murray, created the interdisciplinary department of social relations at Harvard which was to play a major role in the future of anthropology." G. Gaillard. *The Routledge Dictionary of Anthropologists*. New York: Routledge 2003 p. 111.

[195] "Whether the home is broken or not will be regarded by many as of great importance, and housing and general neighborhood conditions will also be deemed

pattern of his instinctive urges, he will go the way of self-determination or self-understanding.[196] Allport proposed that interdisciplinary research was necessary for integral human growth. He said that without integral conception of the person, man could not apply better educational approach to human growth, otherwise, the person undergoes reductionism in being fully human. In the next chapter, we will consider how the anthropology of becoming contributes to integral maturity.

---

factors that must be given serious consideration." Cf. G. W. Allport. *An Experiment in the Prevention of Delinquency: The Cambridge-Somerville Youth Study.* New York: Columbia University Press 1951(co-authors E. Powers and H. Witmer) p. 356.

[196] His understanding of basic personal striving is based on an interdisciplinary perspective; it introduces philosophical anthropology data with secondary science, including the concept of psychological stages of development presented by E. Erikson, A. Maslow, and V. Frankl.

CHAPTER 2

Stages of moral formation

Moral formation is a lifelong process that involves achieving wholesome maturity via the responsible development of emotional impulses, will, and reaction, as well as loyalty to God. Maturity and commitment are revealed in the attitude of holiness. Holiness is not something unattainable and distant, nor is it shared only by a few, is the requirement of the "new man."[197] The essence of mature faith in God is a vocation well accomplished, and man's purposeful pedagogy opens horizons of truth and love of Christ.

Christian formation can provide the fundamentals of man's integration in the person of Christ, enabling him to reform himself at any stage of life. Only then, as John Paul II highlights, will we understand who man is within himself and what the goal of human life is. This correctly and logically provides the solution to the problem of how to lead someone in achieving the real purpose of his existence.[198] Certainly, the aim is to attain the fullness of humanity through socio-cultural self-formation, recovering man's utmost and most reasonable conception of life. For Allport, this integral conception creates the best-possible mature model, which is the task of a lifetime—or longer.[199]

A. The essence of Christian moral formation

The heart of Christian socio-cultural reformation is the self-forming integrity that encompasses the spiritual and emotional patterns necessary to create a "new man in Christ."[200] In addition to spiritual and emotional self-formation, responsible intellectual formation is used according to the age and ability of pupils. To speak of integral ethical formation, it is important to clarify the terms, "formation," "upbringing," and "education." The Greek word formation διαμόρφωση ("modulate, propose a style") will help us define the essence of self-formation and indicate the directions to achieve desired

---

[197] S. Chrobak. *Koncepcja Wychowania Personalistycznego w nauczaniu Karola Wojtyły—Jana Pawła II*. Warszawa: Wydawnictwo Salezjańskie 1999 p. 84.
[198] Cf. Jan Paweł II. *Przemówienie do świata uniwersyteckiego. Poszukiwanie prawdy i kształtowanie młodych do prawdziwej wolności człowieka* (Padwa, 12.09.1982). IN: *Jan Paweł II. Wiara i Kultura* p. 162–163.
[199] Allport. *Religia i Osobowość* p. 156.
[200] Cf. K. Jeżyna. *Moralne przesłanie nowej ewangelizacji*. Lublin: Wydawnictwo KUL 2002 p. 332.

maturity.[201] The process of self-formation indicates individual efforts in expected socio-cultural adjustment.

The term *formation* is derived from the Latin *formare* ("to shape, invoke into being, create, teach, and define"); its etymology involves a continuous process of education by means of institutional learning that shapes a juvenile's unique personality.[202] The idea of any formation is to shape the ethical foundation of the young toward higher values and beliefs. One way in which a well-established foundation does this is by furnishing the right tools and abilities for a cognitive, self-formative approach to life. Another way is by moral formation—a continuous learning process toward living the values of good-minded parents. Such learned self-formation helps to raise awareness in youth that defines mature behavior as the morally good (i.e., holiness of life).

The term *formation* is defined by what comes through hearing and is founded on the parental teaching and catechesis of the Church as well as a pedagogical and educational environment. According to Z. Chlewiński, each growth process has a "formative aspect involving whether the formatter be a person, group or institution in dialog with a person being formed." One undertaking self-formation is always an active and engaging subject, as he takes the effort of its desired good results of formation and individual growth based on his own responsible decisions.[203] In general, the description of a *moral formation* carries the reconstruction and transformation of the personal "I" of man, regarding both the subject and purpose of that formation, as well as how the real self-mature personality is formed.

The concept of the formation can occur both in the general and specific sense. The use of an appropriate terminology allows us to successfully define the problem, which calls for the need of self-formation as a solution to modern life immaturity. From the perspective of ethical reasoning, formation focuses on various integrative aspects of life that generate some perfection. Any educator asks the formatter questions that center around values that modify the student's behavior, positive impacts on their lives, needs that must be addressed, etc. Thus, the juvenile strives for higher good and harmony and knows what price needs to be paid for their full human development. The search for the best model—a pattern of self-formation as an object of desired interest in the interpersonal professional formation—also refers to the art of formation that proposes a development based on the "natural talents" of a student. Natural talents lead to two groups of questions in the process of formation. The first is the question of the ontological (Gr. Οντος) structure of the human person, that is, what

---

[201] H. Hionides. *Greek Dictionary*. Glasgow: Harper Collins 1997². p. 58.

[202] Derdziuk. *Formacja moralna* p. 19.

[203] Cf. *Formacja* IN: *Encyklopedia Katolicka*. T. 5. Lublin 1989. vol. 389.

develops, actualizes, and energizes man personally.[204] The next question is related to the essence of "why?"—the cause and reason for such progression in oneself.

The interpretation of moral self-formation is related to acts of love that strengthen the meaning of life in a broader Christian perspective. Formation becomes permanent when it leads to a perfect state in comparison with the previous imperfect one. Thus, moral self-formation is closely related to the formal education required to remain a disciple of Christ, with respect to one's personal desires. The permanence of such continued education is expressed in Bible studies, inquiry in the classics of Christian thought, ascetic practices, volunteering, and living life filled with moral values. In fact, self-formation is the decent education of man meant to authenticate one's internal leadership under the influence of important virtues. The guiding idea and purpose for self-formation is to fully realize the love of Christ, which is implemented in self-improvement. It is firstly the development of self-enhanced education, but on a deeper level, it is the process of conscious striving for spiritual perfection. Allport uses the concept of co-formation as an alternative of self-education that complements a personalized education.

While working with students of different backgrounds, Allport realized their great need for self-formation and higher values that could protect them from the dangers of losing their faith and integral life at "godless Harvard." Most of the noted problems of ethical deformity, at least to some extent, often lead to increased mental health issues, depression, discouragement, fear, loneliness, despair, and addiction. These symptoms are a consequence of the materialistic conception of life and the decreased inner freedom of youth. Better results of well-planned self-formation extend a person's potential to create capabilities for the reconstruction of his spiritual freedom. In that freedom, ethical reasoning restores the personal integrity and choices of a youth who seeks any form of growth. Only in the sphere of inner freedom can a person build character and lead an emotionally fulfilled, happy life. Besides self-formation, home education provides an effective treatment that corrects fundamental adjustment to social living. Ethical formation by its nature opens horizons to becoming more spiritual and leads to the extended personality. At the same time, ethical formation also creates a higher personal quality of life with others.

The term "education" is derived from the Latin *eroditio*, which also means "to teach, train the human mind, to think culturally."[205] Education has a plurality of social interactions through which a youth learns to live his life in society while developing his personality. Allport particularly praises the

---

[204] J. Piaget. *The Language and Thought of the Child*. New York: Hardcourt and Brace and Co. 1932 p. 152.

[205] H. T. Hionides. *Greek Dictionary*. Glasgo IN: Collins Gem, Harper Collins 1997² p. 13.

indirective methods of home education because of the important process of family influence on the sphere of will and emotions (*formation of in-group*).[206]

The anthropology of becoming entails education. Some educational techniques are centered on training for specific knowledge. At the same time, other techniques are intended to measure the effects of education. In my understanding, the pedagogical purpose of education is to develop a permanent change in the personality of the juvenile. Education has three aspects in terms of an individual: the process, the state, and the result. Through the process of education, one is called to develop unique abilities and skills consistent with social norms. Social embeddedness is often a process of subordinating feelings to reason. The second aspect of education, the state, concerns methods, measures, and conditions. The state of ethical reasoning, for example, impacts individual behavior and promotes appropriate harmony in human perfections. The third aspect of education, the goal of developing permanent change, is seen in the results: a responsible social life.

Modern literature offers many definitions of education.[207] Education can be categorized variously as mental, moral, social, aesthetic, and physical, as well as self-education. The diversity of pedagogical approaches applies to both secular and Christian education. Secular upbringing promotes education without God and emphasizes personal autonomy. It is based chiefly on the secular philosophy of modern man, which reduces literary versatility and attenuates virtue. Secular education, in its materialistic character, lacks Christian knowledge and methods. At this stage, I want to reject the argument that secular education is the only correct education. Like Allport, I recognize the limits of secular education, which does not take into account what religious motivation and mature aspirations provide in the long process of becoming a man. This results in large gaps in the internalization of norms, leaving youth unsocialized for too long.[208]

In contrast to secular education, Christian education highlights that socialization is already available already in the Christian home. It is the process of becoming truly mature and responsible within the larger context of loving that is always informed by divine Revelation. Anyone who meets the challenges of living responsibly attains lasting, transcendent values. Moreover, a person of faith has the potential for interpersonal openness and living with higher spiritual values: a life centered on the beauty, goodness, and life given for another. Human life is a gift from the Creator. In Christian formation, home education leads to self-education, whereby a young man

---

[206] G. W. Allport. *The Nature of Prejudice*. Addison Wesley (Current Publisher: Perseus Publishing). Reading 1979 s. 29–47.
[207] Cf. M. Łobocki. *Wychowanie moralne w zarysie*. Kraków: Impuls 2002 p. 12.
[208] Cf. Allport. *Becoming* p. 28.

efficiently tries to work together with family in the gradual process of becoming. We find school teaching and home formation to be important educational factors as well, because home education encompasses all areas of life. [209] In that process of self-education, the juvenile recognizes the weaknesses of his real self and accepts a well-planned, ideal self.[210]

In the continuous educational process, juveniles discover their real "selves" by learning to achieve their own optimal perfection. So, in fact, we can distinguish formation from education, concluding that education is the initiated process of expanding role models to create a distinct positive change in the juvenile's personality. At the same time, we need to point out the subtle phenomenon of education, claiming that "the important matter is the upbringing," the form of influence, rather than what we want to teach or convey.[211] Thus, the appropriate method of education allows a teacher to persuade educational objectives that are significant to the further development of the whole person in mind, body, heart, and will.[212] The educational process is merely subordinate to human socialization, but already, the pupil is enabled to expand his horizons of cultural dimensions. The process of continual training and socialization techniques complements natural growth, which accelerates integral maturity.[213] Analysis of this process of becoming allows educators to observe the progression of development preceded by certain regressions that depend on the efficiency of internal freedom.

We all recognize that among life events, primary education contributes to human progression, although it is not often an easy process nor is it achievable in the short term of a lifespan. However, primary education can be strengthened through self-formed familiarity, self-discipline, and adherence to ethical imperatives. By that, we urgently postulate for more religious and moral formation outside of general education. M. Pokrywka rightly notes that the problem of self-formation (due

---

[209] Cf. A. Derdziuk *Formacja moralna* p. 25.

[210] Cf. Ibid p. 15.

[211] Allport. *Osobowość i religia* p. 118.

[212] Cf. DWCH p. 1. The concept *formation* is one of the harder terms to define and formulate. Formation consists of a variety of issues that pertain both to the actions of educators and a process of personal growth and progress to maturity. Cf. S. Kunowski. *Podstawy współczesnej pedagogii*. Warszawa: Wydawnictwo Salezjańskie 1993 p. 165–166; A. Gurycka. *Struktura i dynamika procesu wychowawczego. Analiza psychologiczna*. Warszawa: Państwowe Wydawnictwo Naukowe 1979 p. 33.

[213] Cf. DWCH p. 1. The concept *formation* is one of the harder terms to define and formulate. Formation consists of a variety of issues that pertain both to the actions of educators and a process of personal growth and progress to maturity. Cf. S. Kunowski. *Podstawy współczesnej pedagogii*. Warszawa: Wydawnictwo Salezjańskie 1993 p. 165–166; A. Gurycka. *Struktura i dynamika procesu wychowawczego. Analiza psychologiczna*. Warszawa: Państwowe Wydawnictwo Naukowe 1979 p. 33.

to changing socio-cultural conditions) is still an open question and needs new methodology and solutions.

Without the integrative perspective of a personal encounter with the God of infinite love, man remains deformed, dying a scary and enslaved moral death. Without the triumph of the human spirit, a man cannot be truly free. The process of self-formation takes place in a group of holy people. In that evolving context, a man shapes his union with God in free acts to love with all his heart, with all his soul, and with all his strength. Pope John Paul II, in his 1988 Apostolic Exhortation *Christifideles laici*, describes self-becoming as "a continuous process of personal maturation, conformed to Christ, according to the will of the Father, under the guidance of the Holy Spirit."[214] The essence of Christian self-formation is built on the social process of interiorization of the cardinal virtues, because man is not born ready and integrally formed.

The essence of self-formation relates also to what is described by the Latin term *edocere*, as "drawing someone up higher." Etymologically, education, in this sense, means enriching students by imparting relevant knowledge, which can objectify lofty goals. As stated by S. Chrobak, "education is therefore a typically human phenomenon because only a man can be educated."[215] Therefore, human education becomes one's opportunity for socialization with higher humanity. The contemporary concept of education depends on correct understanding of man and his shape. So, the idea of education "refers not only to educational improvement but also to vocational training, as an important factor in the human development and completion of the self-formative task of the person."[216]

In the present theological praxis, education must have the characteristics of integral formation because of the high level of present immaturity. Consequently, in order to improve human behavior, it is necessary for one to know about embeddedness. Christianity has always had the mission of serving disadvantaged people who seek purpose in their lives. As A. Derdziuk notes, this kind of education usually comprises shaping their degraded humanity, which they picked up in their often-sinful initial phase, into the mature phase of self-consciousness.[217] The phase of self-conscious dignity and self-worth is very often a neglected feature of secular education and upbringing. The key to taming antisocial impulses is Christian integral education and healthy motivation that directs one's intent toward healthy activities. In fact, "becoming" a man, from the outset, requires parental

---

[214] ChL p. 57.

[215] *Koncepcja Wychowania Personalistycznego w nauczaniu Karola Wojtyły—Jana Pawła II.* Warszawa: Wydawnictwo Salezjańskie 1999 p. 102.

[216] CV p. 61.

[217] Derdziuk. *Formacja moralna a formacja sumienia* p. 18.

sacrifices, because human nature demands the lifelong physical, intellectual, aesthetic, and ethical influence of integrated people.

Ethical formation, therefore, emerges from a partnership of trusted participants. Their dialogue, based on sound, multifaceted cooperation, leads to a mature personality that is affirmed in active social participation. The very concept of ethical formation, in the broader sense, is closely related to one's moral upbringing. Moral upbringing should inspire young to engage in noble participation—if we want to ensure healthy futures for young people. Re-education must be understood as a desire for harmonious development through mature morality as well as sensitivity to spiritual needs.[218]

We all know it is impossible to form educated and honest people in the laboratory. The task is enormous. Society demands the development of abilities to recognize good and evil. Such integrity allows one to responsibly choose the harder kind of truth and goodness over evil. The impact of formative good should cultivate lasting ability, logical thinking reinforced by examples, and integrity of behaviors.[219]

So, the essence of guided self-formation should encourage juveniles to adopt a vigorous attitude in their earthly lives but also a desire to attain eternal life. The purpose of such guided formation is to establish a lifelong healthy goal. Integral knowledge of life always has a positive effect on the prime motivation to accept responsibility for oneself and others. M. Pokrywka states that many of today's pupils treat the sphere of moral and internal life as a redundant balance, which limits human freedom and makes life difficult.[220]

Meanwhile, without integral formation, there is no way of shaping inner freedom and maturity. Planned internal self-formation, therefore, exposes many errors that prevent the necessary development of a juvenile. The essence of such an education is found in the experience of a transcendent God, rooted in unconditional love for the self-formed. The man who encounters God's love in his sanctifying center knows how to make better decisions about what is good and what is bad. Besides, a moral or ethical education provides the necessary tools for becoming perfect by systematic work and the development of virtues. John Paul II describes this phase of becoming as the state of more loving, "which is sought after reaching a certain level of personal and psychological maturity."[221]

A man who reaches psycho-social maturity is the man of God who stands out among creatures as a co-Creator, and who is distinguished

---

[218] S. Urbański. *Duchowość wychowania w nauczaniu Jana Pawła II,* IN: *Jan Paweł II—Mistrz duchowy.* Red. M. Chmielewski. *Homo meditans.* T. 27. Lublin: TN KUL 2006 p. 128.

[219] G. W. Allport. *Personality and Social Encounter.* Boston: Beacon Press 1960 p. 327.

[220] M. Pokrywka. *Antropologiczne podstawy moralności małżeństwa i rodziny.* Lublin: Wydawnictwo KUL 2010 p. 316.

[221] LdR p. 16.

cognitively, willfully, and lovingly from others (*ens cogitans, ens volens, ens amans*).[222] Therefore, the man of God, through merciful attitudes, manifests his maturity and responsibility for himself and others. The essence of his progress can be seen in respect for life in all its forms, from birth to natural death. For Allport, a man who is integrally educated has the inner freedom to promote and achieve peaceful coexistence with others.[223] Peace education is a necessary and dynamic reality that requires the constant effort of many, but it is an achievable reality through an attitude of the patience and hard work of the man. As M. Pokrywka says, the protection of precious, innocent life restores inner peace.[224] Under the influence of integral education, a man strives for harmony and responds to another person with praise and joy, thus granting himself greater tranquility as well. Peaceful upbringing tends to restore full, harmonious development and also the creation of an ideal.

The core of integral self-education may also be found in the teaching of the Church. In his encyclical *Divini illius magistri,* Pius XI addresses the questions, "who has the mission to educate, who are the subjects to be educated, what are the necessary accompanying circumstances, and what is the end and object proper to Christian education according to God's established order in the economy of His Divine Providence?"[225] Without a healthy relationship with God and others, one can neither function properly nor live with dignity or develop God-given gifts. It is necessary to process internal exercises for the sake of greater good according to the generally accepted rules of society. Every implementation of accepted principles in families should make room for systematic guidance from moral law and order, self-educating respect for ethical conduct.[226]

Moral formation, as a normative discipline, is so much needed today that it is possible through the message of Jesus Christ. Dietrich Bonhoeffer writes that evolved self-formation is born within a unique relationship with the Redeemer. The Second Vatican Council's "Declaration on Christian Education" states that ethical education leads to a higher purpose of existence and therefore, that "true education seeks to shape the human person toward its ultimate salvific goal, but also for the good of the

---

[222] S. Granat. *Teologia osoby ludzkiej.* Poznań: Księgarnia św. Wojciecha 1985 p. 580–582.

[223] "The Allport home was remembered as a 'peaceful but sheltered place with kindness exhibited on every hand.'" (Woźniak. *Floyd Henoy Allport and the Social Psychology* s. V.)

[224] Cf. Pokrywka. *Antropologiczne podstawy moralności małżeństwa i rodziny* p. 353.

[225] DIM p. 10.

[226] Moral norms are understood as elements of culture. They are generally accepted in specific cultural settings like the family, contributing to the development of an embedded culture and general rules required by all members.

community, where the person develops oneself as a member, and whose duties will benefit society when he grows up, with his full participation."[227]

The ethical becoming is the essence in any mature personality.[228] It seems that the concept of becoming can be perceived in two ways. In the first sense, self-formation is understood as the evolving process of an object subjected to external forces of learning, discipline, and actions leading to human growth. On that course of growth, one's "I" requires immense patience. The second important sense of self-formation refers to the way in which the "I" gains its correct and desired form—not only as a matter of external force or formative action but by deliberate interior motivation. In this sense, anyone who undertakes the risk of self-transformation organizes himself according to the desired model of being. In effect, the whole person takes an active role of self-reformation.

Christian-embedded culture appears to be a basic ethical transforming ground to life in which man shapes the dynamic structure of his personality on the following successive or regressive internal growths. The level of that integration or disintegration depends on the logic of deliberate choices or lifespan plans.[229] Christian responsibility of self-formation is expressed in responsibility before God, who is rich in mercy and is always elevating a man, requesting him to respond positively to God's gift.[230] With good reason, the *Catechism of the Catholic Church* speaks of human life in the categories of *gift* and *task*.[231] Dimensions of Christian responsibility are expressed, then, in both meanings as a process and as responsible tasks before God, who seeks positive responses.[232]

The complementarity understanding of self-formation, as a process and task, arises from theological anthropology. In this case, it is the perspective inspired by Christ's motive of loving, which comes from Revelation in Scripture and tradition of the Church. Complementary internal self-formation should, therefore, contain Christian morality lived by natural laws and rules. The first rule of this law is the principle of ecclesiastical morality, which shows the "close connection of Christian morality with the

---

[227] DWCH p. 1.

[228] Allport describes the terms "self" and "ego" more broadly as feelings—things that are one's own—the physical, social, and spiritual entity. Cf. Allport. *Osobowość i religia* p. 38–39.

[229] Cf. J. Flower. *Stages of Faith*. Harper: San Francisco 1995 p. 289.

[230] Cf. J. Nagórny. *Istota odpowiedzialnego rodzicielstwa. Refleksja teologa moralisty w 25 rocznicę ogłoszenia encykliki "Humane vitae."* IN: *Odpowiedzialni za życie i miłość. Materiały z sesji naukowej zorganizowanej przez Duszpasterstwo Rodzin Diecezji Bielsko-Żywieciej.* Red E. Burzy. Bielsko-Biała: Wydawnictwo Wydz. "Duszpasterstwa Kurii 1996 p. 43–44.

[231] Cf. CCC p. 162, 1703, 1,730.

[232] Intentionally targeted Christian faith, with references to God and a meaningful future, allows a man to glimpse his intended integration of personality with mature life purposes, even to the achievement of holiness. Cf. Dziekoński. *Formacja chrześcijanska dziecka w rodzinie* p. 417.

people of faith." By its nature, Christian morality influences the life of community and its co-Creativeness. Community life refers both to Christian and secular society. Yet, the deepest source, from which flows the truth about its ecclesiastical character, comes from Revelation.[233]

In a broader sense, mature self-becoming manifests itself in shaping interpersonal and intercultural traits that are necessary for humanity to absorb higher moral skills at every step of life. Maturity somehow results from ethical life. In a narrow sense, mature self-formation has roots in integral growth (e.g., physical, emotional, and theological-moral growth). Natural or biological maturity has far advanced the development of psycho-spiritual development, and therefore, achievement of psycho-spiritual maturity takes more time. Such internal growth is associated with the sphere of the intellectual, emotional, social, and ethical man. Overcoming immature conditions of any impulsive stage requires a magnitude of work, which can be seen on the higher level of the positive reconstruction of "self" and mature functioning.[234] Thus, the formation of the "self" is born from inner freedom and a better understanding of important ethical principles, universal laws of respect, truth, justice, and general good behaviors. Growth in maturity leads to the adoption of non-contradictory principles that never conflict with the general welfare of others. Internal maturity is often called the intentional growth of a person who takes valuable positive actions that are good for the public.[235]

The essence of being mature, in the Christian sense, is a balance between individualization and socialization, between autonomy and heteronomy. In this regard, adult self-formation is also a sort of suitable social learning that is important to any social conventions defined as the *socionomy*. Social maturity also contributes to the well-developed social conscience.

B. Self-formation of conscience and becoming

Allport notes that embedded social maturity deepens Christian identity in the personal conscience. Therefore, mature identity becomes

---

[233] K. Jeżyna. *Eklezjalny charakter moralności chrześcijańskiej.* IN: ENM p. 163.

[234] "Involves multiple and often interconnecting stairways, each leading to a different ultimate virtue at the summit. One stairway can represent progress toward a commitment to even handed justice, a second toward compassionate caring, a third toward obedience to God, and others toward such values as self-sacrifice, loyalty to one's country, bravery, honesty, humility, and more (...). Growth toward one sort of morality likely involves more phases or steps than does growth toward another." T. Murray. *An Integrated Theory of Moral Development.* Westport: Greenwood Press 1997 p. 263–264.

[235] Cf. A. E. Gała. *Uwarunkowania wychowawcze dojrzałości moralnej.* Lublin: Oficyna Wydawnicza Lew Lublin 1992 p. 45–46.

critical for an individual's conscience (*personalized conscience*). [236] A well-developed conscience helps us undertake the task of self-formation during our school years. Without conscience, the moral center of integral formation is almost nonexistent. The fathers of the Second Vatican Council say that conscience is the voice of God in the human heart that rediscovers the revealed truth: "In the depths of his conscience man discovers a natural law which he does not impose on himself, but which holds him obedient and whose voice calls him, wherever needed, to love and do good and avoid any evil. These movements of the heart are expressed in basic moral principle: do this and shun away from that."[237]

We might theorize that the moral conscience, learned in social embeddedness, has interesting characteristics that help men better recognize what is good and what is bad. For Allport, conscience is an essential force of agency that shapes personal judgment in a man's development because it contains a sense of well-expressed universal duty and responsibility. [238] Conscience is, therefore, an innate ability to recognize good and evil that man should shape throughout his life. In Allport's understanding, conscience figures out moral standards in the process of self-formation and controls the transient impulses for the benefit of long-term goals, consistent with a picture of oneself, or one'd self-concept. Many personalists consider psychological theories for self-growth regarding conscience, especially Roger and Maslow (Roger: "inner life;" Maslow: "an intense spiritual nature"). Based on these interior distinctions, we claim that the phenomenon of conscience develops an opportunistic means of self-formation. Conscience, with personal growth, often goes from the main center of the habit of obedience to the form-oriented and more opportunistic phase of becoming, which is dependent on the ethical stage of self-formation.[239]

---

[236] Cf. M. R. Salvatore. *Personality Theories: A Comparative Analysis*. California: Pacific Grove: Brooks/Cle Publishing Company 1989 p. 333–334.

[237] KDK p. 16.

[238] Cf. Allport. *Becoming* p. 68–79, 92, 99. Allport notes that social conscience has a fundamental element in personality formation that helps realize long=term goals. "Conscience is an important agent in the growth of personality. It is a process that controls transitory impulse and opportunistic adjustment in the interests of long-range aim and consistency with the self-image"

The psychological theory of conscience treats it chiefly as a phenomenon of opportunistic learning. It tells us that we learn conscience as we learn any cultural practice, though in the case of conscience, it is a punishment rather than a reward that seems to be the decisive agent. Allport. *Becoming* p. 68–69. Cf. Allport. *Osobowość i religia* p. 58–59.

[239] The term *proprium* refers to the early, unformed personality of the juvenile. Allport uses this term to describe the personality formation in the following phases: a sense of one's own body-kinesis, a sense of identity, self-love, and an extended "I." Allport. *Osobowość i Religia* p. 39–43.

"Should" is a much better act of freedom and is not the same as "I must."[240] When conflicts and impulses relate to self-image, the sense of duty is not the same as the feeling of compulsion. A sense of need ("I must") is inferior to the sense of "I should." In the anthropology of becoming, "self" continues the vital transformation of "ego" that takes three significant changes under the influence of God's gift and enrichment. First, external sanctions surrender to internal forces. Second, the experience of prohibitions, fears, guilt, and "I must" are subjected to the experience of distinctions, with respect to "I should have done." Such transformation is possible when we visualize the mature self-image (i.e., what self-image should be like).

Mature mental enlightenment seeks higher expressions of God's grace and develops a whole new system of human values. Third, the habits of previous strict external obedience shall lay down any fear to be subjected to the internal reconstruction and transformation that leads to a mature conscience and to a new experience of development: if you do that, you will build a better lifestyle. If not, you will ruin your chance for a healthier and richer way of life. Then, the battled fear expressed in the form of "I must" takes on new meaning under the influence of higher motives, becoming "I should."[241]

The influence of mature conscience becomes the driving force of self-formation. Conscience is born in truth and is the inspiration of God in the heart of a person. Because the human capacity is not self-sufficient and well-developed, a person needs to develop external divine illumination. Like many authors, M. Pokrywka confirms that at the very base of the education of a mature person is the self-formation of conscience, an important duty of every Christian. In the fact, self-formation of conscience is a lifetime task— a daily reality in which God meets with men, and men encounter God in unconditional love. God directly calls for the greater love and awaits man's response, spontaneously and freely. So, I agree with M. Pokrywka's statement that personal formation is the essential art of co-Creating human life.[242] From an early age, children have been introduced to learning and practicing the law of God through their conscience. As Allport confirms, the struggle for

---

[240] The freest act of a man is manifested in the primacy of grace that illuminates his priority ("I should have done") before duty. Cf. Pokrywka. *Antropologiczne podstawy moralności małżeństwa i rodziny* p. 167.

[241] The attitude of a youth, "I must," characterizes a less-mature act and constitutes more dutiful disposition based on an external coercion—as stimulus to the action in contrast to the duty coming from person" structure "I should." "I should" is therefore a normative, self-formed command that encourages oneself to growth and becoming mature.

[242] *Posłannictwo Uniwersytetu.* IN: *Formacja moralna* p. 173.

internalization of the voice of conscience begins at the age of three years, by identifying with the commands and certain prohibitions of parents.[243]

According to Catholic social teaching, the education of conscience proceeds along the various stages of anomy, heteronomy, autonomy, and ideology. Such self-formation "teaches virtue; it prevents or cures fear, selfishness and pride, resentment arising from guilt, and feelings of complacency, born of human weakness and faults. The education of the conscience guarantees freedom and engenders peace of heart."[244]

Furthermore, it allows the development of interior dialogue with God, the author of the natural law, a first beginning and final omega of man. Christian inspiration comes from the inner life and formation of conscience originating in the person of Christ and inspired by the authors of the Bible. St. Paul speaks of this in terms of transformation in Christ (see Gal. 6:1–14; 2 Cor. 5:15). This transformation begins with hearing and responding to God's voice in the heart and is fueled by the supernatural virtues of faith, hope, and charity, which are received in Baptism, the gateway to life in Christ.[245]

Of course, it is possible to transform oneself through dialogue with God in one's own conscience. Just knowing that the love of God is unconditional and given freely becomes a good motive for sharing that same love with others. However, we know that any biological interpretations of conscience are too optimistic. If man born in society can take the self-formation of conscience to heart, he is sufficiently educated. Anyway, a purely biological view of man does not help nor distinguish his conscience for self-formation. It can lead to the narrow individualization of conscience. Indeed, social learning helps to develop professional conscience.

But John Paul II in *Veritatis Splendor* notes that an individualistic notion of conscience lacks the discovery of objective truth: "Only developed conscience has attributes of a supreme tribunal and moral judgment with an infallible decision about what is good and what is bad."[246] K. Kwiatkowski states that an individualistic approach can disappear and that the objective truth as a corollary of conscience develops sincerity and being okay with oneself.[247] Nevertheless, it is not possible to completely eradicate the natural conscience because it is a gift from God and part of human nature. In this regard, we need to comply with natural law.

Especially, parents are required to fulfill an obligatory moral teaching role as the primary social and family educators. On the one hand, the Church

---

[243] Cf. Allport, *Osobowość i religia* p. 59.

[244] CCC p. 1,784.

[245] Cf. J. Bajda. *Sumienie i osoba a autorytet Magisterium.* IN: *Veritatis splendor.* Red. A. Szostek. Lublin: TN KUL 1995 p. 197–205.

[246] VS p. 35.

[247] K. Kwiatkowski. *Formacja sumienia w kontekście sakramentu pokuty.* IN: *Formacja moralna* p. 41.

as a community of believers is the ideal formative school of right conscience and provides support to parents in that regard. On another hand, a school's task should be focused on preserving that natural conscience for future development. This free-given gift comes from God and commits man not to harm oneself or others as basic human ethics. Because it is hard to achieve a properly developed human conscience, everyone needs to be engaged in the self-formation of conscience.

It must be acknowledged that many adults have not completed this task because of an underdeveloped conscience due to the lack of proper cultural change at an early age, and therefore they suffer from unresolved, infantile guilt or conflict.[248] The teaching of the Catholic Church defines proper growth of conscience as follows: "Conscience is a judgment of reason whereby the human person recognizes the moral quality of a concrete act that he is going to perform, is in the process of performing, or has already completed. In all he says and does, man is obliged to follow faithfully what he knows to be just and right. It is by the judgment of conscience that man perceives and recognizes the prescriptions of the divine law." Conscience is a law of the mind but more than that, it warns anyone who can accept liability and responsibility, danger, and hope.[249]

Allport also expresses and postulates the need for the development of a mature conscience among youth. He sees conscience as an internal agency of growth in the process of maturation, which controls the transient impulses and adjusts in the interest of long-term goals. Otherwise, conscience is consistently associated with the phenomenon of adaptive learning from an idealistic image of oneself.[250] In the meaning-making process, the person of faith learns to shape his conscience in almost every discipline of cultural life. The mature conscience recognizes the full truth about humanity, which leads it to a higher level to self-formation. Also, through the mature conscience, a man correctly perceives the real relationship between freedom and divine law. According to Allport, the mature person often has developed proper distance, which allows him to make sound judgments by having an impartial view and vital perspective with understandable objectivity.[251]

According to Z. Chlewinski, the mature, well-formed conscience meets the following criteria:

1. interiorization of good moral standards;

---

[248] "Take the case of an authoritarian family atmosphere. The child who is harshly disciplined, never allowed to pit his will against his parents, can scarcely help perceive existence as a dangerous thing. Life, he is forced to assume, is based not on patient acceptance, but on a power relationship." Allport. *The Nature of Prejudice* p. 316.
[249] KKK p. 1,778.
[250] Cf. Allport. *Becoming* p. 68–69. Cf. *Osobowość i religia* p. 58–59.
[251] Cf. Allport. *Pattern and Growth in Personality* p. 509.

2. ability to distinguish good from evil without application of destructive defense mechanisms;

3. ethical sensitivity in doing good and avoiding evil, for oneself and others, as a pre-decision agency warning (a sense of responsibility for one's own decisions) and the post-decision agency (good action remedying a bad decision, in the sense of regret for evil and satisfaction for sin);

4. application of right laws and appropriate moral standards, which has less to do with legalism than the interiorizing of normative acts;

5. allowance of practical knowledge in applying new moral decisions and behavior;

6. healthy motivation, which grows with emotional maturity, even in the transition from self-centeredness to empathy; and finally,

7. heroic witness in extreme situations.[252]

We view these criteria from the position of moral duty. Conscience, in Chlewinski's understanding, considers a more sensitive part of the human self-control self-assembly, because he defines the moral obligation in the light of the natural law. A person, through conscience, receives a signal telling him if the operation has been performed correctly or not. The conscience of the self-formed man applies physical laws to any situation.[253]

Regarding mature conscience formation, A. Derdziuk emphasizes aspects of the participatory theonomy whereby the pupil recognizes important laws at both the external and internal levels. Rediscovered and revealed, individual law goes through a progression of early formation of conscience and often leads to further awareness of personal weakness.[254] In the theonomy stage, a person discovers God's action, which is discrete in conscience. This discreteness delicately encourages a man to receive what God has established, not in the form of external demand but of internal order and harmony. For Allport, growth begins with the awareness of responsibility for one's own individual motives.[255] Through such a maturing conscience, a man responsible for his moral motivation is socially gifted and emotionally stable—only freer of erratic behavior.

A well-formed juvenile rightly judges things and actions. He is easy to live with and wants to have a positive impact on others. On such a caring

---

[252] Cf. *Search for Maturity: Personality, Conscience, Religion.* New York: Peter Lang Publishing 1998 p. 87–88.

[253] Cf. Chlewiński. *Dojrzałość, osobowość, sumienie, religijność.* Poznań: Wydawnictwo "W Drodze" 1991 p. 81–83.

[254] Cf. *Formacja moralna* p. 26. The term, *participant theonomy*, is often used by John Paul II in the context of his encyclical *Veritatis splendor* No. 41. John Paul observes that the essence of moral law is God acting in the history of man's salvation. God shows man both the external and internal law of God in man's mature conscience. It should be noted that the morality discovered in the mature conscience comes from God and leads to a pattern of ethical life.

[255] Cf. Allport. *Pattern and Growth in Personality* p. 510.

basis, it can be speculated that the self-formation of a mature conscience is subject to the integral growth and moral education of the individual. Mature self-formed conscience dignifies a person and determines the internal order under the influence of an encounter with God.

Any lack of internal growth hinders the development and results from not knowing mature patterns. According to Allport, "Conscience, like other aspects of personality, can be inhibited in one's growth."[256] Thus, the conscience, under the primacy of egoism, is often distorted. In many cases, it should be noted that under the influence of emotional stimuli and authoritarian systems, a conscience may be distorted. A distorted conscience, due to the lack of proper integration of knowledge, has difficulty recognizing truth. Distortion and the darker sense of sin threaten the appropriate exercise of freedom and the search for truth.

The essence of Christian self-formation results from the personalistic nature of the concept of conscience, which shapes, from birth, an expression of being fully human. Such self-formation of conscience leads to the discovery and possession of integrated standards and well-motivated life.[257] Even an adolescent prefers that his authority has direct proceedings. He needs guidance and authority from someone who is admired. But it is hard to offer a backbone of moral character without interiorization, which requires apparent dependence and much time in the process of mature conscience formation. Therefore, it is "obvious that conscience is not formed at birth."[258] It seems equally clear that the task and duty of a Christian require constant interiorization of conscience, so the moral conscience of the person became a causative factor.[259]

The personalistic nature of conscience indicates that the exclusive, personal, formed man, as an entity of moral action, is the efficient cause of mature adults' actions and personalities. An important objective factor of the conscience self-formation of effort is full self-realization and sanctification, as stated by the Magisterium: "The purpose of Christian education is the cooperation with the grace of God in the mined and true perfection of believer."[260] The perfect Christian life always brings serenity and joy even during suffering. From the long-term perspective of eternal life, man may therefore experience that he lives in state of *viatoris* (as a pilgrim).[261]

---

[256] Allport. *Osobowość i religia* p. 62.
[257] Cf. K. Dąbrowski. *Dezintegracja pozytywna*. Warszawa: Państwowy Instytut Wydawniczy Pax 1979 p. 27.
[258] Allport. *The Individual and his Religion*. New York: The Macmillan 1950 p. 87 or *Osobowość i religia* p. 172.
[259] K Wojtyła. *Osoba i czyn* p. 73–149.
[260] DIM p. 6a.
[261] DinM p. 13.

The experience of being called and selected in the plan of salvation makes him feel the presence of God during the earthly pilgrimage to eternal life. With an integral vision of man, as is appointed by God, writes M. Pokrywka, in close connection with both the natural and the supernatural dimensions, man "takes evolving pattern of nature and grace."[262] In this faithful integration process of multiple dimensions and disintegrations, a new self-formation may lead to sanctification. And the purpose of sanctification for the person undertaking formation, is to direct his interest on adopting perfect goals and values.[263] Self-growth is, in other words, proper functioning that improves one's own ways of loving, which covers the love of God and neighbor. Ideally, the process of self-formation through sanctification contains the efforts of parents, educators, and oneself.

C. Socio-cultural stages of self-formation

The comparisons between the stages of self-formation determine adequate methods and educational influence in the vulnerable developmental time of child's ethical grow. Moral formation includes the following stages of development in the life of every human being from the moment of conception until natural death: embryonic, fetal, neonatal, late neonatal, early childhood, childhood, adolescence, middle age, and elderly age. [264]

For a concise approach to the issue of human growth and appropriate ethical self-formation, the author of the book uses the following breakdown: early childhood (ages 1 to 3) and late childhood (3 to 9), interpersonal maturity of youth (girls from age 9, boys from age 12), and early- (ages 20 to 27) and late-adulthood (ages 27 to 65), corresponding to the three stages of personality development presented by G. Allport as childhood, adolescence, and adulthood.[265]

Socio-cultural stages of self-formation show a positive correlation between social self-awareness and appropriately developed moral values related to God, other human beings, and oneself. Human development in the first stage of early and late childhood is characterized by a certain preconvention. At the beginning of childhood, rules are amoral because ethical reasoning is not yet formed. The child, according to Pokrywka, does

---

[262] *Antropologiczne podstawy moralności małżeństwa i rodziny* p. 44.

[263] W. Przybyło ASC. *Formacja Osoby Powołanej Jako Istotny Proces Rozwoju Psychiczno-Duchowego Człowieka*. PERSPEC†TIVA. *Legnickie Studia Teologiczno-Historyczne* 7: 2008 no. 1 p. 161.

[264] Allport expressed this view on the nature of personal formation in his 1964 book, noting that human life is developed in moral phases similar to the phases of theory of Erik Erikson. Cf. *Eight Stages*. J. Bischof, *Interpreting Personality Theories*. New York: Harper & Row 1964 p. 317.

[265] Allport. *Osobowość i religia* p. 115–144.

not have yet any assessments or the capacity to respect ethical standards.[266] This period of development is called "anomie" (Gr. Νομος, *nomos*, "without law") and lasts until sometime between ages two and four. Children then seek only to meet immediate needs. A. Derdziuk emphasizes that the birth of a child is a celebration called into being by the eternal plan of God, even though a person of this stage cannot clearly distinguish it.[267] Allport conveys that early development of intelligence is activated by the surrounding culture that operates without abstract thinking, cognitive concepts, or language. Then, in the "collective monologue," a child is lost in distinguishing among first, second, and third person.[268]

Infants, accompanied by a purely practical intelligence, understand their surroundings and their mom and dad, with whom they are in immediate contact. Childhood development and formation mostly depends on environment. The presence of a caring mother and father is the most suitable environment for healthy development.[269] The educational environment must, therefore, surround the baby with selfless love and warmth. This is particularly important in the case of a mother; the joy of motherhood is a basic expression of early formation in a child's life. Contemporary research by C. Walesa, D. Batson, J. Fowler, and D. Korans-Biela confirm that early records of embedded sensations from the prenatal period of the child (especially parents) are durable and relevant to the self-realization of his whole life. It is simply "the concept of life developed from the experience and motivational thinking."[270]

At an early stage, unconsciously experienced pleasures are good, and the lack of them—evil.[271] Child's behavior, at this stage, rather resembles a hedonistic ethic, but according to many writers such as James Fowler and Jean Piaget, it is not. According to Allport, although the formative influence on a child's personality belongs to parents, the child evolves personalistically rather than in any hedonistic ways.[272] Nevertheless, without the prior

---

[266] *Antropologiczne podstawy moralności małżeństwa i rodziny* p. 321.

[267] Cf. *Teologia moralna w służbie wiary Kościoła.* Lublin: Wydawnictwo KUL 2010 p. 23.

[268] Cf. Allport. *Personality* p. 161. Cf. J. Piaget. *The Construction of Reality in the Child.* London: Routledge 1955.

[269] Allport stresses that life must be maintained at every stage while preserving a common sense of personal values and values.

[270] T. A. Harris. *W zgodzie z sobą i z tobą.* Transl.E. Knoll. Warszawa: Pax 1979 p. 44–45.

[271] Cf. Ibid p. 321

[272] Cf. Allport. *The Role of Expectation.* IN: *Tension that Cause Wars.* Red. H. Cantril. Chicago: Univ. of Illinois Press 1950 p. 73. Hedonistic expectations make the most educational problems in this that a man quickly gets used to the things pleasant, considering or owning them for free without any costs.

exemplary formation, hedonistic behavior may be the source of future behavioral problems.[273]

Children experience a sense of right or wrong, mainly by their surrounding environment and loving support of their family. Children often associate goodness with what they receive, and evil with what they lack. First, they choose good-reinforced conditioning and reject the second. Consequently, they feel a sense of security or lack of it, depending on their parents' reactions. We know well that skillful moral shaping during childhood decisively influences a child's basics expressions of love, hope, and trust in adulthood. [274] Moral reinforcement of the child always needs a loving environment. Only within a concerned embeddedness and environment can a child develop uniqueness. Allport holds the view that the reactions of newborns are conditioned, and we confirm that.[275] The child does not have a developed sense of self. For example, a baby cannot yet determine the cause of his tears, but already, he starts to show his own individuality. It is very important to experience love in the process of differentiation at every stage of development.[276]

Youth who do not experience the warm influence of parents often isolate themselves from others in adulthood. The child has nowhere to run from emptiness and a lack of loving mother, because inside, he feels a painful emotional block to further harmonious development. During the stage of infancy continues the development of the ego or sense of self, which Allport terms "proprium." [277] Infants become aware of their own existence and distinguish their own body from objects in the environment.[278] Concern for childhood formation requires loving care, even prior to birth.[279] D. Kornas-Biela recognizes the criteria that must be met to build a good relationship

---

[273] Allport states, "The quickest way to reduce tension is to commit suicide. Yet most people try to stay alive at all costs, thus maintaining and increasing their desire. To live at all is to have tension." Cf. Allport. *Pattern and Growth in Personality* p. 88.

[274] Cf. Allport. *The Individual and His Religion* p. 107–121. E. H. Erikson presents the characteristics of the virtues of each of the eight phases of the "ages of man" in his book *Childhood and Society*. New York: Harper & Row 1963² p. 110–157, 247–251.

[275] Cf. Allport. *Osobowość i religia* p. 116.

[276] Cf. J. Piaget. *The Child's Conception of the World.* Cambridge: Harvard University Press 1987 p. 27. Compared with the Allport, Piaget specifies phenomenon of the baby's impulsivity, as the lack of differentiation between the world and yourself.

[277] Cf. Allport. *Becoming* p. 41–53.

[278] "Starting life, as a completely selfish being, the child would indeed remain entirely wolfish and piggish throughout his days unless genuine transformations of motives tool place. Motives being completely alterable, the dogma of Egoism turns out to be a callow and superficial philosophy of behavior, or else a useless redundancy." Cf. Allport. *The Nature of Personality* p. 91.

[279] By supporting the culture of life, the Church defends the unborn child in the "duty of human love and protecting life, defending and promoting it." Jan Paweł II. *Komentarz do Ewangelii*. Kraków: Wydawnictwo M 2011 p. 613.

between parents and their conceived child and perceive the child as a separate person.[280]

Very early, starting at 2 years of age, children of the pre-conventional type of moral attitude are unable to adopt perspectives different from their own. This period is determined by having things that may be earned by appropriate learned behavior and obedience to significant people in the near vicinity, including parents and educators. The nascent heteronomy forms an excellent ability to be influenced by authorities, elderly in the life of a child.[281] So there are many important aspects of emotional ties during early life.[282]

Later, the impulsive evolution of childhood, which includes a process of self-identification, leads to the formation of a personality whereby a person defines who he is in relation to others. In other words, this developmental step causes an awakening of identity and pride—early success of becoming a person—which offers satisfaction and a positive perception of oneself. Along with a sense of identity, there is born stubbornness with which the child seeks answers to the question "Why?" Not receiving satisfactory responses from parents mirrors forces of the supernatural world, which have the physical attributes of the father. This is a typical anthropomorphic process of growth during early life. The fact that a child plays different characters and acts as a depersonalized entity in play, using different sounds, proves that being oneself and determining one's own identity does not come so quickly.[283]

Besides, being grateful to the interplay the child develops his personality as a sort of ownership and distinguishes it among many of his collected toys. The child develops his image with high expectations about other members of the family circle. The same happens with the development of the self. The same mechanism of extended perception takes the child in his love for both living beings and animated objects as well. A stranger, in his eyes, is a transitional facility in distinguishing what he has previously learned. The child's development is accomplished via comparative views of the current self-image with new elements.[284] The child sees himself as a unique personal being with individuality, having a unique name, family, etc. The morality of the child, as such, is that there is no specific criterion of good and evil, but he expresses himself exuberantly in his new human life.[285]

---

[280] Cf. D. Kornas-Biela. *Wokół początku życia ludzkiego*. Warszawa: Pax 2004 p. 43–53.

[281] Cf. Piaget. *The Moral Judgment of the Child*. New York: The Free Press 1965 p. 197.

[282] Cf. Allport. *Osobowość i religia* p. 118.

[283] Allport includes waking up the identity of the child, as the more difficult stage of development of personality: a sense of one's own body—the flesh, sense of identity, self-love and extended "I." Allport. *Osobowość i religia* p. 40.

[284] "Because the perception becomes embedded in his personal life, then everything is about the stimulus." Cf. Allport, Postman. *The Psychology of Rumor* p. 145.

[285] Cf. J. Flower. *Stages of Faith*. San Francisco: Harper 1995 p. 290.

We realize any child is indeed a gift from God. Therefore, for his comprehensive development, formation is necessary to stimulate the imagination, which allows for holistic spiritual enrichment that sustains the needs of childhood. Remote is still a stage of construction of interpersonal relationships in the life of a child. Self-centeredness, along with a sense of his own ego (i.e., self-consciousness), is formed at the end of a child's second year. The youth sees his own existence, but he cannot distinguish himself from environment.[286] Soon, the child enters an awkward phase of impulsive evolution when the principle of pleasure gives way to a sense of his own needs.[287]

The child is not yet able to distinguish thoughts from feelings. The feeling of pleasure that comes from being loved is the first formative communication skill that meets the needs of contact and acceptance. Still, until he is four years old, his mother plays an important role in his life; her presence makes the child feel accepted. Religion begins to play a greater role in the child's life when he begins to develop language by watching their parents and environment. Often-repeated operations, such as the sign of the cross, prayer, kissing the image, and tilting the head, which express simple rituals, are only religious, emotional expressions of what the child has encountered. According to Cz. Walesa, this behavior provides an aesthetic function, standardizing and mitigating extreme expressions. These activities create real changes in a child's evolution and transformation that take actual forms.[288]

A child, imitating the verbal attitude of adults, does not have a deeper understanding of the values, but in simple acts, he follows the pattern of developing moral behavior toward a more self-governing conscience. When the child begins making his own decisions, the greatest adventure of shaping an ideal of life of family prayer begins. The great encounter with Jesus leads to building necessary forms of friendship, urgency, and accuracy. A child, mimicking the repetitive prayer behavior of his parents, begins to develop interior, moral life.[289] Further, the more-evolved child's moral attitude, expressed in his perception of environment and still-naive rationality, awakens the creation of its own law for his use. Allport states that in this immature rationality, the child attempts to form autonomous attitudes and perceptions.[290]

---

[286] Cf. Allport. *Personality* p. 159–165.

[287] "A child comes to difficult stage of development: the period around two to four when the ego and the sense of self take their transformation. No longer is the automatic pleasure in affiliation dominant, but the child is marked off from his environment partly because he is punished when he gets in trouble and partly through maturation." Cf. Allport. *The Mature Personality*. PaPs 3: 1952 no. 4 p. 19.

[288] *Rozwój religijności człowieka*. T 1. *Dziecko*. Lublin: Wydawnictwo KUL 2005 p. 36.

[289] Cf. LdR p. 4.

[290] Cf. Allport. *The Individual and His Religion* s. 9.

The fifth year of life marks the transition phase from the impact of the mother to the influence of his father. The bond with the father takes on greater significance. Father introduces the child to the wider world of values, rights, governance, and all the disciplines and arts of living. The child twists to the increasingly aesthetic, social, and ethical values of the father. A relationship between the child's activity and the father's movement is essential to a healthy child's formation. The personal relationships have always significant formative interactions. [291] The subjective relationship between the formal educator and child leads to a greater sense of trust, internal enrichment, and sense of faith.

The spiritual serenity of a moral educator helps overcome the child's impulsivity. Impulsive personality manifests itself in the inability of extreme behaviors, especially when a child plays, making a larger extension of "self" and his image (ages 4 to 6).[292] At this phase, *self-consciousness* is no longer a sufficient form of self-perception but being recognized from other. This impulsive stage of life brings much independence in relation to the surrounding world.[293] But the problematic fundamental manifestation of this stage of development has a similar model to the model of amoral, selfish hedonism, where the feelings of other people are unimportant and unknowable.[294]

That is why it is so important, in guided formation, to play different roles. Through play, children can repeat and deeply remember moral behaviors. Allport states that children are capable of a formative desire to repeat often-practiced roles while playing.[295] The child is gradually gaining a complete picture of his significant people, defining who he is in relation to others. By age five, the child recognizes his status as a member of the group

---

[291] Cf. LdR p. 15.

[292] R. Kegan defines this period (four to six years) with the term "impulsive" (impulsive), perceiving the excitement of the child in satisfying his own reflex needs. Kegan identifies this period (four to six years) as the term "impulsive," recognizing the excitability of the children in meeting their own needs.

[293] Cf. Allport. *Personality* s. 160.

[294] According to Allport, selfish hedonism is a higher form of development, but devoid of the gift of abandoning one's pleasure. As long as a person does not have the right education to take into account the happiness and well-being of others, his hedonistic selfishness brings with him many educational difficulties. According to Allport, selfish hedonism is a higher form of development, without, however, the gift of resignation on its own. As long as the person does not have a suitable lesson, education, also takes account of the happiness and welfare of others, selfishness hedonistic poses many difficulties. Cf. Allport. *The Mature Personality* s. 24.

[295] "We see that children are enormously repetitive. Until a child has something mastered, he wants it repeated over and over again the same way." Cf. R. I. Evans. *Gordon Allport: The Man and His Ideas.* New York: Dutton 1970 s. 31.

and has a sense of ethnic identity.[296] Through the process of socialization, he learns to identify people outside of his family circle and shows kindness toward them, which is extremely important for his image. At this stage, for the benefit of his own image, the child's external voice of authority circle becomes his new inner voice.[297] Most experts on the subject say that this marks a step toward forming a primitive conscience; the child is experiencing an extreme range of emotions, from pleasure to hurt. The child then begins to recognize people and objects in categories of cute or ugly. This, paired with his increasing ability to recognize different emotional states, leads directly to the waking-up of his conscience and proper character formation.[298]

The stage of childhood is when a child needs to be taught tolerance, especially during group activities. Children should be taught very early to respect the rights of others. This is the period during which he is most susceptible to authority and guided formation. Most preschoolers will never respect the rights of others, because at that stage, they are not yet educated in the ability to accept other people's point of view.[299] Allport's studies confirm that it is easier to change group behavior than it is to change a child's individual moral behavior.[300] Group participation at every stage of development can promote sound standards and moral principles within each individual. Then, individual behaviors become more consistent with the moral standards of society.[301]

Just as participation in group play engages the child in experiencing the difference between right and wrong, the same play or imitation of positive behavior becomes an effective method of training the moral self. This child's play period is the beginning of a new awakening of conscience, and so, practicing good behaviors is a necessary element of growth. In late childhood (6 to 12 years), however, a moral opposition arises. It arises out of a desire for arbitrariness and shapes the personality of the child's *imperial phase*. It is expressed in egoistic wants and a still-incomplete internalization of law and moral principles. This imperial freedom is false, however, because it has limits

---

[296] "As early as the age of five, a child is capable of understanding that he is a member of various groups. He is capable, for example, of a sense of ethnic identification." Cf. Allport. *The Nature of Prejudice* p. 29.

[297] Allport. *Osobowość i religia* p. 60.

[298] Cf. VS p. 85.

[299] Cf. J. Piaget. *The Origins of Intellect Piaget's Theory*. San Francisco: Freeman and Company 1969 p. 129–130.

[300] Cf. Allport. *The Nature of Prejudice* p. 29, 40.

[301] Cf. Pokrywka. *Osoba, uczestnictwo, wspólnota* p. 176. The dimension of participation is a valuable feature of human society, which forms a moral commitment to freedom and solidarity. Therefore, the full size of involvement by the freer inclusion in the life of God allows you to see and evaluate everything as if from God's perspective (*omnia quasi oculo Dei intuemur*). Participation creates moral brought up and takes on a mature form.

and prevents the child from realizing many impulsive desires. However, there is considerable freedom of imagination at this phase, and the child develops unfulfilled needs to ascribe human characteristics to the creatures of nature. Such imaginative expression gives him a sense of self-realization and accomplishment when he encounters a priest who presides over younger children. It helps them understand the roles of rulers as well as natural forces of wind or rain. [302] Imperative evolution is an opportunity for moral formation wherein the child turns to Almighty God as a force of all goodness. A child might invent a mystical encounter with someone so great, so loving, and so kind that he can move mountains. With the development of imagination and Christian identity in a child's mind, the positive image of God becomes he who ensures stability, he who is the guardian, and he who is the best Father.[303]

Older children begin to form an image of proper conduct. They can use their common-sense thinking and overcome difficulties, including feelings of inferiority. The basis for the formation of a child's moral attitude can be found in the stories, scenes, and parables of the Gospel that show Christ as the Good Shepherd, full of care and tenderness. The fact is that educators cannot simply order children to be good and leave it at that. Mentors should give positive examples, always exhibiting attitudes of gentleness, trust, and generosity. Allport describes ages 6 to 12 as the *period of rationality*.[304] The intellectual functioning of personality gives the child the ability to cope with various situations, such as the precise enumeration of sins and the process of remembering something important. The child is able to tell the correct time on a watch, count money, and solve simple problems. His thoughts are centered on his own needs.[305]

Although children as young as 6 or 7 years can comply with absolute educational norms and standards, they do not possess the slightest opportunity for the pleasure. (This seems to be characteristic of L. Kohlberg's conventional level.) Practicing good is like a gymnastics exercise for pleasure. If the child wills himself to be obedient, he does so chiefly to avoid punishment. Such obedience without too much love, however, implies detachment of the subject from the structures of self-centeredness. The imperial phase of becoming stands in line with the extension of personality in the direction of having simultaneous feelings of inferiority.[306] It warrants

---

[302] *Rozwój religijności człowieka*. T 1. *Dziecko*. Lublin: Wydawnictwo KUL 2005 p. 166.
[303] Cf. J. Flower. *Stages of Faith*. San Francisco: Harper 1995 p. 153.
[304] Cf. Allport. *Osobowość i religia* p. 42.
[305] Cf. Allport. *Personality and Religion*. New York: Harper Forum Books 1970 p. 47.
[306] Cf. R. Kegan. *The Evolving Self* s. 134. Cf. E. Eriksona fazę określaną na biegunie pozytywnym, w pracowitości i negatywnym poczuciu niższości (4 Industry vs. Inferiority).

instruction in religious morality, which fosters respect for one's personal dignity.

It is a matter of helping the child transition from operational thinking to the ability to distinguish fact from fantasy—what is essential from what is accidental or secondary. [307] For a child, the Resurrection of Christ is something magical (e.g., that same Jesus passed from death to life after taking mysterious pills). The same things happen in moral action, which requires reasonable explanation. If the child lies, he has seen anything unusual; it means only that he cannot distinguish lies from external acts. Children do not associate badness with lies, but they do not have a reason to cheat someone, either. Disobedience, lying, and selfishness are usually accompanied by a sense of guilt and shame.[308]

Evaluation and criticism come only from adults. Young children are more likely to say that they saw a dog as big as a horse as to acknowledge that they quarreled among themselves. This kind of internal inconsistency is caused by a lack of sensitivity, love, and acceptance in childhood. A. Derdziuk states that one of the causes of internal inconsistency is people's astonishing ability for self-deception, to which children are particularly vulnerable.[309] The question is whether educators should pay attention to the child who misleads others or steals something from the store. The answer seems simple: a teacher should talk to the troubled child and support them in addressing the deficiency of love in their life. A child who steals needs more care, much more attention, and above all, the listening ear of the tutor who cares. Hence, at the age of approximately 7, a child perceives a lie through the prism of the material impact it has.[310] Thus, for example, accidentally breaking eight plates is eight-times worse than breaking one plate. The greater offense is denoted by the more significant penalty.[311]

Allport, in determining the heteronomy (Gr. *heteros*, different) of early and late childhood (ages 7 and 8), draws attention to the ethical reasoning of the child, which consists of submitting oneself to the higher authority of parents and educators. Thus, this is an important manifestation of the child's trust.[312] There is no gray space in the moral reasoning of the child. It must be back or white. The gray area comes only from the intentional

---

[307] Cf. Allport. *The Individual and His Religion* p. 29.

[308] H. Malewska i H Muszyński. *The Children' lies.* Warszawa: PZWS 1962 p. 36.

[309] *Formacja moralna a formacja sumienia* p. 17.

[310] Cf. Walesa. *Rozwój religijności człowieka* s. 177.

[311] Cf. L. Kohlberg. *Education, Moral Development and Faith.* ME 4: 1974 no. 1 p. 13, 14. Kohlberg notes that the children understand ethics "of obedience and punishment," especially by identifying morally good act of obedience and the evil as the act of punishment. The weakness of the method, as per L. Kohlberg, was caused by the scarcity of research tools. He failed to scratch the image of children's morality with surprising accuracy, which is presented in *The Moral Judgment of the Child.*

[312] Cf. Allport. *Becoming* p. 34.

level of dependent thinking and intentions. But because, to the child, good and evil manifest only in material and external forms, they can be understood only in quantifiable terms.

However, the child's cooperation with moral authority helps a juvenile address these issues, allowing him to begin a process of self-formation. The dependency of outside authority and leadership begins in child's life during a period of susceptibility wherein he is compelled to work harder on oneself. The minor wants to be addressed by his role models, but he is still sensitive to justice. External standards or rules become the property of the child.[313] This explains his inability to understand adults' expressions and mental states.[314]

The educator's role is to exemplify what he tries to communicate to the child, whose moral backbone is still in development. With older children, the teacher has the daunting task of helping them assess tension-related behavior while transitioning to another stage. In the early phase of childhood development, it is important that the tutor hears from children about right and wrong. The task of formation requires the correction of previous unsure experiences of transition and evaluation based on a wider range of moral judgments. The formator should not, however, interpret their actions and behavior from an adult viewpoint. By listening to the expressions of children, instructors show their respect to minors' personal integration.[315]

There arises the essential question of whether discussions about the moral formation of this age group is appropriate. After all, a child's good upbringing seems invaluable to achieving the benefits of education. The concern of the mentor requires also friendship in times of trial and the work of positive reinforcement. This positive influence (according to Allport, Kohlberg, Rogers, or Erikson) is especially needed when the child wakes up to reconstruct his moral life inscribed in human nature. The educator must

---

[313] Cf. Piaget. *The Moral Judgment of the Child* p. 197–198.

[314] Allport's heterogeneity of coercion is called tribal morality. According to him, it begins with younger children ages three to four and seven to eight expressing themselves in the subordination of the rights of adults, their authority and their submission to the authority. Allport. *Becoming* p. 34. In adolescence heteronomous morality, also under the influence of formative techniques, transforms juvenile into moral autonomy, which Allport calls "individualization." At this stage of individualization, the individual begins to build his own values and moral principles with an inner sense of moral obligation. As a result of maturation, a child ceases to grasp the rule as unchanging; its selflessness disappears, and it begins to understand that people have different views. During this period, the individual evaluates deeds in the context of various aspects of moral situation. According to Allport, the various stages of moral judgment are one continuous process of becoming. *Becoming* p. 35.

[315] Cf. J. Fuchs. *Human Values and Christian Morality*. London: Gill & Macmillan 1970 p. 92–110.

be there when the juvenile attempts to make the transition from self-centeredness to cooperation, even though the child's impulsive behavior does not coincide with heteronomy.[316] But seeing examples of good helps a child learn in the fundamental freedom of choices. When children become aware of their required rules and proceedings, they are inclined to internal self-formation. The growing child looks to solve the problem by doing,[317] whereby his activity forms moral actions. Repeated activity inculcates ethical culture and desired personal patterns of growth. Then, it becomes an enlarged desire to draw continually from the Source.[318]

The youngster slowly begins to think before taking action. Activities that are carried from birth are internalized by repeated actions that perpetuate moral standards. In those internalized processes, children memorize learned images of being positive, which teach them about the durability of patterns. Seven-year-old children direct their thinking to the efficient operation of their thinking.[319] A good image of their little world has become formed in their heads. The cognitive, moral, or mental development represents a big step in adapting to the community. Communal standards empower children to improve themselves through such tools as imitation, imagination, drawing, dreams, fun activities, and especially language as a mean of communication with others.[320]

According to Allport, the child's self-awareness of identified models engages them with play. J. Piaget acknowledges, however, that collective monologues of young children who use appropriate childish language do not serve communication purposes but stimulate the mode of self-expression. Body language is a group's tool, and its principles seem to be imposed on the individual by their cultural environment.[321] According to Allport, that teaching environment evolves a youngster through the use of language. Any playful personification is fun for the child who "becomes," for example, rain, an animal, or an object. This play develops his imagination, through which the child evolves and transcends to next stage of maturation.[322]

---

[316] Cf. B. Häring. *Free and Faithful in Christ: Moral Theology for Clergy and Laity*. New York: Seabury Press 1978 p. 164–208.

[317] Cf. Allport. *Osobowość i religia* p. 118.

[318] A. Derdziuk. *W odpowiedzi na dar miłosierdzia*. Lublin: Wydawnictwo Gaudium 2010 p. 64.

[319] Cf. Piaget. *The Moral Judgment of the Child* p. 191.

[320] Contemporary constructivism is the direction of education derived from the gains of cognitive psychology. This theory assumes that students participate in the process of constructing their own knowledge. Cf. R.I. Arends. *Uczymy się nauczać*. Warszawa: Wydawnictwa Szkolne i Pedagogiczne 1994 p. 377–378.

[321] Cf. *The Moral Judgment of the Child*. Harmondsworth: Penguin 1932. Cf. Piaget. *Structuralism* p. 74–75.

[322] Cf. Allport. *Personality* p. 162–163; Piaget. *Play, Dreams, and Imitation in Childhood*. New York: Norton 1964 p. 230–231.

Growing children no longer are subject to the impulsive behavior but are led by purposeful coordination and their own choices (e.g., giving favorite names for their fish, cats, or dogs and speaking about them with attachment). If asked, they will remember details about them. In the end, the child can express himself and his existence in more meaningful ways. In this period, children cannot yet distinguish between certain categories, for example, the capacities of two containers of different shapes, in which the same amount of water is poured.[323] Years of research and insights of J. Piaget, confirmed by Allport's observations, signify that the youngest among those at the imperative stage of becoming cannot yet think abstractly (e.g., if A = B and A = C, then B = C). A child's ability to concretely recognize combined elements in a structured series (e.g., If A > B and B > C, then A > C) confirms the child's intense evolution in the concrete mechanisms of thinking and acting.[324]

Specifically, they still have no ability to see another point of view, so that when they talk about their favorite dogs, kittens, or unanimated objects (e.g., home, church, and school), they assume that their audience has the same images that they do. For this reason, they poorly distinguish reality from fantasy. These studies are essential for the proper value formation of the child. When small children experience a prohibition ("don't"), they require skillful attention in order to experience inner freedom, releasing barriers, and transitioning to the next stage of development. It is important to form them properly so they avoid unnecessary pains of growing, learning, and training to reach another level. The child sees prohibitions about their initiatives and choices as attacks on their integrity. This offense on their personal integrity often takes aggressive determination: "I do not!"[325]

D. Czyżowska points out that a child's contacts with parents "become the source of the first moral emotions wherein the parents bring the child into a world of principles and norms, and their authority makes the child comply with the rules of the family, thus preparing the child for living in the community."[326] And emotional formation is very important in the immediate educational environment. The emotional influence of popular or mass culture, in its simplicity, becomes more and more understandable for the youngster at every stage of development. However, mass culture based only on mass media saturated by violence and eroticism hinders mature

---

[323] Cf. J. Piaget. *The Origins of Intellect Piaget's Theory.* San Francisco: W. H. Freeman and Company 1969 p. 62.

[324] Cf. Ibid p. 190–191.

[325] Allport. *Personality* p. 165.

[326] *Wychowanie moralne w rodzinie.* IN: *Rodzina w kontekście współczesnych problemów wychowania.* Red. B. Muchacka. Kraków: Wydawnictwo Naukowe PAT 2008 p. 273.

upbringing. For example, mass culture contributes to the sexualization of children and pushes them too early into the roles of adults.

Often, a distorted influence creates a more important personal exterior space with sexual expressions, clothes, etc. Materialistic element becomes more imperative than integrity or any other area of human development. Too much sensual pressure makes integral growth difficult for children seeking to build their ideal world. Often, children cannot understand the content imposed on them, which does not take into account their sensitivity and level of associations. [327] In contrast, higher-learning embeddedness emphasizes the internal and external characteristics of right and wrong, which allow us to explain the complexity of the world and shape feelings and attitudes rather than merely complicate the child's thinking.

Postmodernity has done great damage in terms of children's films because hardly anyone wants to promote classic, easily digestible images of good and beauty to them on screen. Correspondingly, producers of movies and cartoons for children ought to display characters that defend youth against ideologies that paralyze the soul—against the excessive liberalism of the man who exists in a vacuum of hedonism or agnostic beliefs, aiming at the removal of Almighty God.[328] Postmodern ethics complicate images that exist in filmography, which are difficult and blurred in terms of what is good and what is evil. An example of this is the contemporary animation called *Avatar*. The direct contact with the child makes a great impression, likewise illustrated Bible stories that introduce a child to meaningful life (e.g., the story of Daniel calming down hungry lions identifies model of someone with unlimited goodness conquering evil). Also fairy tales create an imaginary door to the realm of mystery. For children, this becomes a possible explanation of a meaningful life. [329] Postmodern culture, however, brutally disturbs children's perceptions of images. More ethically formative are the old fairy tales with clear moral lessons and no unnecessary frills. Wise formation contributes to the moral growth of the child, giving him a proper role model of behaviors.

At the ages of 7 to 8, the child develops further skills of formation at the level of *specific thinking*. At this phase, he constructs the logic of practical thinking in overcoming fantasy as well as in communication with the outside world and acquired experience.[330] If there is no responsible attention paid, by

---

[327] Cf. A. Zadroga. *Wpływ postmodernizmu na postawy religijne*. IN: *Formacja moralna* p. 248–254.

[328] Jan Paweł II. *Przemówienie Wolność, współdziałanie, uniwersalność, służba człowiekowi – warunkami prawdziwego rozwoju kultury (Madryt, 3.11.1982)*. IN: Jan Paweł II. *Wiara i kultura* p. 183.

[329] *Okresy życia* p. 16.

[330] J. Piaget. *The Essential Piaget*. Gruber JJ. Eds. New York: Basic Books 1977.

adults, to moral formation, this transformation will be led rather blindly.[331] In moral formation, moral code is necessary to make the transformation toward greater freedom and liberation from the dependence of the previous phase quite harmonious. Religious practices and ascetic sacrifices prepare the child to think more abstractly. Observance of moral principles, among other ethical practices, affects the transition beyond the child's concrete operational thinking.

Thus, as stated by M. Pokrywka, a true vision of reality allows the child to separate fact from illusion and fantasy.[332] Every religious practice that serves an ethical purpose (e.g. not eating meat on Fridays to commemorate the sacrifice of Jesus) allows the juvenile to accomplish a more mature integration and moral formation. The Christian example is a good ethical system because it also allows a child to build a conscious harmony with others, which raises his obligations to a higher level of moral development.

Although logic is the morality of orderly thinking, morality is the logic of action. So, during late childhood (ages 7 to 12), the objects of a child's perception are focused only on the real matters, and the internalized action has a dual character. The first action forms reversibility, which is repetitive, reproducible, and teaches them to restore the previous art object. This leads to a change in the physical world, for example, the plasticine pattern of a square formed by children's thinking can be easily converted into its original shape through the child's skillful action in the opposite direction. "Playing with plasticine influences the development of fine motor skills." The transformation of the plasticine from the original mold to the secondary form can be reversed, which teaches the juvenile to think creatively.[333] Newly acquired skills give children the mobility of thinking in the real world. But via real analyses of their external world, their thoughts are based on visibility. Nevertheless, the child's intelligence grows quickly. The thinking of children from ages 7 and 8 to ages 11 or 12 is still directed only by the practical operations of the mind.[334]

---

[331] "Personalists see the child as a personality that is self-directing and capable of intelligent decision-making. Children must be actively involved in the responsibility for developing and furthering their formational programs." H. A. Buetow. *Religion in Personal Development: An Analysis and a Prescription.* New York: Peter Lang 1991 p. 46.

[332] *Antropologiczne podstawy moralności małżeństwa i rodziny* p. 320.

[333] Avin Pangestika, Rewinda & Setiyorini, Erni. (2016). *The effect of Plasticine play to fine motor development at preschool children.* Journal Ners dan Kebidanan (Journal of Ners and Midwifery). 2. 169. 10.26699/jnk.v2i2.ART. p. 169–175.

[334] "Two-third of all children are reactive against parental teaching." Cf. Allport. *The Individual and His Religion* p. 32. The opposition to the thinking of others, according to Allport, is the expression of the individualization and practical explanation of the causes for their moral cognition. Cf. Piaget. *The Moral Judgment of the Child* p. 191.

Moral socionomy (9-13 years old) is the acceptance of the norms in the group. It is moral education process of upbringing and developing in the individual traits that facilitate his relations with other people. At this stage of *socionomy,* a child consents to accepted ethical norms, which are enforced in the important group but still have not been interiorized, without recognizing them as a child's values. The teachers should, therefore, use the example of positive images that reveal deeper truths and moral aspects of the internal life. Christian formation needs to be available through teachers because the youth is still too much outside of the compound comprehension. Christianity must be presented as the constant task of bearing witness and living in authenticity. Both educators and youth grow from the source and the experience of faith, "Be ye holy, for I am holy" (1 Pet. 1:15–16). At the same time, embedded culture develops the personality of the child through new institutions, schools, and neighbor children. Morality is an expression of the child's imperial transition to a more mature way of understanding and conquering the world.

Children construct their roles, creating a personal balance between ages 10 and 11.[335] They do very well calculating exactly how to speed on their bicycles, how much money they are spending, and how to control their emotions. There must be the planned work of education regarding the proper interaction between the teacher's and the pupil's culture. Formative environments like the Christian tradition allow the improvement of social norms.[336] A child within a group of kids at school plays a complex social role, and thus, for the first-time, his actions are involved in an organizing culture.

Another important process takes place with individualization of the child. It is progress toward future autonomy which emerges with the school age. The awakening motivation of doing good is the prevailing attitude of an extroverted child about his environment because the child is focused on getting to know the outside world. In the external child's formation of moral idealism, the task is to teach them how to share things with others, because other children also have needs and have a right to attain them.[337] The developed legalistic attitude of a child often does not allow him to cooperate in harmony with the surrounding world, leaving him with a lack of flexibility

---

[335] "New subject-object relation is that child (…) no longer lives with the sense that the parent can read his private feelings. He has a private world, which he did not have before." Cf. Kegan. *Evolving Self* p. 89.

[336] "Learning brings new systems of interests into existence just as it does new abilities and skills." Cf. Allport. *The Nature of Personality* p. 90.

[337] However, since birth, the child's resistance to the pressures and requirements of parents will be a lifelong process of reconciling these two ways of becoming—gregarious and personal—which lights up individuality. Allport. *Osobowość i religia* p. 34.

and inadequate adoption to new peers.[338] A lack of flexibility and commonly accepted conventions prevent a child from maturation later in life. Each step of maturation is accompanied by the development of meaningful relationships; hence, the early parental formation of teenagers inflicts these fundamental questions: Who am I? To which group do I belong? How am I fulfilled by this group associations?

Time, in this last phase of structuring legalistic ethics, continues before the young man reaches self-reliant development toward adulthood. The sense of vocation, aspiration, and its usefulness is somewhat different between the sexes and becomes relevant after age 12.

The ethical formation of girls is somewhat different from that of boys, which is confirmed in a study by C. Gilligan.[339] Girls between 11 and 16 years of age have more difficulty articulating what they know; they feel and live under the influence of emotions, values, and current experiences with the opposite sex. In the educational environment, they are often timid. Their exterior designs become more internalized, and they own it. Girls tend to hide what they know (they prefer to say "I don't know"), so in the moral formation of this gender, educators need to demonstrate great delicacy, sensitivity, and skillful communication.[340]

In communicating with schoolgirls, particularly important is their self-esteem and security, as well as a kind approach that reduces anxiety.[341] The educator ought to alleviate any fear that adolescence imposes, showing the loving attitude of a merciful, good Father. It is not enough that Christian formation identifies social codes. It must also express patience, warmth, and sensitivity without any form of discrimination.[342] John Paul II, an enthusiastic educator, saw a significant formative approach in feminism. Communicating

---

[338] "Authoritarian morality (…) defines goodness merely regarding obedience. The adult, with all his potentialities for growth, is kept at the childhood level." Cf. Allport. *Personality and Social Encounter* p. 170.

[339] "We have come more recently to notice not only the silence of women but the difficulty in hearing what they say when they speak. In the different voice of women lies the truth of an ethic of care." Cf. C. Gilligan. *In a Different Voice: Psychological Theory and Women's Development*. Cambridge: Harvard Press 1993 p. 174.

[340] Evans, K. M. (1965) *Attitudes and interests in education*. London: Routledge & Kegan Paul.

[341] Cf. Allport. *Osobowość i religia* p. 120.

[342] Currently, there is significant support for women's movements. The Magisterium teaches: "Today survived discrimination in the large part of our society forms humiliating experience that seriously offends women, in some areas of United States as childless married, widows, women who live in separation, divorced and unmarried mothers. The Church's Synod expresses grave concern because of these and other discrimination." FC p. 24.

the truth about man and woman, he saw the gentle genius of the female sex in society, which overcomes all forms of discrimination and violence.[343]

The world of the male sex is much different from that of the female sex. Masculinity resonates the opposite values such as independence, autonomy, and competition. Femininity favors dependence based on emotional connection and harmony because girls are not able to create good communication in circles of rivalry in the same way that is possible in men's groups.[344] This lack of soft personal skills in the transformation reveals a lack of concentration in class, a tendency for depression, and starvation. Adults, too, often use this concrete operational thinking without the full exercise of the fundamental dynamics of early childhood. Persons equipped only with immature ego, without hope, willpower, or purpose are plagued with suspicion and doubt.[345] They cannot overcome alone the self-evolving jump and integral development. And their chances of ethical growth outside the heteronomy phase, without a formator's influence and help, are weak.[346]

It seems that a necessary educational tool for pupil's learning is a sense of needed modesty. In present modernity, there is the observable tendency of lowering the age limit associated with shame. Social psychologist A. Cassidy explains that juveniles of immature personality, being insecure, are unable to make a face-to-face contact are mainly capable attracting attention on the Internet. Girls often neglect their self-formation and focus on their bodies, because it is the easiest way to get attention. Under the influence of materialism and decreased inhibition, boys at school do not perceive girls as worthy individuals capable of communication, love, and affection, but as potential objects of sexual gratification.[347] Promoted modesty, according to the teaching of the Church, is "a fundamental component of integral personality, which can be understood—in the ethical—as an awakened

---

[343] Cf. EV p. 99.

[344] "Boys play competitive games with lots of rules. They quarrel a great deal, but they enjoy the disputes and solve them. When girls get into conflicts in games, they tend to end the game. 'Girls are more tolerant in their attitudes toward rules, more willing to make exceptions. Girls subordinated the continuation of the game to the continuation of the relationships.' Of course, in the competitive business world, it is often the boys' rules that dominate, but that is changing in a world 'where women can be astronauts and men can be caregivers.'" Cf. M.F. Goldberg. *An Interview with Carol Gilligan, "Restoring Lost Voices,"* Phi Delta Kappan. 81: 2000 no. 9 p. 701.

[345] Dobson, J. *Preparing for Adolescence: How to Survive the Coming Years of Change.* Grand Rapids: Revell 2014.

[346] "The origin of life is hedonistic, or self-centered if you wish, but a change occurs which makes a person much more aware of others, and extends his sense of selfhood gradually, perhaps to the end of his life." Cf. Evans. *Gordon Allport: The Man and His Ideas* p. 6.

[347] Cf. A. Cassidy. *News Letters.* "Portadown in Turmoil." Belfast: Johnston Publishing Ltd Belfast May 25, 1999 p. 8.

consciousness that defends human dignity and authentic love." [348] M. Pokrywka notes that modesty manifests itself in a healthy response to an attitude of moral depravity and applies necessary brakes to behavior that violates the dignity of the human person.[349] Ethical teaching is a necessary measure to control instincts in the development of authentic love. Learning a true sense of modesty is therefore a basic moral stance in defense of the dignity of the post-modern man. Although self-formative love protects modesty, at the same time, it stands against immaturity, shamelessness, and hedonism.

In situations where the successful transition progresses from the imperial to interpersonal, the pupil's educational needs require educators to support defeating their grown isolation. This guided formation often necessitates more sacrifices to achieve a new sense of freedom in the interpersonal phase, but the price of this growth is loneliness.[350] Educators should, therefore, promote activities, games, and healthy competition for children to help them build close relationships with their peers. Another factor tempering such alienation should be a sport. Every game conceived as a muscle movement is something that helps in the multidimensional development of spiritual and inner life. Such groups work out well when combined with rest breaks, wherein stressful states of loneliness and worrying direct the person toward character development. K. Wojtyła says that man, as a subject embedded in interpersonal relationships, might be submitted to all sorts of alienation.[351] Sport, as an energizing activity, makes a person acquire characteristics of motivation. According to Allport, an active man expects a more robust formula for life—one that will allow him to overcome alienation and suffering. Small victories in defeating developmental weaknesses help individuals grow through social interactions. Entering an interpersonal lifestyle becomes a worthy effort of his inspiration activity. At every stage, overcoming oneself is a deliberate task of integrating talk with

---

[348] PH p. 90.

[349] Cf. *Rola wstydu w obronie godności osoby ludzkiej*. RT 55:2008 z. 3 p. 139.

[350] Kegan's term, describing the "imperial" stage, highlights the lack of reality shared with others. The child (from 6 to 12 years old), in observing his world, feeds suspicion to others. When he sees others in this way, manipulating them, he loses his identity. The person entering this phase of the formation experiences less guilt, looks more at how others will react to him and expects greater acceptance. Cf. Kegan. *The Evolving Self* p. 86.

[351] Cf. K. Wojtyła. *Osoba: podmiot i wspólnota*. IN: Tenże. *Osoba i czyn oraz inne studia antropologiczne* p. 393. Lack of compassion and nullifying the survival entitlement of another human being imposes devastation to that relationship in the layout of "I" and "you." Alienation dehumanizes the person to such degree that does not allow to form any friendly community, as well. Cf. M. Pokrywka. *Osoba, uczestnictwo, wspólnota*. Lublin: RW KUL 2000 p. 76.

good deeds. Some compounds of impersonal life are more meaningful than others because they make human life worth living, as in the words of St. Augustine: "My heart is restless, O God, until they rest in You."[352]

Children ages 10 to 12 do not know what their peers think about them. And there they are, instrumentalists geared to further success and to gaining praise for what they do, creating space for more freedom and responsibility.[353] They no longer passively receive their parents' dos and don'ts. Youngsters use their skillful abilities to predict the responses of educators and their peers in the rules of discipline. In terms of good and evil, these accomplished and competent actors handle more than one role and enjoy playing in everyday situations. They already know how to extort something like making someone laugh; calming fears; or even outwitting, bribing, and blackmailing another. Children age 10 to 12 solve ethical problems according to the law, "an eye for an eye and a tooth for a tooth." At this stage of becoming, they know how to draw parents' attention to the fault of the younger sister, for example. They manipulate their older brother for a reward and will not tattle on him.[354] Schoolteachers should deeply understand the child, always forgiving him and offering him help to repair the evil they committed.[355]

According to Allport, ages 10 to 12 complete childhood. Ages 12 to 16 mark the first phase of self-actualizing needs. Defining vocational needs for growth, especially in the early stages of the educational environment, depends again on support from tutors and other people.[356] The imperial thinking of youth manifests itself in identifying new needs, interests, and perceptions. Personality is expressed in the "essential interacting" and does not imply cooperation with others who coexist in the real world. The teenager is quite introverted; people usually do not know what he is thinking. Teenaged, imperial thinking expresses itself as, "Now I know I have something to say, everything is centered on me."[357]

Youthful *principalism* is visible in examples of their moral understanding and their own inner experiences and perceptions of the feelings of others.[358] Observed external patterns become their attitudes,

---

[352] Cf. Allport. *Pattern and Growth in Personality* p. 59. Cf. C. Valverde. *Antropologia filozoficzna.* Transl. G. Ostrowski. Poznań: Pallotinum. 1998 p. 64–65.

[353] Cf. Kegan. *The Evolving Self* p. 175.

[354] Elements of fairness, reciprocity, and equal sharing are present, but they are always interpreted in a physical, pragmatic way. Reciprocity is a matter of "you scratch my back, I'll scratch yours," not demonstrated loyalty, gratitude, or justice. L. Kohlberg. *The Child as a Moral Philosopher. Psychology Today* 2: 1968 no. 4 p. 26–27; see, Flower. *Stages of Faith* p. 66.

[355] Cf. Allport. *Osobowość i religia* p. 125.

[356] Jeżyna. *Moralne przesłanie nowej ewangelizacji* p. 329.

[357] Cf. Kegan. *Evolving Self* p. 91–95.

[358] Cf. Allport. *Personality* p. 530–532.

defining how their external behavior should look. But external behavior is understood correctly only because different behavioral styles are present, (e.g., what happens when others know about it). The more mature structure begins to emerge when outside-world experiences become more personal. Under the influence of character formation, ethical internalization of norms progresses faster, and adolescents "internalize norms through parents."[359] All objects of interest that were previously used instrumentally now begin to be treated subjectively. The young individuals gradually understand the consequences of their actions and adjust to the principles and norms of their surroundings and society.

By participating in their surrounding culture, the juvenile, in a greater or lesser extension, begins to understand the complexity of his existence, learns to manage interpersonal relationships, and abandons unethical relativism in favor of a positive attitude toward other people. Thus, he hopefully begins self-formation that vanguards interpersonal becoming. These successes, of course, depend on the level to which the teenager was educated as a youth. The juvenile in the socio-cultural stage of relationships begins to create his moral system based on internalized values acquired from the environment. At this stage, he often begins opposing immediate family member. Still problematic is the integration of his personal needs with the needs of the other people. Youth is associated with moral conventions expressed in a desire to be good. Youthful moral education is herein combined with the phase of moral autonomy (Gr. *Autos,* himself, from 16 to 21 years).

Emotional relationships formed on first articulations of loving foster a faster process of internalization of moral codes and life's principles. The young man assesses new knowledge that results from the principles of personal decision-making, in which conscience is still relevant. There appears to be motivational effort involved in achieving desired goals with the aspirations of appropriate striving.[360] Internal self-aspirations become autonomous. The ethical formation of the juvenile can be approached from the perspective of loyalty, which is highly appreciated at this independent stage. A young person seeks answers these fundamental existential questions: Who am I? Who do I

---

[359] H. Gintis. "The Hitchhiker's Guide to Altruism: Genes, Culture, and the Internalization of Norms." *Journal of Theoretical Biology* 220, 4 (2003): 407–418. p. 407.

[360] "Individuals appropriate striving is strongly associated with the other main features of the 'proprium' which is comparable to the 'self' central to Augustine's appropriate striving." Cf. D. Capps. *Historical Interpretation of Augustine.* IJP 4: 1994 no. 4 p. 205–228. D. Capps suggests, using Allport's methodology, that people with well-formed motives develop appropriate striving skills, which play a significant role in the integral personality. These sophisticated features of decent goals are like the personal qualities in the life of Saint Augustine.

want to be as a man? As a Christian? As a citizen? In planning my life, how I want to realize my dreams? How do I respond to emerging passions and vocation? At this interpersonal and autonomous stage, a young man gains freedom in being loyal. According to Allport, independent self-formation stems from the ethics of loyalty.[361] Well-spent teenage time creates intense relationships that require commitment and loyalty, which shapes the teenager's personality depths.[362]

At this period of interpersonal loyalty (ages 16 to 21), a young person encounters their peer group. There is a free commitment to ambitious own goals, passions worthy of reaching. Youthful needs, interests, and desires, which are lively expressed with their peers, motivate them to be self-formed, because reality is created in relationships with others' passions. Thought, at this age, remains uncritical due to the teenager's inability to reflect on himself; objectively, he cannot assume moral obligation or perceive himself critically with his shortcomings imposed by others. His emotional experience does not yet have the necessary depth and maturity.[363] Given the inner voice of his motives, he nurtures a positive attitude in peer relations. Thinking, expressed in the ability to negotiate his needs, leads to reciprocity of his behaviors.[364] An adolescent begins to feel compassion and has a sense of mutual obligation. In relationships, he often expresses guilt and self-reflections like, "How could I let my friend go down, especially when I respect her/his views?" These statements are the first signs of awakening empathy. Empathy for other people is still unformed, but most teenage students feel the need to incorporate this sense to their maturing personality.[365] Creating one's own culture is a part of being young, and may be well taken from the Christian sources of identity.[366]

The external formation of this period depends on the intellectual stimulation conducted by the knowable teacher, trainer, or catechist.

---

[361] "Some psychologists say that the juvenile is 'rewarded' by his memberships and that this award creates the loyalty. That is to say, his family feeds and cares for him, he obtains pleasure from the gifts and attentions received from neighbors and compatriots, and hence he learns to love them. His loyalties are acquired by such rewards." Allport. *The Nature of Prejudice* s. 29. Cf. Allport. *Becoming* p. 29, 45.

[362] *Propriate* from Latin. *Proprius, "own."* All of the "me" or ego functions. Allport proposes to call it pre-eminent password. *Proprium* is not innate but develops over time. Cf. Allport. *Becoming* p. 47.

[363] "There is no self to share with another. Instead, the other is required to bring the person into being." Cf. Kegan. *In over our Heads: The Mental Demands of Modern Life.* Cambridge, MA: Harvard University Press 1994 p. 315.

[364] "We shall see, moreover, that the ideal aimed at is not to give more than one has received, but to meet out its mathematical equivalent." Cf. Piaget. *The Moral Judgment of the Child* p. 295.

[365] Allport. *Osobowość i religia* p. 131. Cf. Kegan. *Evolving Self* p. 165.

[366] Cf. W. Damon. *The Youth Charter: toward the Formation of Adolescent Moral Identity.* JME 26: 1997 no. 2 p. 117–130.

Although individualization increases one's capacity to perceive and understand man's evolution also enters the mature level of motivation.[367] In any case, logical mental development should go a hand in hand with the formative ideal of a decent life and adequate educational desire. For the growth of the Christian personality, it is therefore, necessary to teach moral concepts through discussions, dialogues, and questions and to answer with authority in the educational environment. Young people, often influenced by the culture of death and negative pressures and subcultures, are treated with deformation, belittling, and bullying. They become incapacitated, having no desires to possess higher aspirations and goals.[368] Deformative patterns, weak states of mind, and pressures lead young people to disseminate violence while destroying previously educated sensitivity to the suffering of others. The negative attitude of his peers leads to instrumental treatment and dehumanization.[369]

A characteristic feature of an instrumentalist is objectification through moral indifference, callousness, helplessness in the face of evil, and lack of knowledge. These threats are not conducive to the development of the religious and ethical life of youth.[370] As for the appropriate religious culture, moral socialization helps to build a young man spiritually and create healthy environment. Often, a young person with little spiritual development and an irresponsible sense of using of goods and resources hurts himself by closing his personality into destructive selfishness, or through bad peer-pressure engagement. Religious indifference means not so much a rejection of God, but ignoring God and God's natural laws for evolved meaningful goals in life.[371]

Adolescent personality, stepping into self-formation, is characterized by attaining specified goals and self-perception in mutual relationships.[372] Sometimes, this interpersonal period can be called the search and discovery for his own identity as a young man struggles with other teens under the influence of deeper spiritual questions: Who am I to compare with others?

---

[367] Cf. Allport. *Osobowość i religia* p. 55.

[368] "When a boy gives blow for blow, etc., he does not see to chastise, but merely to show an exact reciprocity. As for collective punishments, they are nearly all of the type 'by reciprocity.'" Piaget. *The Moral Judgment of the Child* p. 295.

[369] The moral attitude is a mature attitude that has been shaped as a result of the many ethical influences and motives that effect the individual to live a disciplined life.

[370] Cf. E. Tocz. *Chrześcijańska formacja młodzieży*. Katowice: Księgarnia św. Jacka 2005 p. 13.

[371] S. Nowosad. *Prawda człowieka—prawda jego działania.* IN: *Antropologia teologicznomoralna. Koncepcje—kontrowersje—inspiracje.* Red. I. Mroczkowski, J. Sobkowiak. Warszawa: Wydawnictwo UKSW 2008 p. 64.

[372] Cf. Allport. *Osobowość i religia* p. 120–121.

How do I want to live my life better in the face of the discovered truth about myself? Learned moral codes and principles allow young people to self-form their moral climate for the benefits of all humanity. The virtue of justice in the context of learning places each growing person where he rightly belongs based on right and fair consciousness. Teens discover that equitable treatment of others' needs requires virtues, without which his human existence is degraded. The only life worth living is truly filled with justice and permanently reflects the virtue of loving. A teenager realizes that he cannot limit his life to the love of God only in the theological aspects, but should be open to an authentic life of love.[373] The young man figures out that becoming a real man is a big task for him.

According to Allport, sensitivity in the ethical life of a young person tests his previously accepted principles. The adolescence who carried out significant self-reorganization reveals significant educational and adaptive patterns to new environmental problems.[374] Persons at age 17 experience all sorts of difficulties in their new peer environment. One of the biggest problems is revealed in school when a young person is subject to a confrontation with different educational climates than that of his own family. Frequent use of vulgar language by peers confirms its deformational influence. More support in that regard belongs to schools that ought to help with etiquette problems. Now, the adolescent enters interpersonal relationships, both positive and adverse—especially desirable training in social virtue and imagination.

Fortunately, a higher efficiency of grown intelligence leads a teenager to distance himself from conformist behavior to the views of parents and educational institutions.[375] This autonomy condition arises from the need to think for the teenagers in the school environment. The teen's personality in this period comprises more distrustful and skeptical traits. He is less susceptible to formation on the part of educators and catechists. Young people, who build autonomous beliefs, often oppose and rebel against the direction of parents and the culture of their education environments. Some young adults continue the process of individualization and reconstruction of thinking. Allport argues that many teens express forms of belief from

---

[373] Cf. B. Migut. *Antropologia teologiczna w odpowiedzi na współczesne wyzwania wychowawcze.* IN: *Kościół—naród—rodzina. Nauczanie Jana Pawła II w praktyce duszpasterskiej.* Red B. Migut, D. Capała. Lublin: Polihymnia 2004 p. 194–195.

[374] "One study reports that 80% of responders indicated they are more concerned about a comfortable life on earth, and 54% admit that their religious beliefs do not have an effect on the way they conduct their daily affairs." Allport. *Personality and Religion.* Red W. Sadler. New York: Harper & Row Publishers 1970 p. 81. Allport notes that extrinsically expressed faith becomes a formation problem for young people.

[375] Cf. Allport. *The Individual and His Religion* p. 39–42.

animism, deism, agnosticism, and atheism—"in the world of young mortals show their religious inclinations."[376]

Identity or self-identification difficulties arise from the lack of an inclusive life conception, lack of personal formation, and an inability to solve existential problems. Recommended are actions in favor of raising self-esteem, (i.e., praise, understanding, and appreciation). In the process of formation occur common but significant changes in thinking and emotions that disturb a young man's correct functioning, such as a nagging sense of guilt or shame derived from the conflicts or sexual awakening and interests. Young people at this stage of development cannot cope with high pressure, impulses, and variables feelings.[377]

Especially in adolescence, a person makes some reconstruction in the way he perceives himself, his faith, and moral behavior. J. Bazylak, in exploring the attitudes of young people, notes more consistent search toward religious morality. The stronger relationships that youth establish, the better they are at maintaining correction and controlling themselves. They have precise command and inhibit their impatience or anger. Through their religious reflections, they form better behavior, control their impulses, and act in compliance with the applicable rules of coexistence. When young people exhibit a greater intensity of their ethical patterns, the greater is the severity of their cognitive curiosity connected with needs of association, subordination, or caring for someone. They also display interest in harmony, order, and readiness to overcome their weaknesses. Similarly, their reflective religious intensity goes hand in hand with their tendency to reduce aggressive patterns.[378] But the young man cannot yet have a higher autonomous motivation. Educators see a youngster's moral transformation from selfish interests to different higher altruistic ideals as a very long process of meaningful self-formation. Allport points out that a moment of this transformation must come as "the day the decision."[379]

A young person's moral decision-making can be inclined in one of two directions: toward self-development and improvement of his humanity (including what St. Paul calls God's instrument of justice: "Do not offer yourself to sin as some instruments of wickedness, but rather offer yourselves to God, as those who have been brought from death to life; and offer every part of yourself to him as an instrument of righteousness" (Rom. 6:13), or else toward personality deformation and the dubious love of God that leads to a skepticism and even the denial of faith.

---

[376] Allport. *Osobowość i religia* p. 115.
[377] Cf. Allport. *The Individual and His Religion* p. 33.
[378] J. Bazylak. *Postawy religijne młodzieży i ich związki z wybranymi elementami osobowości.* Warszawa: Pax 1984 p. 178–179.
[379] Cf. Allport *Osobowość i religia* p. 120.

Young people often treat others objectively, for example, as an object of sexual desire, enslaving personal beauty imbued with love.[380] The grown juvenile's objective look at another person destroys God's order of values of mutual self-giving. Each case of a too-restrictive offense on an immature person triggers reactivity. Similarly, reactive opposition to the order of moral values awakens youth's rebellion in the educational process. Allport says that without professional attention, the same reactive external reaction may be formed when there is opposition to relevant standards and general human values.[381] After a great emotional and identity crisis, young people experience stabilizing peace and a moral revival. In this state, young people begin to appreciate moral and spiritual values.[382]

Although through the hard work of self-formation and education youth personality may become more integrated, stubbornness still locks him out of deeper internalized levels of executing what God or people expect from him. The juvenile's job performance still has a low maturity. His expressed externalist morality is regardless characterized by excessive austerity and a certain perspective on accepted principles. Because of that, the externality personality of the young man needs the continued support of professional education and stimulated external formation.[383] When it seems that God is only a means of meeting their egoistic wants but not principles, the personality of college students are still immature and show only utilitarian ethics.[384]

The particular morality of grown adolescents is often characterized by utility—but achieving only psychological comfort and solace of one chosen way of life presents many challenges. Simple moral utilitarianism also leads to immature forms of prejudice and a continued regression in the development of loyalty.[385] Utilitarianism creates formative problems because the assessment of moral actions depends on pure effects. The young man

---

[380] P. Góralczyk. *Wychowawcza etyka seksualna.* Ząbki: Apostolicum 2000 p. 105.

[381] "He's often religious, but in a turmoil." Cf. *Reactive formation.* IN: Allport. *The Nature of Prejudice* p. 312, 382, 427, 440, 442. Reactive formation arises in the supervised juvenile embeddedness, who protests immaturely against the true content of ethical life. Cf. Allport. *Osobowość i religia* p. 188.

[382] Cf. Ibid p. 121.

[383] Benedict XVI notes that due to the relatively small presence that religious education has, it has a great ability to integrate life. Christian education has also an effective way of teaching a new generation to be peaceful and live in harmony with another, from which no one should be excluded. Benedict XVI. *Wolność religijna drogą do pokoju.* SDP (1.1. 2011). OsRomPol 32: 2011 no. 1 p. 5.

[384] Allport. *Personality and Religion* p. 85.

[385] Utilitarian ethics is a system of values in which the central theme of deliberate behavior is deemed to be valuable from the perspective of usefulness in reference to morality. The secondary approach in this system is the egoism that altruism gives collective utilitarianism. Cf. E. Spranger. *Types of Men: The Psychology and Ethics of Personality.* Halle (Saale): M. Niemeyer 1928 p. 210.

wants to adopt absolute moral principles but only because they serve his personality. He believes that "God exists to guarantee the moral values of his choosing in which he believes."[386] A youngster, at this stage of growth, acquires necessary skills after being taught empathic behavior, especially under the influence of strong feelings like falling in love. The young man thinks by accepted values but also evaluates them according to his mindset—whether or not the new experiences can be incorporated into the precinct of his anthroposphere, socio-sphere, and ecosphere.[387]

Another reason for becoming morally better at this stage of adolescence is rationality, which challenges one to embrace authority patterns and have, according to Allport, "mental acuity."[388] By clarity, systematization of concepts, and principles, proper discipline in moral growth becomes a tool in objective self-realization and becoming an independent thinker.[389] The independent being is a higher form of manifestation in that he can overcome past obstacles of development. The youth independent also evolves from less-refined structures of thought, away from the former child's personal dependence on others.[390]

In the sociocultural formation aspects of expecting is more visible. Maturing individuals begin to reach their highest potential. They are looking for new visions of better designs and are consistently striving to achieve real successes—whether professional, educational, or social. Although the task of self-formation becomes a process to open new possibilities and widen the personality (allowing an extension of the self), the process itself requires proper stimulation of intellect, emotions, and motivations. Everybody knows that without carrying out the tasks of life—without achieving more ambitious goals and learning appropriate judgments and personal patterns—a young person cannot count on self-achievement and spontaneous integral development.[391] The impact of the public might intensify self-formation as well. Media personalities who live by faith often shape the young man's attitude toward a meaningful life. For example, many young people who have observed the life of John Paul II have learned a testament of how to live a personal and integrated life.

---

[386] Ibid p. 122.

[387] W. Andrukowicz. *Sześć szczebli rozwoju wrażliwości na prawdę, dobro i piękno*. IN: *Wychowanie moralne w szkole katolickiej*. Red. A. Sowiński, A. Dymer. Szczecin: Kwadra 2003 p. 248.

[388] Cf. Allport. *Osobowość i religia* p. 123.

[389] Cf. Ibid.

[390] Cf. Allport. *The Individual and His Religion* p. 55.

[391] J. Piaget identifies a period in adolescent life, at the early as the age of 13 years old, when a person starts learning the ability of abstract thinking. The ability of abstract thinking comes with the help of education systems in which a person learns the logical use of reason, deduction, and systematic planning.

Studies show that during adolescence, girls and boys differ in their susceptibility to education. People under age 20, Allport observes, are seldom guided by the wisdom and ethical motivation that seniors have.[392] Puberty is a time of "emancipation" from the parental way of life. Simply putting it, young people easily forget the experienced warmth, parental pietism, and moral reasoning of their parents. But by age 30, these same children, having struggled to develop some meaningful modus, observe that the educational model of their parents does not have to go into oblivion. Thus, almost half of the subjects studied by Allport adopted parental morality as a correct direction in their lives. However, at this stage of maturity, it becomes clear that the parental path in life is best. Seven out of 10 of Allport's students answered affirmatively to the question, "Do you feel that in achieving a fully mature worldview you need some form of ethical guidance?"[393] Of course, different people require unique types of guidance through marriage and life. Young people, especially, recognize the loving relationship of a husband and wife as a covenant.[394] The self-formative phase of interpersonal relationships also becomes a maturity test of the readiness of young people for marriage. Most of us agree with Allport's statement that "marriage is for mature adults."[395] At the same time, he sees that only some are completely ripe for the responsibility of marriage. Nevertheless, that readiness can be achieved—presumably by all—in continues process of self-formation.

In analyzing the interpersonal period of youth, we can see the need for external brainstorming and stimulation that involves interactive, mature thinking. That's why many educational systems involve a brainstorming phase. Therefore, the invitee motivates and shapes himself to have a more attuned life, because a moral, thoughtful approach will not form itself. The culmination of this interpersonal stage comes with autonomous motivation, which engages young professionals in the management of their personal lives.[396] But given their still-low personality integration and multitude of intensified feelings, young professionals encounter moral and development crises that arise with new force. But overcoming crises shape self-esteem for better integration. M. Majewski points out that misunderstanding of this integration process among educators or parents who struggle to tolerate these challenges often leads to emotional tensions.[397]

---

[392] Cf. Allport. *Osobowość i religia* p. 124–125.

[393] Cf. Ibid p. 124.

[394] Cf. F. Adamski. *Rodzina między sacrum a profanum*. Poznań: Pallottinum 1987 p. 35.

[395] "Few people are wholly mature before marriage—maturity I achieved through marriage; through its strains." Allport. *The Mature Personality* p. 19.

[396] According to Allport, *propriate striving* is expressed in the capacity of active "ego involvement." Cf. Allport. *The Ego in Contemporary Psychology*. PSRev 50: 1943 no. 5 p. 451.

[397] Cf. *Wychowanie domaga się zaufania. Katecheta* 34:1990 no. 4 p. 68.

In the early stage of adulthood (ages 21 to 27), the individual accepts general social norms on the level of post-convention.[398] Because his early adulthood reveals a more mature perspective of understanding social rules, a man's challenge ought to motivate him to seek profound self-formation. In adulthood, a person chooses real solutions. Allport emphasizes that the transformation process of developing toward the self-formation of external sanctions is subject to moral imperatives. Only through high moral imperatives does man live in greater freedom and responsibility for himself and others. The transformation process thus includes the reorganization of previously approved constructions in favor of moral imperatives toward more positive thoughts and actions. Moral life of a mature person is much more objectified.[399] In fact, morality matures in the formed self through a conscious and reflective extension of "self." At this stage of adulthood, the self-forming man experiences corresponding intuition and self-insight.[400] The man accepts the good in God's truth, writes John Paul II: "The Supreme Good and the moral good meet in truth: the truth of God's creation, and the reality of man redeemed by Him."[401] Through the influence of human and divine authorities, one adopts altruistic personality traits. And although he is devoted to higher values, now the Christian opens himself up naturally to self-formation.

Both in early and later adulthood, the education of conscience is linked to the science of ideas, or "ideonomy" (Gr. *idea*, pattern). The ideonomy of spiritual development continues almost to the last years of one's life. It sometimes causes a transition to a more in-depth faith, morality, or righteousness of conscience, even though chronological age is an inadequate measure of emotional and religious maturity.[402] Personal maturity is often associated with a mature self-esteem—an accurate assessment of one's positive and negative attitudes. Nevertheless, deeper reflection with achieved freedom allows adults to read their own internal states of mind in different situations. Such a person wants to live more meaningfully in the love of God that gives him the inner strength to overcome vanity, coldness, anger, and impurity. J. Bajda notes that the mature stage of life bases all acts on entrustment rather than control, wherein actions stem from genuine love. At

---

[398] Cf. Kegan. *Evolving Self* p. 190–191.

[399] "Characteristics of the mature personality: extension of the self—self-objectification, insight and humor, the Unifying Philosophy of Life." Cf. Allport. *Personality* p. 213–235.

[400] "Somewhat similar is the trait of self-insight. Knowledge of oneself, research shows, tends to be associated with tolerance for others. People who are self-aware, self-critical, are not given to the ponderous habit of passing blame to others for what is their responsibility." Allport. *The Nature of Prejudice* p. 436.

[401] VS p. 89.

[402] Cf. Pokrywka. *Antropologiczne podstawy moralności małżeństwa i rodziny* p. 322.

the adulthood level, the whole human being focuses his own energies for God's sake.[403] Otherwise, all educational effort would make no sense. Finally, the man finds equilibrium and dialogue with God. As a reflective Christian in his adulthood, he experiences harmony with God through the Sacrament of reconciliation.

In the stage of early maturity, the self-formed man continues in truth, freedom, and autonomous and healthy motivation to perfect his roles. Man not so much undertakes the attitude of a servant but realizes how to fulfill and meet different roles and expectations to collaborate in God's Creation. Allport observes that man, growing at this stage of autonomous self-formation, not only reduces anxiety but also activates vital functions of this experience to become a more independent thinker and a leader of a more dignified life.[404]

But he most mature Christian life is expressed in *theonomy* (Gr. Θεός, "God" and νόμος, "law"), which refers not only to an external law but also to all norms and forms belonging to people in everyday life.[405] God's law becomes individually adopted internal legislation expressed in God's law of creation as well as in the experience of indefinite mercy when a man admits to being weak. And here, before Christ, man humbles himself, acknowledging before God that he acted imperfectly. And then, during deeper conversion or confession, something unusual happens. [406] The inspired Christian appreciates asceticism, identifies the causes of things, strengthens his character, and shores up his tender conscience, all of which help him get rid of deception and seek long-term solutions. Deep faith reduces ignorance and shows him what is fair and valuable. Often, the period of early maturity is about life organization and formation of institutional personality. [407] An overseeing personality now knows how to professionally take care of other people, how to take responsibility for subordinate employees, and how to administrata social organization, for example, in his local church. Although the man at this stage knows how to responsibly manage a group of people, he often lacks continuous ethical self-formation to gain a much higher integral life.[408]

---

[403] Cf. *"Chrystus odwołuje się do serca." Wokół problemu interioryzacji.* IN: Jan Paweł II. *Mężczyzną i niewiastą stworzył ich. Chrystus odwołuje się do serca.* Red. T. Styczeń. Lublin: RW KUL 1987 p. 160.

[404] Cf. Allport. *The Individual and His Religion* p. 52–53.

[405] Cf. VS p. 41.

[406] A. Derdziuk. *W odpowiedzi na dar miłosierdzia.* Lublin: Wydawnictwo Gaudium 2010 p. 29.

[407] Cf. Kegan. *Evolving Self* pp. 226–227.

[408] Similar to Allport's way of reasoning is M. Dziewiecki, who sees that human crises are caused mainly by a lack of concern for upbringing and self-formation. Cf. M. Dziewiecki. *Kształtowanie postaw.* Radom: "Ave" 1997 p. 14.

The socio-cultural stage of late adulthood (from 27–40 to 65 years) is the period of adult life in which the reasonable, mature person draws from the models of true interior freedom. Therefore, we characterize the late adulthood in respect for all and what an adult can be in heroic responsibility for others and their humanity—even culturally distinct people. A person at this self-seeking moral development phase retains the ethical intercultural principles that have been universally formed in and around him. His mature personality, which is expressed in the deep wisdom of his moral self, is about reaching interdenominational cultures. Allport supports the hypothesis of Jung, saying that a person will not develop a valuable sense of moral self until he reaches, at least, middle age. The high values triggers intellectual pursuit of self-formation and being better a version of oneself. Continuation of transformations in adulthood tend to widen an individual's personality and interconnected harmony (through the extension of interests and higher goals).[409] The developed self, in mature adulthood, sees another person not as an object but as an important subject, so the person, according to Allport's theory of mature personality and motivation, is autotelic. Being autotelic stands in contrast to the effective treatment of another human being. The law of God becomes internal legislation of individual multiple acts of mercy.[410]

The personality of the mature man comprises a deep moral responsibility to others and God's Creation. Allport specifies that "the Knower," in man's cognitive functions, has more compassionate significance. [411] A man forms his new attitude toward society out of spirited compassion for his community and the whole world. Hence, he has a sense of institutional responsibility (he who knows what is right, good, and beautiful). [412] The self-formed individual, at this stage, has identification abilities: the person manages the organization, others. His progress manifests itself not so much in the ethical administration and the management but rather in the internal responsibility for the organization (e.g., the common good of all). A mature person has well-established relationships. A grown man, as an adult, is made responsible for others through deep self-reflection; a higher level of self-criticism; and an understanding of his roles, norms, and tasks. Often, he behaves defensively on behalf of others when chaos threatens the order of the community for which he is responsible.[413]

---

[409] Cf. Allport. *The Mature Personality* p. 24.
[410] Hedonism is derived from the theory of reducing human determinism in which feelings of pleasure and the unpleasantness are key components of ethical life.
[411] Cf. Allport. *Becoming* p. 51–54.
[412] Cf. Allport. *Osobowość i religia* p. 46.
[413] Cf. Kegan. *In over our Heads* p. 314.

A full-grown person identifies himself through the expression of moral autonomy and his ability to distinguish between good and evil with the depth of experience. He draws on learned experiences, available resources, and ethical knowledge to fix developmental matters much quicker than he could before. Maturity in adulthood, which occurs through the self-formation of cognitive and emotional structures, is well-manifested in the stable control of the whole sphere of self-expression. Higher emotions include, among others, moral, aesthetic, and intellectual beliefs, which activate a person for any moral action. A mature personality is much different from an immature one in that allows the person to control his feelings, both positive and adverse.[414] The task of socio-cultural self-formation is to realize universal human capabilities and essential values in a balanced, mature way. Continuous and ongoing self-formation is particularly valid when it encourages and strengthens further efforts from higher-volitivity movements and emotions. Internal self-examination of these states does not come spontaneously but often through contemplative life, reflection, and prayer by which an individual moves to a desired state of mind in harmony with his surrounding reality.[415]

In adulthood, the sociocultural self-formation of consciousness is uttered through the universal call to holiness, thus carrying the willingness to become more involved in spiritual life and active charity and better managing feelings and values. Man does not exist for oneself in any society, and therefore, he has the task of moral self-actualization through his consciousness and free moral acts. Man's inner freedom is not only a sign of co-Creation with God but is shaped in God's likeness. Therefore, the higher duty of every human is to improve one's life and become a close co-Creator of a better world.[416]

This growth approach restores the inner harmony and paves a smoother road of reintegration with God. Human integration in late adulthood is associated with the ability to smooth disproportions and bring them to a higher moral level of being. Allport argues that deeper tolerance requires more time and reflection in terms of achieving mastership and better self-control. Even the most integrated personality does not always work in harmony with its believed values.[417] And that's why the mature man needs the Person of Christ. The human person creates harmony only in Christ, his Savior, who sacramentally opens the compassionate way for man to return to the fullness of truth about himself and master his sinful nature. The nature of God's salvation includes the imperatives of a deeper level of self-control.

---

[414] "Feelings of guilt suggest poor personality teamwork." Cf. Allport. *The Individual and His Religion* p. 87.

[415] "Through prayer one simply moves oneself closer to the state desired." Cf. Ibid p. 134.

[416] Cf. A. Just. *Osobotwórcza funkcja religii*. STV 13: 1975 no. 1 p. 176.

[417] Allport. *Osobowość i religia* p. 65.

A higher standard of restraint and mastery makes a person better integrated and refuted to his negative emotions, primarily uncontrollable and sudden, like wrath and anger. This mature level of self-control leads to the experience of self-giving, enriching interrelationships. Mastered self-control comes to the believer as the fruit of the Spirit of God. K. Wojtyla states that the man maturely formed is precisely a man truly integrated.[418] The individual becomes capable of such a self-giving gift, because in the model of Jesus Christ, the redeemed man has been returned to his full ability of self-ownership, which allows him again to become an offering to God or neighbor. Such grace allows a man to get rid of various forms of selfishness. Rightly, points out M. Pokrywka that "peace of heart" is not only the natural knowledge of eternal truth "of the beginning," but also man's capacity and mature acts of free choice.[419]

At the stage of mature personality, the fundamental basis of Christian morality comes from obedience to moral truths, higher principles of life, guided virtues, and noble intentions. A unique role in the integral formation of a mature personality is abided by self-formation. Self-formed personal decisions are volatilely-based and come only with deeper self-knowledge. When the personality is open and relational (i.e., has a widened personality, as Allport says), the person chooses good over evil, seeks beauty, goodness, love, and complete truth about himself. This is the quality of heart that enriches human existence. John Paul II draws attention to this aspect, saying that "the educational process leads to the phase to which one when after reaching a certain level of psychophysical maturity begins his upbringing updated in self-formation." Over time, self-education somehow surpasses the formal educational process.[420]

According to Allport, a mature person is a wise person, able to deliver significant judgment about himself, others, and actions resulting from internally formed principles of love, guaranteeing a generous gift of self for others, for the Church, and for a great cause. Adult's human existence reaches a so-called socio-cultural maturity at the stage of mature adulthood. Such maturity consists of heroic responsibility for others, even when they are culturally different.[421]

---

[418] Cf. *Miłość i odpowiedzialność*. Lublin: Wydawnictwo KUL 1986 p. 130.

[419] The biblical notion of "heart" is the deeper dimension of humanity that directly connects a sense of the human body with the true sense of the higher order. So, Christ not only evokes the "truth of the beginning" but puts her in front of man's eyes as a mirror so he can see the state of his heart. Pokrywka. *Antropologiczne podstawy moralności małżeństwa i rodziny* p. 163.

[420] LdR p. 16.

[421] According to R. Kegan, the interindividual stage of evolving is a higher stage of maturity. Higher maturity fulfills traits of being more humane. As R. Kegan notes about this juncture: "it's almost something beyond maturity, and it's usually a

In the service of new evangelization, only the mature man can respond to God's call. The person in mature adulthood has a unique ability of essential knowledge that determines desired changes in his behavior, and similarly, "intense faith can change character.[422] For the self-forming man, the most important task is to realize one vocation received from God—to live by the highest motives and good intentions inscribed in his heart." For that reason, to act well, Gilson writes, it is not enough to believe that what we are doing is pleasing to God; it must also be proved as—according to the will of God—what a man should do.[423] An adult in every act not only fulfills a real goal but also seeks God, who ought to be his ultimate desire. The Christian morality of adulthood ought to be, then, an art, and the theory of his interior life should be based on the fundamental thesis of the existence of the loving God. For the mature Christian adult at this stage, God is the ultimate source of goodness and the criterion of human ethics and morality. At every human stage, Christian life is shaped by the principles and timeless values that are aimed at the good of society.

According to John Paul II, the "pastoral activity of the Church must inspire everyone to discover and appreciate the role of the elderly in secular and the ecclesiastical community, especially in the family life."[424] He recalls in *Familiaris Consortio*: "How many children have found understanding and love in the eyes and words of the elderly!"[425] Reliable knowledge about man and his goal-realization leads a person of mature age to take thoughtful initiatives. The harmonious life of a mature person allows continual internal development in the form of continuous self-formation. [426] Allport emphasizes that motivation in late adulthood results from the depth of one's autonomous faith. It means that religious values can mobilize all energies and involve the whole personality. John Paul II rightly notes that "each of us is the goal, and the starting point of autonomous self-formation."[427]

The mature personality of the adulthood stage is characterized by a settled sense of integrity and internal freedom of loving. There is no superficial exteriority of imitated behavior like there was in the previous

---

precarious state to be in. I mean, we loved Jesus, Socrates, and Gandhi after we murdered them." E. Debold. *Epistemology, Fourth Order Consciousness, and the Subject-Object Relationship or…How the Self Evolves with Robert Kegan.* "Enlighten Next" 22: 2002 no. 1.

[422] Allport. *Osobowość i religia* p. 152.

[423] É. Gilson. *Historia filozofii chrześcijańskiej.* Transl. S. Zalewski. Warszawa: Instytut Wydawniczy Pax 1987 p. 148–149.

[424] FC p. 27.

[425] FC p. 27.

[426] K. Wojtyla notes that mature self-formation is "the evolution of the human person in the direction of the final destination, and at the same time, for the good of the Church and society by the harmonious development of the congenital physical, moral and intellectual spheres." Wojtyła. *Miłość i odpowiedzialność* p. 124.

[427] ChL p. 63. Cf. PDV p. 69.

stages. [428] The attitude of a mature person is the direct result of deep reflection—man knows who he is in the final perspective. This phase of growth into mature adulthood, as indicated by Allport, can be called a transition toward deeper morality in the Christian's life. More consciously lived morality (intrinsic), is manifested in the communion of persons and has a mature attitude toward the commitments that arise from faith, creating—as defined by John Paul II—"a school of deeper humanity."[429]

According to Allport, mature people with adequate positive self-esteem are usually happy and moral. By analyzing the biography of many saints, we learn they experienced happiness in union with God. This stage of ethical self-formation has an integrating nature. It means that an educator must see the potential capabilities and weaknesses at various stages of human development in the implementation of different avenues to harmony. It is necessary that the Christian recognize steps that are reasonable, useful, and relevant so that he can be the best version of himself. It seems momentous that the freedom of well-implemented choices lead to fulfilled transitions at every stage of life. The dimension of liberty helps a person cross the threshold of one stage of personality development and into the next stage of maturity and morality. Therefore, the sociocultural becoming of meaningful formation requires the use of adequate educational methods of influence in the most vulnerable time of ethical reasoning.

---

[428] Cf. Allport. *Personality* p. 156.
[429] FC p. 21. Cf. LdR p. 52.

CHAPTER 3

Formative environments

The process of one's fulfillment is grounded in the uniqueness of each person and takes place in civilized society. One of the most essential dimensions of the fully formed person is his humanity. Humanity of formative environments creates certain values, enriching the potential of each person in the capacity of loving and having meaningful brotherly relationships. So, in the climate of freedom, the evolved man grasps the compassionate essence of his humanity to become an icon of God. In that sense, the human being, as a subject of intelligent, free, and responsible decisions, grows while actively participating in the process of upbringing. M. Pokrywka states that due to human dignity—which is not attributed to man but with which he comes into the world—a person is recognized as a distinct entity from any other creatures, the world of things, and the world of objects.[430]

Humanity is freely given to the man, and at the same time, it is God's gift that comes with co-Creating tasks for every person. The self-realizing man, conscious of his dignity as a child of God, therefore, has the capacity to undertake the work of integral formation. Allport also points out that an intellectual breakthrough in the perception of humanity is valuable in terms of eradicating anthropological misconceptions that enslave and objectify human life.[431]

The subjective formation of youth considers their obstacles in growth, and that a mature person cannot be built only "from outside." John Paul II explicitly highlights that the art of formation requires that every man creates his integral humanity from within the toil, perseverance, and patience.[432] Without realistic education, young people go astray and "depart from an objective order of values. Therefore, as M. Pokrywka says, even "education is reduced to the extreme mode of socialization or individualization."[433]

This notion of socialization assumes different avenues. The most harmful is that which imposes on the pupil's political power, which has less

---

[430] Pokrywka. *Antropologiczne podstawy moralności małżeństwa i rodziny* p. 284.

[431] Cf. Allport. *Personality and Social Encounter* p. 348.

[432] John Paul II. *Przemówienie do intelektualistów "Kultura i perspektywy przyszłości świata" (Coimbra*, 15.05.1982). IN: DzZ T. 10 p. 657.

[433] Cf. *Antropologiczne podstawy moralności małżeństwa i rodziny* p. 326.

to do with education than with taming or dressage. Examples of totalitarian dressage reflect the *homo Sovieticus*: the depersonalization and passive acceptance of everything the government imposes. A man exposed to such taming runs from any true freedom into various forms of slavery. For example, one becomes deprived of responsibility and independent thinking. Totalitarian socializing in the form of dressage causes excessive dependence toward the stronger imperator and aggression toward the weaker.

Another radically opposed approach to socialization is individualism, which leads to the disintegration of education through relativism and subjectivism. M. Pokrywka stresses that a direct consequence of individualistic behavior is subjectivism, which pushes the student down the road of moral relativism to arbitrary action, ultimately destroying any process of ethical reasoning and self-formation.[434] The integral sphere, which includes moral and spiritual spaces, is treated as being an unnecessarily imposed burden from the outside, preventing egoistic self-fulfillment in formative activities. The subjectivist concept of formation, flowing from secular or atheistic anthropology, leads in principle to anti-pedagogy.[435] We must strongly emphasize, once again, that human formation cannot be one-sided or superficial. Subjectivist conception leads directly to liberalism.

In this context, of great importance is the formation to the fullness of humanity, which restores the natural rights of God in human life. The attainment of the "measure of the stature of the fullness of Christ" (Eph. 4:13) entails love of Christ on the part of the disciple or ward. Without Christ, it is hard for a man to discover the fullness of truth and live the fullness of humanity. It should be noted that the veracity of moral education is based on a realistic vision of man approached from personalistic anthropology. Allport points out that personalistic formation in Christian anthropology is derived from the source of all personal dignity in the educational process.[436] Human entities engaged in self-formation truly restore the natural law of God in their lives and thus magnify the dignity of each human life. The Christian

---

[434] Cf. Ibid p. 288.

[435] Cf. M. Dziewiecki. *Osoba i wychowanie. Pedagogia personalistyczna w praktyce*. Kraków: Wydawnictwo Rubikon 2003 p. 12.

[436] "The anthropology of good morale is shown by the stamina with which people stand up under punishment and by the energy with which they strive to realize their ideas (...). The first essential for good morale is a definite goal. People who have nothing to look for will show poor morale. One of the most destructive consequences of our prolonged economic depression was that so many young people came to feel that there was no hope ahead." G. W. Allport. *Civilian Morale*. Red. G. Watson. Boston: Houghton Mifflin Company p. 30.

formation of enriched humanity through the person of Christ is possible only by preserving the subjectivity, respect, and dignity of the pupil.[437]

Examples of disrespect and objectification are visible in unjust secular legislation that deprives people of fundamental human rights. As we read in *Christifideles Laici*, "when the individual is not recognized and loved in the person's dignity as the living image of God (cf. Gen. 1:26), the human being is exposed to more humiliating and degrading forms of 'manipulation,' that most assuredly reduce the individual to a slavery to those who are stronger." [438] Through moral self-formation based on Christian anthropology, it is possible to live at a level worthy of man, as a child of God. J. Gocki rightly underlines that "the defense and promotion of human dignity and their rights will only be right when one accepts the full personalistic concept, not reduced only to the idle humanism."[439]

Any self-formation toward living in the fullness of humanity teaches individually integrity that give realistic convictions of one's unique position in the humane world. As such, personalistic formation contributes to the fact that humanity unifies, expands, and enriches the person, leading people to higher education through prayer, theater, books, or meeting with friends. The man, living in the fullness of his life, is truly free in union with Christ while acquiring the best values. When the modus of ownership enslaves man, the opposite human modus triggers the dimensions of values and peace.[440]

---

[437] Dignity and respect are important to integral personality self-formation. Allport notes: "Respect for each person is the right formation of the personality. A program is good if its aim and practice are intended to further the well-being, growth, and integrity of each personality. A democracy believes that the maximum development possible in each is for the best interests of all, and it imposes respect for the person is not altogether a principle of leniency. It engenders a sentiment of great hatred of oppression.

Compliance with the person is the motive power behind Jefferson's often quoted pledge, 'I have sworn upon the altar of God eternal hostility to every form of tyranny over the mind of man.' Especially in wartime is it well to stiffen the militant fiber of the nation by arousing this very sentiment. Already strong, it can be stimulated and augmented until it becomes the dominant factor in winning the war. Militant and psychologically active, it is at the same time entirely consonant with the ethics of democracy." Cf. Allport. *Civilian Morale* p. 8–9.

[438] ChL p. 5.

[439] *Wychowanie w służbie praw człowieka*. T. 1. Red. R. Sadowski IN: *Biblioteka Towarzystwa Naukowego Franciszka Salezego*. Warszawa: Towarzystwo Naukowe Franciszka Salezego. 2008 p. 34.

[440] E. Fromm notes that the man engrossed in materialistic orientation and consumption must go to the level of the spiritual values of truth and justice. This process is the formation of the moral self. "I have no need to be aware of myself as myself because I am constantly absorbed with consuming (...). He must emerge from a materialistic orientation and arrive at a level where spiritual values-love, truth, and justice-truly become ultimate concern to him." E. Fromm. *The Dogma of Christ: And Other Essays on Religion, Psychology and Culture*. London: Routledge 2004 p. 88.

The actualization of the moral self sees the potential of humanity in the acquisition of human qualities—known within natural and revealed law—which remarkably characterize development utilizing a perfect language, feelings, and behaviors that are worthy of a loving image of the Creator. The formed self, as the subject of its social setting, occupies a unique place in the universe. "The human person who is and ought to be the principal, the subject, and the object of every social organization has the obligatory duty of human fulfillment."[441] The human person has principles and is therefore required to actualize humanity. All of the most-valuable human traits are common to most people and manifest from the beginning of man's creation. The task of integral self-formation directs the man toward realizing his higher personal goals that are in line with ultimate objectives. John Paul II notes that the fullness of humanity has been achieved in response to the call that everyone must "enrich according to the gifts (…) which were endowed upon him."[442]

The formation of the moral self, inspired by divine Revelation, serves us in building humanity using literature, arts, body, figurative language, and speech to strengthen the Christian identity of the student. An important role in integral formation toward experiencing the fullness of humanity, says John Paul II, is Christianity and non-Christian religions. Referring to the teaching of the Second Vatican Council, he said: "The Fathers of the Church rightly saw in the various religions' reflections of the one truth, seeds of the Word, which testify to the fact that although different the roads, one human spirit directs to the deepest aspiration, which is expressed in the searching for God—and at the same time in searching through the pursuit of God—the full dimension of humanity with the whole meaning of human life."[443]

Moral self-formation toward the fullness of humanity thus discovers the meaning of life in two ways, one inherent and other supernatural by the grace of God, especially in an adult who is fully mature. The natural road to sincere desire and developing personal qualities is expressed in the realization of spiritual values, thinking, and actions. The self-realized man gains humanity by doing good and avoiding evil. Through orderly, loving development and formative self-discipline, humanity awakens to the responsibility of tolerance and positive socialization and learns to be properly expressed, in speech and writing, in the language of love. The Church draws her vision of full humanity from divine Revelation (Scripture and Tradition), using the classical systematization of the Fathers in the integral interpretation of truly human life, based on the cardinal virtues of prudence, justice, fortitude, and temperance.

---

[441] CCC p. 1,892.
[442] LdR p. 9.
[443] RH p. 11.

Drawing on the thought of St. Thomas, John Paul II defines virtue as a constant trait by which the human being becomes real.[444] Orientation toward the fullness of humanity by means of acquired virtue shapes human morality and stability.

Prudence is the first of the four cardinal virtues. It does not belong to someone who can cope with life but to the man who lives according to the requirements and voice of an upright conscience. Justice disposes one to respect the rights of those whose dignity may be threatened, relying on firm devotion to the will of God, to who, they are associated.[445] M. Pokrywka also stresses that this is about creating a wealth balance of material nature but also privileging honor, respect, and reputation. The personalistic, full dimension of humanity is vital because of a person's legal rights.[446] The *Catechism of the Catholic Church* defines fortitude as "the moral virtue that ensures firmness in difficulties and constancy in the pursuit of the good. It strengthens the resolve to resist temptations and to overcome obstacles in the moral life."[447] Finally, the virtue of temperance moderates the love of pleasures, ensuring the will's mastery over instincts and subordinating human desires to the spiritual ideal. The moderate man, says John Paul II, is master of himself, a man in whom passions do not overtake reason, will, and "heart." In other words, he can control himself. It is easy to see how indispensable the virtue of temperance is in self-formation.[448] Moderation demands abstinence from behavior that degrades one's humanity.[449]

The different cardinal virtues are interrelated. The research of Kegan and M. Dziewiecki in developmental psychology confirms the necessity of continuous formation without unduly postponing it to later stages of life. Similarly, Allport links systematic formative work to the development of healthy habits.[450]

Internal discipline and self-improvement activities are essential to shaping character. In Allport's terms, "character" is often interchangeable with "personality." Character is the personality evaluated, whereas personality is character devaluated.[451] In general, character describes the developed characteristics and personal qualities that distinguish one person from another. Allport draws attention to the potential of citizens to combat delinquency and ethnic prejudice. Faithful people know that good is always stronger than evil, for goodness comes from Him, who is the perfect Good. M. Pokrywka stresses the necessity of persistence in doing good and taking

---

[444] LE p. 9.

[445] CCC p. 1,807.

[446] Cf. *Antropologiczne podstawy moralności małżeństwa i rodziny* p. 327.

[447] CCC p. 1,808.

[448] *Katecheza "Cnota umiarkowania"* (22.11.1978). IN: DzZ T. VI p. 26–27.

[449] Cf. KKK p. 1,809.

[450] Cf. Allport. *Osobowość i religia* p. 55.

[451] Cf. Allport. *Pattern and Growth in Personality* p. 32.

individual responsibility. Educational tasks should never be discouraging but should always awaken in the trainee pro-social identity and the mature feeling of being special and well-integrated into the social system of references through a unique, satisfying role.[452]

Well-planned formation, engaging good practice, allows a person to fill exemplary roles in society, and in the embedded environment, they develop interpersonal skills toward being more human that protect them against selfishness. An altruistic model of life orients a person toward valuable relationships and long-term goals. The Church's Magisterium states that "real education strives to shape the human person toward its eschatological goal."[453] Christian moral formation aims at the improvement of human character, even though (as M. Poznańska has shown) it often requires the hard work of adopting interpersonal and cultural norms and values.[454] Getting to know one's personality through a pupil's reflection becomes an important goal in the ability to use internal forces and work together, according to the image of God found in the student's heart. As Benedict XVI affirmes, a person's authentic, integral development has an important transcendent dimension, without which it is much harder to achieve enriched humanity.[455]

Commitment to seeking humane development is significant for each stage of the integral life. True self-realization has a basis of education in supernatural qualities—hope, love, and faith—which not only prepare a man for the transcendent enlightenment of his intellect but also move his will to positive territory because of his affiliation to God.[456] Christian self-formation, therefore, is the essential process of becoming a perfect disciple of Christ. An ethical model is found in the Person of Jesus Christ, who introduces the lost man to the right path of good decisions. His ideal realism perfectly fits the harmonious model of humanity. The person focused on Jesus can discover, in Him, the eternal design of God. As John Paul II writes, young people look in His direction because youthfulness means a "demand" for a model of humanity that is complete, simple, and transparent. At the same time, Jesus's humanity is "exemplary." Meaningful life demands moral humanity that activates young people. Young people going through identity crises are most interested in these questions: What is it to be human? What

---

[452] Cf. M. Suska. *Tożsamość a system wartości i postawy współczesnej młodzieży.* IN: *Tożsamość osobowa a tożsamości społeczne. Wyzwania dla edukacji XXI wieku.* Red. T. Bajkowski. Sawicki. Białystok: Elan 2001 p. 111.

[453] DWCH p. 1.

[454] Cf. M. W. Poznańska. *Tożsamość jako element kultury pedagogicznej współczesnego wychowawcy.* ED 2: 1995 no 1 p. 64–65.

[455] CV p. 29.

[456] Cf. KKK p. 1,805–1,809.

kind of person should I be? How am I to be truly myself while filling a real gap in human civilization?[457]

One of the most important tasks of spiritual self-formation can been seen in the mature patterns of the lives of saints. A. Derdziuk highlights three of its characteristics: common sense models of the knowledge of life, accurate assessments of situations, and the ability to consider the future. [458] Hagiography shows the ideal posture of humane moral life for the implementation of these models. If hagiography teaches ideals for human activity, integral self-formation offers a humane road to fulfilling these ideals. Then, the fullness of humanity can be achieved through respect for the sanctity of every human life. Hagiography comes from the principles of God as its donor. D. Kornas-Biela states that with respect to any form of given life from God, personal dialogue ought to meet the essential conditions of mutual communication.[459] In the name of humanity, no one can deepen the state of human cynicism in any form—a lack of communication, destruction of one's good name, war, and enslavement—as the supposedly necessary means of resolving aroused conflict. Therefore, every immoral activity evidences the need for intentional human self-formation toward honorable values and good human behaviors.[460] We claim obvious and explanatory humane reasons for intentional self-formation in the following question. What would the state be with degraded culture, or the family without morality, if people did not believe in the moral superiority of humanity?[461] Together, within an international community, promotion of the value and sanctity of life is possible through education, self-formation, and the integration of life.

---

[457] Jan Paweł II. *Niedziela Palmowa. Homilia na zakończenie Jubileuszu Młodych* (15.04.1984). IN: *Nauczanie Papieskie*. VII 1. 1984 (styczeń-czerwiec) p. 481.

[458] *Formacja moralna a formacja sumienia* p. 32. Cf. Pokrywka. *Antropologiczne podstawy moralności małżeństwa i rodziny* p. 320–321.

[459] Cf. *Wokół początku życia ludzkiego* p. 42–54.

[460] The intentional self-formation expresses, in its noble intention, the moral action, to achieve the intended moral purpose. The self-formation of the moral impulse, to be intentionally oriented, should contain a fundamental rather than the formal concept of life. The contemporary use of the term "intentional formation" requires self-formation of good intentions that shapes a student's vocational needs. This middle term is closely related to the time concept self-formation, which is a form of rational thinking, so the student has a better understanding the world in which he lives, how and for what he lives his life.

[461] "Mankind, shattered by discord though it is, is now seen as a single family. Its problems of human relationships are no longer merely local but are becoming increasingly universal. Even if our interest happens to center on some single region of the world, we now know that we cannot properly understand that region without drawing comparisons between it and other regions. As the adage says, 'No one knows his own culture who knows only his own culture.'" Cf. Allport & Gillespie. *Youth's Outlook on the Future: A Cross-National Study*. Garden City: Doubleday 1955 p. 1–2.

The whole Christian community is dedicated to humanity's creative output, which triggers every person toward something or someone above. Understanding this shows how the meaning of each action defends the dignity and culture of life through its duration and beyond.[462] To live in the fullness of humanity, all human life, including the precious life of the unborn and the frailty of old, a person should be treated with dignity. Human life, at every stage, has a meaning and is a gift from God. This argument should give rise to an attitude of gratitude to God as the source of life. For the above reasons, the Council fathers, especially in *Dignitatis Humanae*,[463] write about the Christian call to live with the dignity of divine affiliation.

In the Council's teaching, normatively important is the right of the human person which stems from religious law which ought to be respected, because every human has been given a natural task. So, self-formation is sufficiently linked to the principle of promoting humanity and the dignity of the person as an end. Thus, people in their free humanity and dignity must not be used to another end. In this way, the person is guaranteed to be a subject with its natural autonomy.

We must strongly emphasize that given the current human condition, self-formation to the fullness of humanity is always possible. Therefore, it requires strong intentions on behalf of each person. A few people are spontaneously free from fear and enslavement, which means that their real intentions are hidden from them. A "possessive mother," says Allport, can claim that her real intention is the welfare of children, but a deeper examination can prove that her objectives are much more selfish.[464] A person aimed at achieving the fullness of humanity, in a worthy ideal, should employ mature feelings that are not at the mercy of unconscious motives and cannot be understood. Honorable motives that are clearly defined and worthy of living often help one achieve emotional maturity and self-formation. Shaping moral experience expresses a better style of conscious existence, which becomes a means of linking himself to authentic life and mature humanity. According to Allport, when the person is well-integrated, human life, under the influence of good intentions, positive factors form harmony and emotional maturity.[465] Moral self-formation

---

[462] J. Mastalski. *Zarys teorii wychowania*. Kraków: Wydawnictwo Naukowe PAT 2002 p. 125.

[463] The Magisterium of the Church emphasizes that "all men are obliged to seek the truth, especially in all matters concerning God and God's Church, and to know it, to receive it, and to keep it." DWR p. 1.

[464] Allport. *Osobowość i religia* p. 208.

[465] Cf. Allport. *Osobowość i religia* s. 74. According to Allport, long-distance goals and healthy intentions affect learning and well-done work.

through reflection is therefore able to build humanity, healthy intentionality, and a harmonious life.

Self-actualization toward the fullness of humanity and moral anthropology forms man as *ens cognitas, ens volens, ens amans*.[466] W. Granat sees the primary value of a person as distinct from other creatures in terms of being self-aware and capable of transcendence. Man, in his transcendence, realizes that he needs not only economic or technical means to grow but also better pedagogical methods and approaches to support him as a person in the full realization of humanity. A man observes the meaning of his activity, and in this perspective of the integral sense of the person, as embodied in his whole being, he perceives the fullness of humanity in communion with God.[467] Although man often loses a lifelong goal, the meaning of life has a much-dependent relationship on his carnality. It is through self-formation in more humane environments that one has an opportunity to build richer integrity.

A. The formative embeddedness of the Christian family

The Church's Magisterium repeatedly emphasizes that the primary educational and formative embeddedness belongs to the family. Considering the responsibilities of parents toward children in the transmission of moral values, the Second Vatican Council teaches that it is the parents who have the first and absolute duty to help children in the harmonious development of all humane values. They become the first and most important teachers and catechists of their children in the "richer humanity." With this obligation, no one can replace or slow parents down.

Among other educational environments, they play a large role in school influence. In this context, the Declaration on Christian Education stresses that "among all means of educational and formative structures, significant growth belongs per se to the school environment."[468] It is the school that completes the formative task of the family. In school, children and young adults develop their intellectual abilities; create a beautiful, moral way of thinking; form their will and affectivity; develop self-esteem; and strengthen attitudes, convictions, and rational behavior, which are essential elements of the cultural heritage to which they belong.[469]

The harmonious development of the moral sphere arose from the stage of integral formation—as already noted—which is possible only if unified efforts meet the demands of all educational environments. For the

---

[466] *Personalizm chrześcijański. Teologia osoby ludzkiej*. Poznań: Księgarnia Św. Wojciecha 1985 p. 580–582.

[467] Cf. CV p. 61, 70.

[468] DWCH p. 5.

[469] Cf. Kongregacja do spraw Wychowania Katolickiego. *Świecki katolik świadkiem wiary w szkole*. Poznań: Pallottinum 1986 no. 12.

formation of moral self, the primary responsibility belongs to the family but also to the school and church. Close cooperation among these communities is thus required to shape implemented ethical principles in the individual sphere. It is crucial because moral formation can never comprise rivalry or unhealthy competition. Social communication also has an impact on human development, especially the Internet and television. The cooperation of all these means of influence affects the young man and women, the family, school, church organizations, youth associations, the state, and the media as an essential power for integral self-development.

An essential home educational environment surrounding the young man is the family. According to the Second Vatican Council, parents are the first and principal educators of their children. Children's relatives, in the highest manner, are called and committed to their moral development.[470] Family plays an important educational function that belongs to its natural role of loving in a community of love and life. The Council also recognizes the family in the basic community of human society that most corresponds to the nature of man.[471] After all, the doctrine of the primacy of family formation over educational institutions stems from a deep concern for human life. The natural responsibilities of parents come from their being procreators. That is why the family is the natural environment for the upbringing of children in love. Also, family becomes their first school of life, preparing them for personal and societal responsibilities.[472] The mutually freeing, enriching gift is necessary to create lasting relationships and subsequent moral development in children. Parenting and family life strictly belong to the family due to complementary aspects of endowment. Parental procreation comes from natural law. Therefore, the first home message is a transmission of physical life in the deepest sense of loving, and the second signal is providing a meaningful way of life from a moral stance to the supernatural.[473]

The deep need for integral self-formation in the family comes from a long process of becoming and takes the form of generous self-gift-giving by each household member. From a theological point of view, the formation

---

[470] "The parents, because they gave life to children, in the highest degree, are required to raise their offspring and therefore must be considered as the first educators (...). Parents create an atmosphere of a family filled with love and respect for God and the people, to foster the entire personal and social education of children (...). There, children experience first a healthy humane society and through the family slowly are placed to the civic community obligation and integrated with the people of God." DWCH p. 3. Cf. FC p. 36.

[471] Cf. KDK p. 25.

[472] Cf. Jan Paweł II. *Do wychowawców, katechetów i rodziców*. Kraków: Wydawnictwo "M" 2000 p. 25.

[473] Cf. FC p. 28.

of any moral man as a person in the household can signify two things: on the one hand, it stimulates a life of good seeds, which the Creator made in the man. On the other hand, it removes any bonds with evil movements that paralyze spiritual, good morale, and it eliminates aberrations that occur because of unnecessary and destructive actions. [474]

The bestowal gift of humanity is the right and honorable duty of every person. Father and mother, in their love for their child, must complement their biological parenthood attitude in religious and spiritual fatherhood and motherhood. [475] These complementary roles in formative education are significant. John Paul II, in his *Letter to Families,* states that procreation according to the flesh marks the beginning of further internal "birth," which is the gradual and multi-lateral birth process that occurs through the whole process of education. [476] Parenting is the transfer of physical life, and internal formation is the procreation of moral, spiritual, and supernatural life. [477] Parents that give a child physical and spiritual life participate in the Creative act of God, and through the formation of their children, they participate in the divine pedagogy of education. The family becomes a real educator unit, mapping the pattern of God. Bodily birth marks the entrance to the path of multilateral delivery through the entire process of integral formation. It is about the higher level of education and intentional self-formation of the person in the family, which should be both bright and subtle.

In any family's upbringing, there should be a mission of moral programming. Of course, it is not a mere transfer of knowledge about life but a presentation of its original and integral meanings based on the wealth of the whole person—body, emotions, and spirit. As M. Pokrywka says, the family, as the primary subject of formation, is responsible for a new life, and this excludes any forms of family replacement or appropriation by others.[478]

Based on the undeniable law of the Christian family, Christians should be freely allowed to send children to schools that can educate their children in conformity with the convictions of their parents. Through respect for their moral and religious beliefs, a child may be formed by permanent, prominent figures who can verify their values. Often, the rights of parents are violated to prevent the moral development of the child (this phenomenon takes place in a secular school system), which should, rather, forge of character formation as *ars Scientia, artiumat scientiarum.* This is not about

---

[474] S. Dziekoński. *Formacja chrześcijańska dziecka w rodzinie w nauczaniu Kościoła od Leona XIII do Jana Pawła II.* Warszawa: UKSW 2006 p. 230.

[475] Cf. Chrobak. *Koncepcja wychowania personalistycznego w nauczaniu Karola Wojtyły—Jana Pawła II* s. 90

[476] LdR p. 16.

[477] Cf. FC p. 28.

[478] Cf. *Antropologiczne podstawy moralności małżeństwa i rodziny* p. 293.

protecting the religious freedom of families by the state but the appropriate recognition of parental rights.

One of the major tests of actual progress is to respect the rights of freedom for each religious family. Parents, Benedict XVI stresses, should always be able to teach young people freely, without coercion and with responsibility to their heritage of faith, values, and culture.[479] In the family, which shares natural love, no one refers to codes because the basis of their relationships is their genuine love for their child and concern for his welfare. As M. Pokrywka explains, parents bring a child into a world of rules and standards, and their authority makes the child comply with family principles and values.[480] Parents should not only shape the body of the child, but indirectly, all of his humanity in the climate of love, too.[481] A child's formation must be organized so that the family favors the realization of the child's personal goals and helps him form an integrating personality. Parents, therefore, fulfill a significant role in formation; they give their children not only food and water but also, most importantly, affective support and approval.

The family fills a critical gap in a child's care, paying attention to the environments in which he is brought up. Any praise and prohibitions in the family home should be educational and contribute to the integral development of the child. This also applies to the use of the media, which often become a threat to the educational process. Easy access to degrading content in the media often falsifies a child's model for happy life. According to John Paul II, postmodern parents do not care enough about this aspect of children's integral development.[482]

A skillful parent who attends to the needs of his family distinguishes a child's spontaneity from media-driven fantasy. Media and technology can cause a child to lose interest in contact with others, including family. Parents must teach their children important family-unifying values and discipline, while not discouraging curiosity and the satisfaction of overcoming the fear of others. Drawings especially inspire a child's imagination because they provide active models of coping with and overcoming evil. Today, this kind of interaction is highly desirable because a lack of contact with loved ones creates a dangerous, deformative emotional vacuum. Verbalized feelings of

---

[479] *"Orędzie na światowy Dzień Pokoju Wychowanie młodzieży do sprawiedliwości i pokoju."* OsRomPol 32: 2011 no. 1 p. 5.

[480] *Antropologiczne podstawy moralności małżeństwa i rodziny* p. 322.

[481] K. Jeżyna. *Wychowanie istotnym przesłaniem nowej ewangelizacji.* IN: *Formacja moralna* p. 162.

[482] Orędzie na XIV światowy dzień przekazu. Rodzina wobec środków przekazu społecznego (1.05.1980). IN: DzZ T. 4 p. 869.

parents and grandparents, via tales, yield fantastic solutions to childhood distress.

Ongoing family dialogue strengthens the moral development of the child. In the context of family discussions, Allport emphasizes that verbal exchanges constitute, for the child, an important lesson in adapting to different situations. Dialogue helps children develop valuable communications skills, engaging and enriching them with new experiences that modify their moral sensibility.[483] Any interfamily dialogue activates good and helps children internally sensitize it. No doubt, both father and mother must carry out the well-planned formation of the child to authenticate his faith and moral behavior. This process relies heavily on the quality of the parents' mutual relationship of marriage. D. Opozda rightly notes that inappropriate marital relationships hinder a child's education and consequently lead to irregularities.[484] Dignified and responsible actions on the part of both husband and wife are equally critical to children, although these roles are implemented in different ways.[485] Spouses, given their gender diversity, provide complementary growth to fulfill developmental roles in their child's life. The evolution process within the family requires that both spouses demonstrate positive attitudes. These positive standpoints should always be characterized by a qualitative and joint effort to determine appropriate penalties and rewards for their children. There is no doubt that upbringing gives children appropriate paternal and maternal models.[486]

In the process of ongoing self-formation, God-given talents help children, including inherited genes. The factors that influence them the most—those factors that help them evolve into a young man or woman — also depend on innate qualities. Often, aspects of self-development are neglected, whereas mature actions speak lauder in self-upbringing. According to Allport, a child mainly inherits his life philosophy from his parents.[487] The habits of children reference the behaviors of their parents and are, to some extent, inherited from them. In this sense, we can talk about inheritance, patterns, norms, roles, and social attitudes. Allport emphasizes that the mature and benevolent vision of life might not be possible if insecurity dominates the psyche of the child.

---

[483] Cf. Allport. *A Secondary Principle of Learning*. PSRev 53: 1946 no. 6 p. 335–347. Cf. Allport. *Osobowość i religia* p. 55.

[484] Cf. D. Opozda. *Charakter i specyfika wychowawczej funkcji rodziny* IN: *Wychowanie w rodzinie chrześcijańskiej. Przesłanie moralne Kościoła*. Red. K. Jeżyna, T. Zadykowicz. Lublin: Wydawnictwo KUL p. 36–37.

[485] Cf. B. Mierzwiński. *Mężczyzna istota nieznana*. Warszawa: Oficyna Wydawniczo-Poligraficzna "Adam" 1999 p. 30–35.

[486] Cf. Pokrywka. Antropologiczne podstawy moralności małżeństwa i rodziny p. 300.

[487] "The child's philosophy of life grows chiefly from the seeds planted by his parents." Cf. Allport. *Personality and Social Encounter* p. 341.

If, inner restlessness is the dominant factor in the personal perception of the external environment and if parental authority delivers a young man something that threatens the work undertaken by him or that threatens his special way of life, the pupil will react aggressively, or at least will become more suspicious in interpreting such environment. [488] Few parents are aware that their children often have distorted attitudes that contribute to their inadequacies, lack of self-security, and difficulty adjusting to the environment. Allport argues parents must develop of an approach built on positive expectations. Greater expectations for a child's behavior in constancy and self-confidence from parents leads them to be better prepared for mature adult solutions.

The child has the right to a loving family and the full personal growth that comes from the fundamental truth of the human person. [489] Without proper formation, a child ends up being socially maladjusted, suffering from poor socialization, reactivity, aggression, and many forms of addiction. In this case, one might apply specialized counseling. The moral formation of a child can only exist in the context of familial love. Coming into the world as a helpless creature, man needs both paternal and maternal love, given and received in a loving family. Undoubtedly, the love in the moral authority of father and mother helps their child create a positive image of God. Positive childhood fantasies and images of God often come from a loving blood father, whereby a child creates positive self-image, adopts family roles, and builds aspirations that motivate him and let him set good goals in life. In shaping his self-image, a child looks for his ideal self. At the same time, he determines the direction of many of his realistic activities.[490]

The healthy family provides the child with security, teaching them how to be a son or daughter and allow them to grow. To make secure growth possible, parents should create an environment of love and understanding. In their sacrificial love, parents have duties to satisfy the mature needs of their child. The verbal, mature spirit of love and sacrifice teaches children strong will and self-reliance, leading them to freely adopt moral attitudes. The education of the moral self in the family strengthens the good will of its members.[491]

---

[488] Cf. Allport. Personality and Social Encounter p. 342.

[489] Cf. Evans. *Gordon Allport: The Man and His Ideas* p. 251.

[490] Cf. Allport. *The Individual and His Religion* p. 31.

[491] The *will* and *character* are not the same. However, the personality tests at the beginning associated the *character* and the *will* of the human person with *aptitude*. Nevertheless, according to Allport, this approach is inadequate because presents the problem much too generally.

"Tenacity is the persistence in a certain line of activity in the face of obstacles and discomfort. 'Will power' is the term popularly employed, especially when the

Negative emotional relationships between parents and their child are not conducive to the formation of the family. Over time, negative feelings can get worse because of separation anxiety or the temporary lack of a parent. Erikson calls this state of moral anxiety in a psychosocial crises as a phase of "trust vs. mistrust," or a lack of confidence. [492] I am convinced that confidence derived from the family gives a sense of faith and certainty of moral principles. Children form their behaviors in relationship with the closest embeddedness or vice versa; mistrust sometimes causes a barrier in the shape of a lack of confidence.

The experience of children is often different from the experience of mature adults. In many cases, the attitude of children causes great concern to parents. This does not mean that the child experiences feelings differently than his parents do. This results in different interpretations of their emotions, especially as affections become more intense and individual to parents on the impulsive stage. Allport illustrates this idea by the following example: what, for an adult, is a twig or a piece of wood? The child comprehends it to be something of greater value. For a child, it might be the most expensive, magical twig and his favorite toy. What an adult considers nearly miraculous, for a child, it is something obvious and vice versa. [493]

The internally formed family leads to the development of mature personalities by meeting a child's needs for love, belonging, security, and friendly relations. A family life rooted in community derives values from the living tradition. Socially grown, this basic unity of society also takes its resources from culture, patriotism, and civic values undermined by the liberal environment. We need to recognize that the evolved family allows the child to feel secure, and that by these means, an infant learns religious and patriotic values faster. Similarly, Allport notes that a healthy, happy family creates a prosocial state of complete physical, spiritual, and social well-being with attitudes of inclusion. [494] A particularly valuable role in this respect - as is rightly observed by M. Pokrywka—is to meet older people who, through their own wise experiences of life, teach their grandchildren smarter ways to look at global events. [495] Responsible family dynamics contribute to the future self-formation of mature morale, which is responsible for the culture of life and love. J. Nagórny names the virtue of responsibility as most important in the integrated family life. [496]

---

tenacious behavior takes the form of resisting an evil habit." Cf. H. Allport. *Personality—The Social Man.* Boston: Houghton Mifflin Company 1924 p. 106.

[492] Cf. E. Erikson. *Childhood and Society* p. 250.

[493] Cf. Allport. *The Individual and His Religion* p. 28.

[494] Cf. The *Individual and His Religion* p. 32.

[495] *Antropologiczne podstawy moralności małżeństwa i* rodziny p. 298.

[496] Cf. *Istota odpowiedzialnego rodzicielstwa. Reflesja teologa moralisty w 25. rocznicę ogłoszenia encykliki "Humane vitae."* IN: *Odpowiedzialni za życie i miłość. Materiały z sesji naukowej*

In the self-formation of mature love, religious education plays a significant role.[497] The Church, which has the "real charism," contributes to the formation of a mature religious outlook within family life and faith. By its very nature, the family strengthens the relationship between God and man and protects against the practical materialism, individualism, and hedonism of its members. The family becomes the community of people wherein their personalities are also formed in the spirit of Christian virtues such as honesty, justice, sincerity, kindness, and the strength of mind. Those qualities are of crucial importance for the future of the peaceful world.[498] It is thus evident that any family man filled with faith is characterized by social maturity. [499] Allport believes that a healthy, happy, and self-realizing family contributes to the basis of every society because the sanest and happiest people are raised in families.[500]

Self-gift giving, as an example of God's cooperation and understanding, should work within the family as a responsible moral trait, expressed in readiness to positive reactions, whether intellectual, emotional, motivational, or behavioral, to its subject matter.[501] All family reactions find their base in deeper personal relations, shaping other people in mutual co-Creation and cooperation. Z. Marek characterizes the relations of the religious person in the family as a well-learned personality trait that determines the behavior of the individual to appreciate and approve another person.[502] In the family's embeddedness, he learns to be loved and love his

---

zorganizowanej przez Duszpasterstwo Rodzin Diecezji Bielsko-Żywieckiej. Red. E. Burzy. Bielsko-Biała: Wydaw. Wydz. Duszp. Kurii 1996 p. 43–44.

[497] J. Bazylak defines religious self-formation within the family as a constant pursuit of something meaningful, a goal and direction difficult to grasp through specific impulses, and primitive urges. *Postawy religijne młodzieży i ich związki z wybranymi elementami osobowości*. Warszawa: ATK 1984 p. 16.

[498] Cf. ChL p. 60.

[499] Cf. R. Kahoe. *The Development of Intrinsic and Extrinsic Religious Orientations. Journal for the Scientific Study of Religion*. 24: 1985 no. 4 p. 408.

[500] "For one thing, familism is a universal foundation for individual and group life. It is the essential framework within which students view and plan their futures. Attitudes toward the family of orientation and aspirations respecting the family of procreation are much alike. In our samples the philosophy of child-training seems relatively uniform. Basic moral values and ethical codes of conduct are everywhere prized. They provide a foundation for international understanding and amity that remains even while specific political conflicts may hold the center of attention." Cf. Allport and J. Gillespie. *Youth's Outlook on the Future: A Cross-National Study*. Garden City: Doubleday 1955 p. 37.

[501] W. Prężyna. *Funkcja postawy religijnej w osobowości człowieka*. Lublin: RW KUL 1981 p. 20.

[502] Marek. Podstawy wychowania moralnego p.103.

siblings and himself until he gives up his life and can give no more. Through family support, he learns to love his neighbors as well.

There is a widespread belief in today's society that the religiosity of children and young people is an absolute luxury in the family home. Add to this the fact that the contemporary family neglects "to be" in favor of "to have." It is easy to prove that this way of thinking leads to a dangerous stance or a thesis in favor of the dichotomy between secular and Christian life.[503] The present irrational fashion is a stumbling block for family members who try defining what is and what is not of value or in vogue. Another limitation is that school is expected to reflect social values and teach children meaning only within the existing materialistic social frameworks. In the modern family, the weakness of this less-effective method is its absence of required goals centered on excellence.

Allport states that home embeddedness is far greater than any other environment but often lacks the creative forms of learning.[504] Creative ways of learning provide the communion of persons. According to *Familiaris Consortio,* the Christian family, through expressions of religious faith, is geared toward the inclusion of both supernatural and moral values.[505] The integral and universal aspects of Christian formation creates harmony in the believer in terms of what is natural and what is spiritual. Paternal and maternal interactions create a community of people capable of mutual evangelization and holiness based on accountability and delicacy taken from the image of the Holy Family. The happy family, as the *communio personarum,* stems from a proper relationship that enables complementary internal formation. Therefore, marriage is the mature Sacrament of Creation and redemption that leads to the communion of persons united on a deeper level as God's people.[506] Through co-educational communion, the child naturally accepts his gender, which allows him to imitate traditional patterns of family roles. So, the family, being the original basis of embeddedness, teaches both the self-formative paternal and maternal relationships.[507] Allport notes that a good parent is a better teacher, not because his paternal authority is accepted by all but because the parental realization of the required objectives are objectively right, leading a person in the co-formation of the household.[508]

The well-being of the family requires that individuals are subordinated to the common interest as the first effect of a healthy and

---

[503] Cf. J. Bagrowicz. *Edukacja religijna współczesnej młodzieży.* Toruń: UMK 2000 p. 18.
[504] "A home that infects the child with galloping consumption, which encourages only canned recreation and has no creative outlets, can only with difficulty be offset by the school." Cf. Allport. *Person in Psychology.* Boston: Beacon Press 1960 p. 161.
[505] Cf. FC 17.
[506] S. Chrobak. *Koncepcja wychowania personalistycznego w nauczaniu Karola Wojtyły—Jana Pawła II.* Warszawa: Wydawnictwo Salezjańskie 1999 p. 88.
[507] Cf. Pokrywka. *Antropologiczne podstawy moralności małżeństwa i rodziny* p. 300.
[508] Cf. Allport. *Becoming* p. 31–32.

essential unity of the simple social structure. Unfortunately, contemporary postmodern transformations are often used to meet the needs of individual at the expense of the general good of the whole family. Individualizations and a lack of unification lead to difficult upbringing and mature loving within the household. Allport points out that only a healthy home environment creates the climate needed to combat self-centeredness, antisocial behavior, and depravity.[509] Despite the many anti-social and negative trends in today's notions of the family, still, the Christian family takes up the challenges to be a community of persons who form the sacrificial character of their members via higher values and love. Of great importance are accurate models of a "loving father," naturally accepted by sons and daughters toward a further self-sacrificial way of life.[510] A loving father's tedious work and responsibility contribute to children's formation.

Undoubtedly, valuable traits and talents are created within the family community. Thus, a unique role of the teaching parent is to help a child identify tasks for growth.[511] Although Allport does not say much about vocational aspects, his writings emphasize the value of parental help in discovering the exceptional talents children have for the sake of future society. Parents can find some superior skills in their child simply by providing continual inspiration to achieve their desired goals. Apparently, postulated dreams help a child discover important humane values that are unique to each person. In the loving family, members work together to acquire meaningful ambitions for their entire lives.

Gaining valuable lessons often takes place during "difficulties and sufferings" that present a concrete, subjective idea of how to be better formed.[512] Christian subjectivity in the family helps a man discover the mystery of who he is and who he should be to meet the divine endowment. In other words, moral self-formation takes place in a loving home that teaches a child how to choose and how to share the good, so that everyone in the family contributes to the best personality. The integrating influence of persons is expressed in a genuinely Christian love pattern.[513]

The family's moral formation is also expressed in the transfer of personal culture to each of its members. Family embeddedness provides the child with many valuable sources of knowledge and the practicality of repeated good experiences that enrich the process of becoming.[514] Because

---

[509] Cf. Ibid. p. 32.
[510] Cf. Allport. *Osobowość i religia* p. 145.
[511] Cf. ChL p. 58.
[512] Cf. Marek. *Postawy wychowania moralnego* p. 113.
[513] Cf. Jan Paweł II. *Mężczyzną i niewiastą stworzył ich. Chrystus odwołuje się do początku. O Jana Pawła II teologii ciała* p. 73–75.
[514] Cf. Allport. *Becoming* p. 82.

the person grows in different cultural contexts, ranging from family to school to the professional environment, the impact of good etiquette is crucial for creating a desired hierarchy of values.[515] Help offered to a child from a cultural world of good convictions, includes the use of the words "sorry," "thank you," or "please." Evolving a child's experiences allows him to enter a new world, often better in subjective valuation, respectively mature in its complexity. So, any courtesy in interpersonal relations, expressed in the habit of good manners, of being polite and "asking and giving thanks" is of great value and importance.[516]

Christian culture plays a significant role in family education, which creates the right conditions of bringing up a child with the necessary convictions and triggers their potential to do good and protect themselves against pseudo-choices. As J. H. Anderson states, social growth carries a child's language development and introduction to the family's culture of being. The sensitivity of a child's needs requires that parents offer a careful selection of educational materials, like reading to children and involving them in necessary chores to connect culture and family life.[517] Family formation promotes the opportunity to play family roles and engage in practical solutions. Parents, in challenging their son or daughter at school, develop his or her respect for privacy and autonomous identity, awakening the child's self-respect.

More freedom in this regard is reflected, for example, in giving children consent to decorate their rooms according to their fascinations, ideas, likes, and dislikes. A parent might also offer them a pocket watch so that they can better organize their time. In that spirit of responsible acceptance and inclusion in the family, engaged children experience integrating feelings of consistency and subjectivity. An appropriate climate of freedom leads a child to a mature life and morality. Such freedom builds a trustful relationship that allows them a faster transition of growth within the family.[518] Respect for acquired morality, trust, and freedom becomes an incentive for self-forming, ideal goals and their promotion. The family allows for more inner freedom and moral integrity from its members.

But many post-modern family attitudes and relationships can be instrumentalized. M. Pokrywka offers many examples of instrumentalization, who notes that the reduced position of a father or mother who only secures

---

[515] "It is important to recognize that neighborhood gangs, mass media, and the lie does have predisposing influences." Evans. *Gordon Allport: The Man and His Ideas* p.16.

[516] Cf. R. Niparko. *Oryginalność metody wychowawczej Sługi Bożego Edmunda Bojanowskiego.* "Poznańskie Studia Teologiczne" 1986 t. 6 p. 200.

[517] Cf. J. H. Anderson. *The Role of Storytelling and Personal Narrative in Cognitive, Moral, and Oral Language Development.* Olympia: The Evergreen State College. Master's in Teaching 2007 p. 19.

[518] Cf. CCC p. 2207.

the material needs of the child is not true parenthood.[519] Contemporary studies remind educators about the higher non-material obligations of parents toward their children that often become redundant. This philosophical materialism practiced by some parents equates the education and ethical formation of children exclusively related to their maintenance, and therefore, their obligation to protect their only material needs. Without moral integrity, parents instrumentalize and deform their offspring. Manipulative relationships in the family that avoid deeper questions make the family ties weak. In this case, the educator cannot provide a more in-depth life, and the child adopts a less meaningful hierarchy of values. This attitude of manipulation and laziness has only a menial task: it leads the individual toward selfish interests. The apparent lack of Christian morality expresses the materialistic makeup of an individual. The fact that the child does not need to stand for higher authentic faith remain the outer gestures of selfishness and apparent morality.

This type of personality is expressed in a lack of insight into others and thus manifests in the absence of moral and religious characteristics. The attitude of superficial religiosity or its extension is often supported by a lack of realism.[520] Although irrationality destroys a realistic approach to life and self-formation, there are many similar detriments to the family, destroying its core identity. Because the family is an essential social organism of national strength, any lack of a good morality or integrity contributes to the destructive force of societal order. Once family identity is lost through individualization, the young men therein do not strengthen their relationships with the culture of their ancestors. Because of detachment, self-maturation loses its meaning as well. T. Kukołowicz notes that the reason for this current crisis of identity lies in the lack of a long-term perspective and outlook on life. The road, without realistic goals, imposes a sense of human loneliness that breaks the links of the future with the past, thus rejecting classical upbringing.[521]

The formative activity of parents and teachers, preparing young people to participate in the secular community, is not always an easy task. Shaping a child's internal characteristics requires tireless work by the undertaker of self-formation as well. The young person is likely influenced by many destructive internal and external factors like harmful substance

---

[519] Family integrity is threatened by many external ideological factors supported by apparent contradicting values and anti-family models. Both phenomena externally lead to deforming family, and the lack of internal life contributes to the family crisis. Cf. *Antropologiczne podstawy moralności małżeństwa i rodziny* p. 287–290.

[520] Cf. Allport. *Personal Religious Orientation and Prejudice.* JPSP 5: 1967 no 4 p. 433.

[521] Cf. Budzenie zmysłu religijnego u dzieci w wychowaniu religijnym. "Pedagogika Katolicka" 1: 2007 no. 1 p. 56.

abuse (e.g., alcohol and drugs) and widespread subculture. Subculture advises illusory ambitions and momentary pleasure, often giving little joy in the long run and destroying the personality of the young man, leaving on them permanent scars of personality deformation.[522]

There is no doubt that parents who use and abuse different harmful substances, including tobacco, drugs, and alcohol, rain destructive patterns on the family. These substances destabilize the family priority, both materially and morally. An additional degeneration of this basic social unit is the loss of a true source of income, which can direct the family toward pathological criminal activity. At the same time, it leads to the negligence of children and future generations.[523]

Requirements expected of children can only be fruitful if they meet the proper attitudes of their parents. As M. Zając states, when children acquire mature decision-making skills earlier, they are more likely to make alcohol-abstinence promises in later years.[524] A decisive factor of this is commitment from the family to keep abstinence promises, too, giving younger members examples to follow. This is the right approach taken by a child literally toward responsibility. A. Derdziuk points out that parents and the Church have a positive influence in teaching young people to sacrifice for the greater good and empower independent, free, moral decisions. When second-grade children prepare for First Communion, parents may strengthen a desire of abstinence from alcoholic beverages and smoking. This way, they have a chance to realize the object of their promises. But in this modeled process of parental preparation, there is a huge commitment to abstinence, which should avoid any grounds of petrifying children.[525] Children imitate a parents' moral and spiritual way of life. A family school builds a community of persons.[526]

At an earlier stage of a child's formation, parents have strong control over the impact of television on the internal life of their youngsters. Television and the Internet should serve the child's true development and contribute to a pro-social education. John Paul II expresses this position of the Church, stating that dependence on television can deprive family members of opportunities to interact with one another through conversation,

---

[522] Cf. M. Babik. *Rodzice, niezastąpieni wychowawcy – w poszukiwaniu optymalnego środowiska wychowawczego.* IN: *Pedagogika wiary.* Red. A. Hajduk, J. Mółka. Kraków: WAM 2007 p. 109–117.

[523] Cf. T. Kamiński. *Parafia wobec problemów społecznych.* "Chrześcijanin w Świecie" 2: 1997 no. 1 p. 107.

[524] Cf. *O wielkich postanowieniach małego dziecka w przygotowaniu do I Komunii Świętej.* IN: *O wielkich postanowieniach małego dziecka.* Warszawa: Parpamedia 2009 p. 10.

[525] Cf. *Moralny wymiar przyrzeczeń pierwszokomunijnych.* IN: *O wielkich postanowieniach małego dziecka. Profilaktyczne aspekty formacji rodziców i dzieci do I Komunii Świętej.* Red. P. Kulbacki. Warszawa: Parpamedia 2009 p. 21–34.

[526] Cf. I. Kraińska-Rogala. *Rodzina wspólnotą miłości.* Kraków: WAM 1999 p. 2.

joint exercise activities, and common prayer. Wise parents know that good television and Internet programs should be supplemented by other sources of information, entertainment, education, and culture.[527] Allport confirms the effect of unhealthy and negative mass media on the morale of the family. For instance, people are subjected to the often-repeated glorification of different interests, experiences, lobbying, propaganda, blindness, and deafness of judgment. Frequent dependence on social communication threatens healthy evolution. Parents have every right to protect their children from the harmful influence of the mass media. Christian-oriented media is required to serve objective truth, strengthening the values espoused in the family. Often, among the noise of advertisements, intrigue, war, hatred, and crime, the family loses precious time to grasp the message of brotherhood.[528] Hence, John Paul II's statement is still relevant today; he considers the specific requirements of the vast group of "customers," or children and the consequences of responsible adults, in the service of the conservation and development of the family and society.[529]

It can be argued that Christian media develop formative tools that have a decisive influence on multidimensional growth, supporting the family or at least not causing division. Nevertheless, from my experience, Christian communication within the family entails the fostering of values such as solidarity and local communities of peace and cooperation. The media that invites parents to share their knowledge, promote the word of God, and encourage moral and spiritual life are truly Christian. Public mass media should, therefore, bear greater responsibility for the preservation of good ethical standards that disseminates the values of family life. The family, as a necessary form of embeddedness, ought to be enabled to use the resources of media communication. Media can perpetuate pro-life arguments and other religious and cultural values. At the same time, media can promote a version of humanity that shapes their own identity.[530]

The family shapes a child's cognitive ability to comprehend different outlooks of the world. Family self-formation follows a simple conclusion; manhood comes from a stable family. Quality formation of their offspring strengthen the nation. All environments of formation must therefore

---

[527] Jan Paweł II. *Orędzie Na XXVIII Światowy Dzień Środków Społecznego Przekazu* "Telewizja w rodzinie: kryteria właściwego wyboru programów." Vatican. (24.01.1994) p. 48.

[528] Cf. Allport. *Personality and Social Encounter* p. 249.

[529] Jan Paweł II. Orędzie Na XIII *Światowy Dzień Środków Społecznego Przekazu „Środki społecznego przekazu w służbie ochrony i rozwoju dziecka w rodzinie i w społeczeństwie".* Watykan (23.05.1979) p. 85.

[530] Jan Paweł II. Orędzie Na XXVIII *Światowy Dzień Środków Społecznego Przekazu "Telewizja w rodzinie: kryteria właściwego wyboru programów"* p. 2.

recognize that the "family is the fundamental unit of healthy society."[531] The family as the very small cell of society is the truest community older than any state institutions. The Second Vatican Council called the family a "school of deeper humanity." The rich inheritance of the family, due to its responsibility for the upbringing of children, gives her a higher status of humanity. The family creates the future of the world and should be endowed with special care. The well-embedded values of the self-formed family is therefore the root of the nation and the state.

B. The school in sociocultural formation

The school, as a social institution, has an educative and formative purpose. The Second Vatican Council teaches that the school shapes its mission through faculties, developing students' ability to issue correct judgments. The school introduces cultural heritage and important values, and it prepares the child for professional life. The school supports dispositions of conductive mutual understanding while building a close interrelationship of students with their different character and the nature of their origins.[532]

Any school, as an important institution of sociability, beyond the possibility of forming pupils with their personalities, also provides canons of good morale and socially acceptable standards. All over the world, the basic mission of the school, according to education bills, is to support the educational role of the family.[533] This educational act promotes important laws within different countries that parents have the right to educate their children according to their beliefs and values. The school therefore requires greater cooperation with the family home. Any school—in addition to the family—should ensure that a young man or woman becomes a fully-fledged and socially altruistic adult. The school's obligation should be to fight against the selfish attitudes of deficient families to adjust young people to society so that they can become valuable citizens.

According to Allport, school must meet, in its formal curriculum, a few basic conditions, namely to recognize the equal status of all students.[534] Any teacher, through verbal and non-verbal contact with students, has a duty to educate them and provide professional care for them throughout their entire education. Formators must consider the educational plan that's appropriate for each child's curriculum, increasing not only the pupil's logical

---

[531] Cf. DA p. 11.

[532] DWCH p. 5. Cf. Jan Paweł II. *Wychowanie człowieka do wartości moralnych*. OsRomPol 15: 1994 no. 5 p. 16–17.

[533] M. Pilich. *Ustawa o systemie oświaty. Komentarz*. Warszawa: ABC 2012⁴ p. 29.

[534] "The tradition of fair play and equal educational opportunities teaches authentic values" Allport. *The Nature of Prejudice* p. 479.

and conceptual thinking but also deepening ethical perceptions and reasoning.[535]

A great concern is that many public schools provide students guidance on how to get funding for homosexual behavior, premarital sex, abortions without their parents' acknowledgment, teach students about alternative sexual behaviors. That alternative demoralizes students. These ineffectual liberal education reforms have adversely affected contemporary education. For example, early national reports from the Carnegie Foundation for the Advancement of Teaching did not pay enough attention to school discipline. I found that it is mentioned only in one paragraph out of a 300-page report. Some state school teachers lack the minimum support they need to maintain discipline and respect in their classrooms.[536] It is not about a restrictive approach but the lack of decisive moral authority in schools. Understandably, it seems that in the context of the post-modern influences, educators, teachers, catechists, and experts of moral formation think that their view is needed now more than ever for better education for young people and not just more education.[537] And teachers require to have more courage in the use of appropriate methods of real education. Teaching in schools should lead pupils to integral maturity in the search for truth to serve the common good. Various forms of laxity and abandoning the teaching of ethics harm young people and the whole society. By learning integral formation, youth pay more attention to the impact of home and the family.[538]

Hope is born, however, when teachers ask: What can be done to fulfill the formative task of the school? Anyone interested in integral formation agrees that there is a clear demand for specific values that students need to acquire, namely self-control and intellectual exercises.[539] Intellectual exercises cannot be separated from moral elements, because the classics teach that goodness, truth, and beauty are inseparable. The task of each educator is to carry pupils to discover the gift of self and help them achieving worthy goals set by God, excluding any abusive instrumentalization. A part of this instrumentalization is visible in utilitarianism. "Utilitarianism seems to be a consistent program of selfishness without any possibility of transition to self-

---

[535] Cf. Allport. Personality and Social Encounter s. 276.

[536] R. Arum. *Judging School Discipline: The Crisis of Moral Authority*. Cambridge: Harvard University Press 2003 p. 189.

[537] S. Wielgus. *Pedagogika i formacja młodzieży. Pedagogika Katolicka* 1: 2007 no. 1 p. 12.

[538] Cf. E. Mitek. *Dom rodzinny środowiskiem młodego pokolenia*. "Wrocławski Przegląd Teologiczny" 3: 2005 no. 1 p. 109.

[539] "It is especially about the formation and development of human personality that we need to open doors (…). One of the capacities most urgent is the formation of a style of life that is self-aware, self-critical, and self-enhancing." Cf. G. W. Allport. *Becoming*. New Haven: Yale University Press 1983 p. 18.

formation." [540] The school—it must be strongly restated—provides an environment to support the ongoing formative function of the family. Allport's thoughts on human formation are consistent with the Congregation for Education, which states in Section 69: "(...) the task of the school is to support and complement the work of parents."[541]

School formation can be divided into two processes. In the first area, formative action should be related to the care of moral security, perceiving and understanding a student's thinking with a skillful response to aroused issues. In the formation of moral self, secular schools and their educational programs ought to aim at eliminating abuse, violence, and lack of tolerance. All schools must develop programs devoted to preventive prophylactics. The second area of guided formation in the school is directed at the proper self-formation of moral attitudes toward other people and the tasks of citizenship. J. Wrobel says that in the process of learning arises respect to ideals and to fidelity.[542] This is school formation, which has relevant examples in role models including the primarily paradigm of the principal. As A. Derdziuk affirms, there is a need not only for moral principles but also willingness among pupils to implement them into their lives with an attitude of responsibility.[543]

Continuous formation in the school system depends on how many principles are rooted in the personal structure of pupil's motivation. It is therefore clear that raising an honest person who is guided by mature motives of conduct always results from the internal, intrinsic structure of the human personality.[544] A recent study, "Self-Discipline and Catholic Education: Evidence from Two National Cohorts," by M. Gottfried and J. Kirksey, shows that the private school does a better job.[545] Private education might have a better chance of teaching pupils psychological integration because man does not develop autonomously. Moreover, moral maturity is not an automatic process. Besides, the central element of the mission of the school is to instill ethical human interactions with other people. In such a case, a person of good character is formed by societal qualities, or—regarded in

---

[540] "Utilitarianism," observes K. Wojtyla, "is a civilization of effect in use—the culture of "things" rather than culture of "people," and the civilization in which persons become subject. *Miłość i odpowiedzialność*. Lublin: TN KUL 1986 p. 39. Cf. LdR p. 13. Utilitarianism, adds A. Zadroga, is a moral decision that depends on results of its usefulness or harmfulness. *Współczesne ujęcie etyki biznesu w Polsce*. Lublin: Wydawnictwo KUL 2009 p. 158.

[541] PH p. 69.

[542] *Antropologia ludzkiej płciowości: powołanie do życia w komunii prawdy i miłości*. IN: *Ocalić obraz człowieka. Antropologiczne podstawy moralności*. Red. P. Morciniec. Opole: RW WT Opole Uniwersytet 2003 p. 89.

[543] Cf. *Formacja moralna* p. 26.

[544] Cf. Allport. *Osobowość i religia* p. 156.

[545] M. Gottfried and J. Kirksey. *Self-Discipline and Catholic Education: Evidence from Two National Cohorst*. Thomas B. Fordham Institute. May 2018 p. 5–8.

theological language—as being blessed with virtues of good will and the glory of God by love.[546] The person is spiritually formed in a sense that he has enough mature personality to construct responsible schemes of adulthood identity.[547] Also, this early identity helps the young adult establish central commitments. The education of a mature personality is not an independent process, but it is—as defined by T. Domaniewska—a long-term process of integrating student's variety of experiences.[548] Other authors emphasize varieties of moral experiences as the clear motivational effect of the person (G. Allport), educational environment (J. Piaget), or embedded culture (R. Kegan).When an educational program or pedagogy proposes a vision of man, it must consider the practical and philosophical conceptions of man within one's existence. The school environment, although it helps to extend a richer dimension of humanity, applies to every person undertaking formation. Outgoing human formation at school thus shapes humanity by making students able to meet and pursue their personal goals and a meaningful life, according to the principal values.[549] The primary purpose of human upbringing is to use the talents given to one by God. Jesus says, "Be ye therefore perfect, even as your Father is perfect" (Mt 5:48). Often, the Christian school, under the influence of the traditional culture of the Fathers of the Church, constructs meaningful reality in the context of an eschatological perspective. All purposeful relationships in school teach the art of life, which is indispensable from shaping identity and personality.[550] But, as A. Krapiec and B. Kieres affirm, the school should build that identity from an eschatological perspective. According to their personalistic theory, human nature has features that distinguish a personal entity from any other created being, and those human traits are love, freedom, and religiosity. Therefore, human nature demands general formation even within the school.

The requirement of integral formation at Catholic schools is confirmed by the Church's Magisterium. Pius XII, in his Apostolic Constitution *Sedes Sapientiae* (31 May 1956), indicates the great need for social education to "shepherd the flock of the Lord."[551] This idea is also expressed in the *Ratio fundamentalis institutionis sacerdotibus* by the Congregation for

---

[546] Cf. VS p. 78.

[547] Cf. D. Lapsley& D. Narvaez. *Moral Development, Self and Identity*. Mahwah, NJ: Lawrence Erlbaum Associates 2004 p. 207.

[548] Cf. Marek. *Podstawy wychowania moralnego* s. 245. Cf. T. Domaniewska. *Wychowanie społeczno-moralne*. IN: *Podstawy pedagogii przedszkolnej*. Red. M. Kwiatkowska. Warszawa: Wydawnictwa Szkolne i Pedagogiczne 1988 p. 264–267.

[549] Cf. W. Dłubacz. *Pedagogika Katolicka? Uwagi filozofa*. "Pedagogika Katolicka" 1: 2007 no. 1 p. 52–54.

[550] Cf. Chrobak. *Koncepcja wychowania personalistycznego w nauczaniu Karola Wojtyły – Jana Pawła II* p. 108.

[551] KSS p. 6.

Catholic Education (6 January 1970). The same Vatican congregation requires educators to attend to the psychological and sociological sciences, which contribute to a better knowledge of people and things.[552]

A certain dynamism is visible at every stage of school formation, whether in emotional or personal interactions, when its sources are self-knowledge, self-control, and the desires of becoming more human.[553] Well-integrated schools animate more personal dynamism by loving every dignified aspect of school life. At every stage of schooling, it is necessary to influence procreative perception, whose source of the natural law is found in God's Creation. The educative absence of this sphere is felt in the child and expressed in speech delay or lack of attention. Difficulties caused by a lack of parental love are also caused by weak cooperation with the classroom teacher, characterized by poor vocabulary, poor listening skills, and little capacity to memorize information, among other factors.

An adult's altruistic expression of positive feelings arise from the psychodynamics of prior periods, when a child is portrayed by appropriate loving patterns of life. It should be noted that personal dynamism cannot be reduced only to the processes of perception, facial expressions, gestures, and dynamics of behavior. The momentum of development and human self-formation is first encoded in the biology of any organism that has a true purpose to develop. Their dynamic nature, apparently, conditions not only the human biological realm, which is a step ahead of mental health self-formation, but is also combined with structures of spiritual formation.[554]

Personalistic dynamism in the mission of the school is born of higher feelings. Loving, the so-called dynamism of self-giving, engages a Christian in different areas of personal relationships. That autonomous energy manifests itself in the human character, drawing strength from reservoirs that restrict impulses, fear, hunger, and lust of the flesh.[555] Dynamism arising out of selfless love is always activating, as Saint John says: "There is no fear in love, but perfect love casts out fear" (1 Jn. 4:18). New interests, abilities, good ideas, and the development of a vocation—everything is included in the expanding sense of humanity, manifested in a deep commitment to life and attitudes far beyond the selfish ego and its protections.

Growth for self-sacrificing love cannot occur without a qualitative freedom of thought in school. The education of the moral self involves fostering the interior freedom of a student to nurture the objective truth. Such truth dynamically improves people's life and conscience. The self-

---

[552] Cf. RFIS p. 94.

[553] Cf. E. Smołka. *Filozofia kształtowania charakteru.* Tychy: Wydawnictwo Maternus Media 2005 p. 185.

[554] Cf. M. Wójcik. *Specyfika ludzkiej płciowości.* IN: *Człowiek. Osoba. Płeć.* Red. M. Wójcik. Łomianki: Fundacja "Pomoc Rodzinie" 1998 p. 117.

[555] Cf. Allport. *The Individual and His Religion* p. 63–64.

formed, gaining inward freedom, can now return to higher values to shape others, reaching maturity in the moral sense.[556]

According to Allport, the school exists to educate a student in six values: the theoretical, economic, aesthetic, social, national, and religious. These values, adapted in the formation of a mature personality, can be expressed in the following ways: first, theoretical: the values that allow you to shape yourself empirically, under the influence of criticism, rationally, and interest in discovering the truth. Second, economic: an interest in what is pragmatic, practical, and feasible; third, aesthetic: the internal interest in self-education is the search for higher values, seeking harmony, grace, symmetry, and mental and physical health. An educated man of aesthetic values perceives the truth as being on par with beauty. Fourth, social: altruistic values, expressed in loving people and oneself. Fifth, national values: personal interest with the ability to influence others. Sixth and last, religious values: a focus on selecting transforming mystical themes, solidarity, and unity of being with the Creator.[557]

The mission of the school, besides implementation of these values, is important because the young person has the right to a basic knowledge of these gifts. When a personal ward structure is more flexible and sensitive to positive change, educational formation around sexual life occurs through mature dialogue between teacher and students.[558] The role of educators should allow young people to deeply understand the sphere of sexual morality, because they have the right to essential information. This right is differently perceived today, often isolated from values. In many ways, a secular school opposes student's extended outlook, addressing only his personal functions and omitting whole concept of Christian person.[559] Thus, the laic school misses integral aspects of education in its personalistic dimensions.

The most effective period of self-formation that should be considered in the mission of the Catholic school is after-school programs. In his spare time, the child may indulge in creative pursuits and wise choices suited to his talents, needs, and interests. Skillful teachers use these breaks for higher co-education, developing the positive traits of their clients. Proper use of spare time for a child brings extra opportunities for them to grow. Many publications show that children often use their free time incorrectly and need assistance in this area. Another primary task of schools is their

---

[556] Cf. DFK p. 22.

[557] "No doubt (…) aesthetic, social, and religious values are still more decisive in the formation." Allport. *The Nature of Prejudice* p. 440.

[558] Cf. PH p. 70.

[559] Cf. E. W. Boecenfoerde. *Wizerunek człowieka w świetle dzisiejszego porządku prawnego.* IN: *Człowiek w nauce współczesnej.* Paris: Editions du Dialogue 1988 p. 117–125.

intellectual extension at all levels of education. Intellectual education incorporates the expansion of interests and the desire for knowing more—a search for truth and the truth telling. Only by reaching the truth can intellectual formation contribute to the development of students' thinking and memorizing moral norms. When a child is engaged in good practice he or she better organizes learned knowledge that has been coming from the general environment.[560]

A child's education is based on imitation of the authentic patterns of their teacher's behavior. Therefore, obligation and commitment is implicit in the imitation.[561] T. Zadykowicz states that commitment leads to the student's adoption of the creative thinking with the effective conformity of learning. Formative education also depends on the frequent use of memory exercises for clarity of mind. A good memory of well-done deeds engages is part of the learning process in that it teaches various mental functions. Those efficient exercises of the brain functions in developing thousands of creative behaviors. In many situations, educators affirm that by studying geometry and passing Latin tests, student's memory is extended logically and importantly contributes to their good will. So, these ongoing practices help children not so much to be honest, but in the longer run, frequently mobilize them to have positive reactions and do good in most situations.

The human being, as an intellectual, spiritual unity who is, at the same time, autonomous, despite a weakened freedom, can imprint their unique talents on everything. For this reason, according to Allport, any intellectual person "directs toward the infinite" and not only changes its existential subjectivity but builds relational implications to the infinite.[562] In the Christian school setting, children play repeated roles, measuring their impact according to competence with others and the order and rules of camaraderie. In a group of peers, children develop the ability to negotiate and share their needs, so they can practice their behavior more maturely and subjectively. Good motivation plays an important role in self-form retention and inspires all acts associated with intelligence. Otherwise, tendencies to steal and lie, according to many studies, including those of H. Hartshorne M. May, are more closely related with less intelligence, then age.[563]

---

[560] "Typically, a person learns when he is trying to relate himself to his environment, under the combined influence of his motives, the present requirements of the situation, active participation and knowledge of relevant facts, including a memory of his previous success and failure." Cf. Allport. *A Secondary Principle of Learning.* PsRev 53: 1946 no. 6 p. 346–347.

[561] *Sequela Christi et imitation hominis. Paradygmat naśladowania we współczesnej refleksji teologicznomoralnej. Źródła i perspektywy.* Lublin: Wydawnictwo KUL 2011 p. 273.

[562] Cf. *The Individual and His Religion: A Psychological Interpretation.* New York: Macmillan 1950 p. 142.

[563] Cf. D. Graham. *Moral Learning and Development.* New York: Wiley 1972 p. 239.

Intellectual practice, although it rests on cognitive ability, is a very complex phenomenon in human development. In the view of American psychologist H. Gardner, intellectual training involves at least six components: linguistic intelligence, musical, logical-mathematical, spatial, motor, and interpersonal social skills. Intellectual education allows children to gain ideal tools to better understand the consequences of their behavior and the behavior of other people. Gifted children mature much earlier in moral judgments than children with lower intelligence, for example, because they rely more on the results of their well-motivated actions rather than their intentions. Allport's research proves that intellectual self-formation is dependent on information determined both by genes as well as learned from interacting entities.[564] However, educational programs should involve a code of ethics and ways of learning ethical standards for humane proceedings through integrity, liability, participation, and quality of a pupil's work.[565] The aim of the multi-level continuing education process is to develop intellectual capacity of the individual regarding both the natural and the supernatural competence complemented by an integral formation of the self.[566]

Engaged students ought to be invited to the continuous development of the intellectual sphere and the process of overcoming human weaknesses. Integral education seems possible through the motivated interests in theoretical, economic, aesthetic, political, religious, and spiritual values.[567] For good morale in school, the most important thing is education that strengthens the will of the ward. For better self-formation, education ought to include external formation exercises that discipline the will in its ability to manage freedom and the inner-self-formative interests specified above. Well-informed will, through values, contributes to a pupil's intellectual direction and positive attitudes. [568]

Often, school education should be concerned with the development of patriotic attitudes. The patriotic aspect of education is one of the natural divisions for the deliberate and conscious development of the juvenile.

---

[564] Cf. Evans. *Gordon Allport: The Man and His Ideas* p. 78.

[565] Cf. M. Beaty and D. Henoy. *The Schooled Heart: Moral Formation in American Higher Education.* Waco: Baylor University Press TX 2007 p. 34.

[566] Cf. S. Mojek. *Formacja moralna.* IN: ENM p. 206–207.

[567] Integrative learning within the theoretical and practical values is a necessary part of a competent school. "Topic of values is a recurring thread all the way through Gordon Allport's career of writing. (…) The theoretic type accords with the ethics of general legality and the value of objectivity; the economic type with utilitarian ethics and the value of utility. The aesthetic model shapes harmony; the ethics of the love and loyalty." Cf. R. I. Evans. *Gordon Allport: The Man and His Ideas.* New York: E. P. Dutton 1970 p. 123–124.

[568] Cf. W. Chudy. *Charakter jako wartość antropologiczno-etyczna.* IN: *Wychować charakter.* Lublin: Gaudium 2005 p. 44.

Patriotism is a needed call "to assume responsibility," and this call to stand for others has formative and educational dimensions.[569] Of course, patriotic education promotes social attitudes to live more responsibly in the spirit of freedom. The mission of the school ought to have a sense of belonging to national traditions linked with respect and affection for the home country achievements and culture of their people. Particularly essential in the school is the integrated process of becoming a man and this characteristic should be best developed. It is no less important for pupils to realize that communities such as family, social environment, and homelands give great goodness and value in the life of every individual. With the privilege of being involved in the community, pupil's learning combines social virtues and duties. So, patriotic education in school should not just be talk about the rights of freedom, social life, and solidarity, but should also pay attention to the social duties that are integrally connected with patriotic ethos. In this regard, the patriotic love of country is a derivative of Christian self-formation.[570] In terms of love of country, school should be a community that participates in the collective good of the fatherland. Besides, the obvious normative duty of any school that teaches patriotism includes paying taxes as a general righteous obligation of all citizens.

An important function of the teacher, beyond school assignments, are teaching lessons. These lessons may carry the message of the ancient wisdom of the community, to which the pupil rightly belongs. Shaping students' thinking through the advantages and disadvantages of his national identity should enrich each juvenile inwardly, and extended reflection further betters understanding beyond the common consumerist obsessions with material things. In the long run, it should have much to do with a high standard of consciousness. An important step in the formative function of the educator are these questions: Does the school genuinely respect the dignity of students and teachers? Does the engaged student have personal freedom for initiatives like philanthropy and compassion? What should be done to strengthen the student's precious gift of liberty? The Church states clearly that "the man can turn to good only in freedom."[571] The educator's role to nurture self-formed freedom, indeed, is a prerequisite in the election of fair and equal treatment. Allport states that the pupil, being a free participant in a discussion group, becomes less inclined to reactivity because it educates his own sense of respect in interpersonal communication that is valuable and desirable. [572]

The school largely prepares pupils for professions and enables the acquisition of relevant and necessary qualifications or skills for the common

---

[569] Cf. Nagórny. *Wychowanie do patriotyzmu.* IN: *Formacja moralna* p. 143.

[570] "Values derived from Judeo and Christian ethics, are about the finest mankind has yet formulated." Cf. Allport. *The Nature of Personality* p. 162.

[571] KDK p. 17.

[572] Cf. Allport. *The Nature of Personality* p. 148.

interest. So, the mission of vocational training must be linked to an upbringing in the family that strives for higher partnership. Good professional training makes a person ethical and developed at work, whereas the school aids in the formation of social virtues in the service of God and other humans.[573] Each social virtue is acquired in great hardship. So, paying attention to the ethical dimension of professional development is also an opportunity to improve not only moral but also some human standards of a trainee.

Vocational training, as one of the instruments of human activation, considers the personalistic, anthropological, theological, social dimensions of work. Such ancillary work improves skills and is a significant factor in the formation of a mature personality.[574] A. Biela warns, however, that unprofessional training may intimidate the employee and cause excessive stress, like an overloaded computer.[575] Ultimately, schools ought to be real apostolates of character that form individuals "in the image and likeness of God." Therefore, the school has an obligation to promote God's universal truth and human goodness.

The primary task of school is the pro-social education of a young man in truth and love. The school is the place of learning interpersonal cooperation. The cooperating object of prosocial teaching must be concerned with the theological and moral disciplines.[576] The pro-social dimensions of morality derive from the principle of selflessness with an attitude of altruism, founded for both the material and the spiritual wellbeing of the trainee. So, to educate in ethical sphere, the school ought to prepare pupils to have an active community life and concern for the common interest. The Church expresses this truth in these words: "A person ought to rediscover lived values, which will have a substantial social impact in the process of forming a better self. Since it is, in this case, the common good, civil society must ensure that schools provide a secure atmosphere of physical and moral growth."[577]

The opposite of prosocial attitudes, like any form of aggression, comes from low self-esteem, which is an educational concern. Most often, antisocial behavior has negative consequences (e.g., incurred losses, injustices, pain, and suffering for individuals and communities affected by

---

[573] Cf. Jeżyna. *Moralne przesłanie nowej ewangelizacji* p. 341.
[574] Cf. Allport. *The Nature of Personality* p. 149.
[575] Cf. A. Biela. *Stres decyzyjny w sytuacji pracy zawodowej*. IN: *Stres w pracy zawodowej*. Red. A. Biela. Lublin: RW KUL 1990 p. 173.
[576] Cf. T. Rostowska. *System wartości rodziców i dzieci jako zadanie rozwojowe*. IN: *Rodzina – źródło życia i szkoła miłości*. Red. D. Kornas-Biela. Lublin: RW KUL 2001 p. 217–229.
[577] PH p. 64.

it.)[578] That pro-social barrier even constitutes financial or organizational deficiencies. Therefore, the school should complement gaps and combat mental pathology by teaching universal and moral standards. The cause of the student's pathology is often ignorance, preserved in the deformed attitudes of a few parents toward their children. Most likely, the excess of visualized violence distorts a child's personality and good manners and embezzles a system of values.[579]

With school intervention, prosocial thinking teaches the pupil better mastery of fear, doubt, and negative thinking. This stimulated self-control challenges them to achieve something meaningful in life.[580] A pro-social attitude is a necessary feature that teaches sharing with others—in other words, an altruistic commitment to social solidarity, oriented toward the common good.[581] Pro-social education, then, both at school and at home, teaches the values of right judgment so that man demonstrates an attitude of empathy that is not limited to the transmission of pure knowledge.[582] Eventually, a self-formed person believes in higher values that emphasize human integrity, equality, dignity, justice, and responsibility for others. School systems also educate man in acting positively, in a way he can help others. It might be through empathy, which is the ability to adopt the status of another person or persons,[583] that schools could understand the feeling of a pupil. Allport notes that this school mission is possible by expanding the teacher's personality, interpersonal relationships, emotional stability, good perception of self, and self-acceptance. At school, there is a chance to be distanced from tension, stress, anxiety through engaging humor and shared virtues.[584]

Pro-social formation of the school requires an altruistic culture capable of activating society standards, values, and socially desirable motives, aware of its consequences. It is education that allows engaged students to act

---

[578] Cf. W. Okoń. *Nowy słownik pedagogiczny*. Warszawa: Wydawnictwo Akademickie "Żak" 2001 p. 15.

[579] Cf. J. Izdebska. *Mass media i multimedia – dominująca przestrzeń życia dziecka*. IN: *Pedagogika społeczna*. T 2. Red. E. Murynowicz-Hetka. Warszawa: Wydawnictwo Naukowe PWN 2007 p. 520.

[580] "We must demand unequivocally that our children practice self-control and self-restraint in all areas of human temptation." D. Lapsley. *The Challenge of Pluralism: Education, Politics, and Values: Pluralism, Virtues, and the post-Kohlbergian Era in Moral Psychology*. Red. F. Clark Power. Norte Dame, Indiana: University of Notre Dame Press 1992 p. 169.

[581] Cf. M. Łobocki. *Altruizm a wychowanie*. Lublin: UMCS 1998 p. 157.

[582] Cf. Pokrywka. *Posłannictwo uniwersytetu w integralnej formacji człowieka* p. 182.

[583] Allport describes empathy as a higher feeling in action. "Imaginative transposing of oneself into thinking, feeling and acting of another." Cf. Allport. *An Experiment in the Prevention of Delinquency* p. 466.

[584] Cf. J. Wilson. *Personality in the Social Process*. Hillsdale: Lawrence Erlbaum Associates 1985 p. 56.

humanely and socially. So, we can predict that for those seeking perfection, schooling can provide appropriate assistance. It seems reasonable to assume that a good personality has a significant influence on pro-social behavior. The idea of pro-social education is closely linked to learning generosity, systematic responsibility, altruism, and love of neighbor. In pro-social education, the teacher, as the creator, deliberately and consciously "molds" the pupil from the outside through formative education, which is, in this sense, the whole art of influence. Such positive impact enables the pupil to undertake formation and be properly equipped for coexistence and interaction with others. [585]

The lack of pro-social attitudes is caused by individual isolation, as well as the loss of sensitivity for others and a lack of dialogue. A lack of social interaction may also result from a failure to listen. The school appears, here, to fulfill a huge educational gap, teaching students the ability of sensitive listening. The art of listening is lost by the demoralizing Internet and television. Nearly three per hour noisy television programs are associated with violence. Less than 5 percent of these programs teach pro-social patterns.[586]

Therefore, the mission of the school is to prepare students to listen, absorb, integrate, and associate with necessary knowledge, skills, and attitudes that will help them become responsible citizens who are effectively interactive with a changing world. With fewer role models, it is much harder for a young person to reach integral maturity. Other factors result from a lack of interpersonal relationships, loneliness, escapes into cyberspace, and violent computer games. Now more than ever, school should inspire creativity in the community and classrooms. Hence, the critical mission of the school is to teach one to live in harmony with all of Creation.

Pro-social skill training demands intensive listening. Nothing hurts the young adult more than not being heard by his tutor. Hurt feelings, even by misunderstanding, lead to amoral attitudes. Therefore, the empathic ear of an educator is an important tool in emotional formation.[587] Just like talking without listening, listening without understanding is a serious obstacle in inculcating moral principles. Too often, the attitude of the ward, due to a lack of listening, leads him/her on the path of alienation and separation from the

---

[585] Cf. P. Tyrała. *Bliżej uniwersalnych wartości i realnego życia.* Torun: Wydawnictwo, "Adam Marszałek" 2001 p. 68.

[586] "The prevailing passion to live for yourself, not for your predecessors or posterity. We are fast losing the sense of historical continuity, the sense of belonging to a succession of generations originating in the past and stretching into the future." Cf. C. Lasch. *The Culture of Narcissism: American Life in an Age of Diminishing Expectations.* New York: Norton 1991 p. 5.

[587] Cf. M. Nichols. *The Lost Art of Listening.* New York: Guilford Press 1995 p. 1.

influence of the school environment. Integral teaching requires real hearing. It is a unique personal relationship in which both formator and pupil interact with each other, changing roles and learning to maturely expand their personalities into empathic behavior. Interpersonal dialogue accompanies a bearing witness. Hearing a pupil gives him a signal that he is being treated like a person.[588]

With a mature sense of being heard, a young person develops more mature stances involving his feelings and will to act in a more responsible fashion. Allport sees, in the social tone of this interactive impact, educative self-formation toward human perfection, which is fulfilled in the idea of brotherhood.[589] The ability to listen also shapes tolerance and mutual respect between children and parents and communication with loved ones in the world of values. The school should pay close attention to cooperation among parents, teachers, and youth. Such cooperation is formed by better listening, which is child's a natural experience of his mother's approved values.[590] The school requires teachers who expect a lot, but also students who are actively heard and understood in the interpersonal culture of becoming more mature. It can be assumed that mature pro-social traits would not be kept up only by those who teach. But the type of contact a student has with his teacher affects the student's characteristics and ethical behavior; thus, in the case of Christian education, of great importance are optimism and respect for teachers.[591]

Allport recognizes that a lack of personal lived experience in the real world (e.g., making friends, living in new conditions, developing passions) rather narrows the personality down to the simplified forms of conservation.[592] The abundance of technology in today's schools can also significantly delay the integral development of youth. Most young people experience the shock of information related to the Internet. The irresponsible use of a computer or a global network can be difficult not only for children but also for adults. Unlimited Internet access, deliberate disinformation, online pornography and violence pose threats to all. No socializing technology can completely replace the personal impact of the trustful environment, indicating right concepts, philosophies, or life values. While the still-immature young person loses the ability to select information, the good

---

[588] Cf. Ibid s. 17.

[589] Cf. Allport. *The Individual and His Religion* p. 57–58.

[590] Cf. M. Nichols. *The Lost Art of Listening*. New York: Guilford Press 1995 p. 24.

[591] "The first ingredient of morale is the possession by the individual of a robust set of convictions and values which for him make life worth living. Because he believes that he can meet whatever emergencies the future has in store for him, his emotional tone is high. He is prepared to put forth a zestful defense of those values that to him engender meaning in life." Cf. Allport. *Nature of Democratic Morale*. IN: *Civilian Morale* p. 4.

[592] Cf. *Osobowość i religia*. Transl. H. Bartoszewicz, A. Barktowicz, I. Wyrzkowska. Warszawa:Pax 1988 p. 32.

teacher provides a sensible and worthy criteria. He or she helps to select which messages are decent and which are wicked.[593]

Through cooperation with educators, school teaches etiquette, and the pupil learns to build proper relationships. The Catholic or private school better controls sources of any immature behavior and teaches right expressions of freedom.[594] Immoral attitudes are clearly challenged in the context of objective truth. Willfulness of the still-unformed person, succumbing to instincts, depends on purely sensual desires and power. Often, their apparent lack of understanding of their inner experiences and the feelings of others, notes Allport, is seen in a lack of compassion. At the same time, there is the sensitivity factor, impeding their ability to listen to other (i.e., a lack of empathy).[595] The school has the mission of shaping compassionate relationships, especially the Catholic School, which teaches moral valuation based on the gospel of Jesus Christ.

The integrative process of schoolwork—as I already mentioned—is not free from risk. Relativist, anti-educational systems aim to "reduce human life to the level of an animal consuming."[596] Anti-educational systems combined with permissiveness, undermine God's natural law of objective good and truth. Often, such relativism leads to self-disintegration of person.[597] Today's trends, due to cultural transformations, direct one's attention to more individualistic and self-centered lifestyles than any family or communal system of values provides. This process of personal deconstruction frequently leads to a crisis within family and the school system as educational and formative institutions. Relativism contributes to all educational levels we see today; when selfish behavior is permitted, it weakens the relationship of human society to faith and moral life.

Rarely, deformative patterns can come from negative stereotypes the educators might have, which manifest as incorrectly transmitted feelings.[598]

---

[593] Cf. W. Dębna. *Komputer jako zagrożenie dla rozwoju dzieci klas I-III* (the unpublished M. Div. manuscript). Wyszków 2001 p. 13.

[594] Cf. J. Galarowicz. *Spór o człowieka a personalizm Karola Wojtyły*. IN: Servo Veritatis. *Materiały Międzynarodowej konferencji dla uczczenia 25-lecia pontyfikatu Jego Świątobliwości Jana Pawła II* (Uniwersytet Jagielloński 9–11 października 2003 r.). Red. S. Koperek, S. Szczur. Kraków: Wyd. Nauk. PAT 2003 p. 391–392.

[595] Cf. Allport. *Personality and Social Encounter* p. 530–532.

[596] B. Kiereś. *Wychowanie a wychowane. Wspomaganie czy kształcenie*. IN: *Wychować charakter*. Red. A. Piątkowska, K. Stępień, Lublin: Fundacja Servire Veritati Instytut Edukacji Narodowej 2005 p. 92.

[597] B. Kiereś. *Wychowanie a wychowane. Wspomaganie czy kształcenie*. IN: *Wychować charakter*. Red. A. Piątkowska, K. Stępień, Lublin: Fundacja Servire Veritati Instytut Edukacji Narodowej 2005 p. 92.

[598] "For example, men who are self-assertive will seldom repeat successful acts but will see new means to satisfy their mounting level of aspiration. Men who like novelty

Personalists and Allport state the same: that mature stability creates a mellow personality—the personality of someone who is calm, cool, and free of harshness. The task of integral formation is to help a man grow in the freedom of divine affiliation. Systems and manipulative mechanisms—whether financial, emotional, or pseudo-educational—that do not care about the wellbeing of the person enslave man. The riskiest threats come from the relative systems themselves because the relative outlook stems from confusion in the mind of man, distorting the harmony of life and knowledge of God.[599]

Illusory patterns of conduct hinder proper understanding of one's world, experiences, and emotions and become destructive advisors that shape a selfish existence. Anti-value attitudes are intrusive and make a person less mature, representing almost childish behavior that blames others for one's own powerlessness and confusion. The school must alleviate any lack of justice. The application of moral principles has universal value and comes from the principles of justice, regardless of the culture or environment. Allport, too, encourages schools to fight ignorance and build a personal philosophy of life based on the acceptance of human values.[600]

Every school, in assessing the behavior of a juvenile, should not desensitize his conscience. Any of these desensitization techniques are extremely dangerous social mechanisms that relativize thinking. They reduce sensitivity, harm growth, increase indifference and callousness toward other human beings, and diminish human dignity that comes from God.[601] When there is visible arrest of ethical values, growth is threatened, even when intellectual or physical maturity has been maintained. Failures to comply with the norms and standards of ethical behavior are most noticed in schools.[602] Deficiencies in a young student's moral growth often leads to difficulty later in life. Thus, the deficit of holistic formation at school leads to delinquency that makes the pupil's integral growth stop. Often, educators ignore or understate the integral formation of youth for selfish reasons. The greatest obstacle to a healthy upbringing is a regressive educator, who Allport associates with convenience, selfishness, promotion of pleasure, a lack of

---

will deliberately shun a repetition of acts; so too will men who are set to solve new problems (since stereotyping of acts cannot contribute to new solutions)." Cf. Allport. *The Nature of Personality* p. 170.

[599] Cf. EV p. 70.

[600] "The principle of justice is always the same ideal form regardless of climate and culture." Cf. J. Davison Hunter. *The Death of Character: Moral Education in an Age without Good or Evil.* New York: Basic Books 2000 p. 206.

[601] Cf. Allport. *The Nature of Personality* p. 187.

[602] Cf. M. Pokrywka. *Wezwanie do formacji sumienia w świetle nauczania Jana Pawła II.* RT 48: 2001 z. 3 p. 53–54.

interior development, and a lack of insight into others, which is reflected in the lack of going beyond common routine.[603]

C. The educational influence of the Church

Ethical formation is the primary task of the universal Church, in which Christ serves as the main educator of Christians. The Church, since its inception, has been interested in the integral growth of men based on the classic patterns corresponding to the needs of time. Christian civilization centers used to be housed in monasteries. The community of believers cared for the growth of moral life, high art, scriptoria, crafts, and libraries, which helped raise the culture. The tradition of the Christian faith is a renewing tradition. Today, as in the past, the Church has an important, often unappreciated role, serving man in the transmission of civilization and the arts of writing and reading that ensures the continuity of the Greco-Roman culture. John Paul II portrays that truth by writing "is the way of the Church." The Godly man justifies his participation in the community of believers as part of the formation of man.[604]

The Church of Christ undertakes authority in matters of faith and morality, dating back to God's covenantal love communicated through the Bible. The Church of Jesus Christ is a loving community motivated by genuine faith and Sacraments that have formative influence. The Church, as a favorable growth environment, calls for the discovery of Christ's message and creates a civilization of truth and love based on the principles of the Gospel. The educational and formative process of the Church is, therefore, a chain of connections and successive harmonious reconstructions.[605] Just to refer to the *Redemptor hominis* encyclical in which John Paul II states: "The man who—(individually as a person)—has its history of life, and above all its own 'history of the soul.'"[606] The spiritual man, who has so many diverse existential needs, writes his personal history through numerous bonds, contacts, and social structures. He links himself with other people and begins interconnected growth from the first moment of his existence on Earth— from the time of conception to his natural death. That man, living in the full truth of his existence, is still "the community" within own family and within so many different environments—within the nation and within the whole of mankind. Therefore, this man is the primary route by which the Church must travel in fulfilling her mission. The Church, adapting only the worthy patterns

---

[603] Cf. Allport. *The Nature of Personality* p. 172.

[604] Cf. Chrobak. *Koncepcja wychowania personalistycznego w nauczaniu Karola Wojtyły – Jana Pawła II* p. 95.

[605] Cf. Kunowski. *Podstawy współczesnej pedagogii* p. 181.

[606] RH p. 14.

of the secular world, acquires and integrates various threads of culture into the Christian tradition. This pattern allows the faithful trainee to build identity within a rich heritage of Christianity and the collective mentality of many.[607] Thus, the Church remains open in communion with the national and patriotic values led by individual, local Churches and their pastors. The community of faithful is visible in the dimension of international dialogue, whereas the local Church is the primary cell structure, filling the gap between the high and low cultures of Christian life. Another network of parochial schools, cathedrals, and universities permit young people to know the truth and experience the impact of high culture and holistic education.[608] Every religious community conducts a cultural dialogue with the world on the most important matters. By speaking up in the matters of morality, elementary justice, and the alleviation of conflicts, the faithful continue self-formation. Technology helps solve the moral problems of the unprivileged in the undeveloped world by offering them the latest scientific achievements to improve their lives according to humane and ethical standards. But technology creates enormous destructive power, not necessarily equipped for transformation according to God's plan of goodness, truth, and respect for life. In this reductionist approach, man loses full awareness of the meaning of life.[609] Because of incorrect understanding and a reductionist, minimalistic approach to each person, the human being becomes "himself objective," acting against dignity, good, and harmony with God, especially if the man wants to be like God, but without God.[610] The man, left alone, does not establish a personal relationship with God and misses the chance to form experiences of true happiness, because without reference to God as the Giver of all life, he loses his humanity. One reason for the extinction of man's hope is destructive anthropology without God.[611] The Church, as a community that forms meaningful life, strongly emphasizes that "religious indifference and a complete lack of practical references to God are phenomena no less

---

[607] Cf. VS p. 91. "The European Union, as it enlarges and deepens, should regard the Catholic Church as a model of essential unity in diversity of cultural expressions, a consciousness of membership in a universal community which is rooted in but not confined to local communities, and a sense of what unites beyond all that divides." Cf. P. Manuel. *The Catholic Church and the Nation-State: Comparative Perspectives.* Red. L. Reardon, C. Wilcox. Washington: Georgetown University Press. 2006 p. 111.

[608] The Church seeks the dignity of man at every stage of life and sees the human dignity of man. The dignity of the person is due to the fact of being the person himself. Allport refers to personal dignity, which depends on an ascetic or good character. Such dignity is a fundamental value in Allport's educational ethics.

[609] M. Pokrywka points out that only integral formation can protect a person from the reductionism that comes from the misinterpreting of the human vision. Cf. *Posłannictwo uniwersytetu w integralnej formacji człowieka* p. 171–172.

[610] Cf. *Catechism of the Catholic Church.* LEV 1994 p. 100–111.

[611] Cf. EE p. 9.

disturbing and mostly destructive than overt atheism."[612] In her teaching, the Church wants to defend the truth about the dignity of every human person who struggles with the reductionist currents of thought of modern societies.[613]

The growing problem of the moral decadence of societies and nations requires more routes to individual self-formation to become the honest image of God among others. Living the standards God's law allows one to experience his faith community as a harmony of better choices. All responsible decisions shape not only the quality of life but also the harmonious development of the individual and humanity. The best path in life, consistent with the natural law of God, sets a person in the proper, meaningful direction. Although regression often precedes the progress of enlightenment, from the previous stages of development, the trainee cannot belittle the need for the moral and spiritual formation. The Church claims that without integral education, as Pius XI points out, an "unhealthy culture of young men unaccustomed to respect God will not be able to endure the disciplined life or accept honest desires easily following subversive action."[614] The fundamental mission of the Church is found in the thesis that self-formation is possible and socially desirable. There are three communities of formation that are necessary and different, teaches Pius XI. God bound these communities into a harmonious whole, where man is born for the family and the state in the natural order. Above these two, the Church's community is a supernatural order of dignified human life.[615] Nevertheless, the most relevant environments for mature self-formation are the family and the Church, who, together, form one temple of Christian upbringing. The Church has paid attention to the educational role of the gift of love, which has been always a faithful witness. [616] Particularly, post-conciliar teaching states that the conjugal love of parents culminates in the educative and formative development of children, especially when relationships are built on the road of true love and not domination.[617] "Parents and educators—called John Paul II—are to help all children, young people, to experience peace in the family and school daily activities." The teamwork activities, relations, and sport competitions always establish and restore (…) friendship."[618]

---

[612] ChL p. 34

[613] Cf. Dziekoński. *Formacja chrześcijańska dziecka w rodzinie* p. 204.

[614] DIM p. 1.

[615] DIM p. 1.

[616] Dziekoński. *Formacja chrześcijańska dziecka w rodzinie* p. 136.

[617] FC p. 13.

[618] Jan Paweł II. Orędzie na XII Światowy Dzień Pokoju "Osiągniemy pokój wychowując do pokoju" (1 stycznia 1979 r.). Watykan (08.12.1978) p. 2.

The Church supports the development of the family modeled on the heroic love of Christ and underlines its significance as the smallest unit of society. Christ's teaching takes many forms: once during stabilization and restraint and other times by failure. Human formation in the Church develops and cultivates respect for God and emphasizes deeper humanity, without which life loses its meaning. People grow up most fully in relationships with others. Hence, there is a great demand for the creation of a simple, traditional education. Education guided by the principle of "the domestic Church" allows parents to educate themselves through other relatives and teach children with the co-presence of other children. [619] The Church encourages one to enter the path of co-participation and the visible, salvific influence of the community of believers in the process of integral formation.[620]

The other important supernatural influence of the Church comes from Christ teaching young people who seek the meaning of life. Adoption of Christ's message opens young people to the formation of their personalities by the Church and in the Church. The community of faith goes on to meet young people in charitable actions that speak loudly in maturing their personalities: "Dear young people, where is a better place for the development of your character than within the Church? In the community of faith, you may discover the Word of God that gives life meaning; action of Christ who makes all men brothers, children of one Father; a force capable of unleashing the creative energy in you to build a new just, fraternal world.[621]

Therefore, it is necessary that the Church's educational path is conducted at various levels, as well as through Christian media, to achieve a greater impact on family, neighborhood, and individual behavior so that respect, dignity, and other values persevere. Without Christian environments, a young person probably does not develop ethical awareness and value. The Church has always supported man, understanding well the weakness of fallen natural forces, giving Christians the generous help of God's grace. Therefore, in the Sacraments, Christ sanctifies man to transform human beings.[622] Most important for the Christian is internal transformation. The Church aids not only through the Sacraments but through a variety of forms of education and institutional associations with the aim to shape a man from a Christocentric source. In the Apostolic Exhortation *Catechesi Tradendae* of 1979, a reflection on moral education, John Paul II sets the formative tone of the "Christocentric" character of education. [623] Centered on Christ, we are grateful to the influence of many environments of growth including

---

[619] Cf. LdR p. 16.

[620] Cf. Pokrywka. Osoba, uczestnictwo, wspólnota p. 19.

[621] Jan Paweł II. *Przemówienie "Chrystus jest odpowiedzią na wasze pytania."* (Caracas, 18.01.1985). OsRomPol6: 1985 no. 1 p. 25.

[622] The sacrament expresses the presence that God is with us. Cf. Jan Paweł II. *Przekroczyć próg nadziei.* Lublin: RW KUL 1994 p. 27–28.

[623] Cf. Ct p. 5.

catechists as the true "teachers of man and human life in the faith."[624] Integral formation in the ecclesial community is often a complex process that impacts the human person. This takes place in stages, because "the ultimate moral maturity requires mature solutions and questions about the meaning of life.[625]

Allport, too, repeatedly stresses the important role of the community of faith in the formation of valuable human qualifications. The community of faith, based on principled moral norms, interiorizes the structure of the individual and creates a well-established assessment of facts and mature reality. The code of the Bible, brought forward by the Person of Christ, contains a lot of information about the human person, making him a more authentic being.[626] Authentic multicultural participation from members in Church activities strengthens man's integration, making their personalities ascetic. Allport recognizes this as a fundamental task of the Church—its institutional contribution to the safety of the family. For example, the Christian community provides value exercises in ecclesiastical activities for youth organizations and associations.[627]

The fundamental role of the Church is to discover the truth so that moral formation, based on Christian anthropology, can elevate the human person (rising out of life to Revelation, from wounded human nature to heavenly perfection). The space of "heaven" ("ideal" me) and the space of "Earth" ("real" me) determine the realization of proper formation in the Church's ministry. "Heaven" is also the realm of the perfect (the *sacrum*), whereas "Earth" is the realm of effort and continuous work on the profane. The area of perfection and authority, according to Allport, emanates from the ascetic personalities at the bosom of the Church, among the creative environments of the parish. These creative and educational environments build the Kingdom of Heaven and the family as the smallest cell of the Church within a parish. Ultimately, there is "the forefront of catechesis."[628] The parish is also a place of character education and personal identity. Within the Church, as the intermediary community of faith, many experience a call to the formative communion. The *communio personarum* of the Church forms the unity of all persons in Christ. *Communio personarum* is one of the educative concepts that John Paul II discusses.

The Church has a threefold role corresponding to man's threefold nature as body, soul, and spirit: she is the temple of human formation (body); she assembles and integrates the faithful (soul); and she presents God and

---

[624] Ct p. 22.
[625] Cf. Kohlberg. *Education, Moral Development and Faith* p. 14.
[626] Cf. Allport. *How Shall We Evaluate Teaching?* IN: *A Handbook for College Teachers.* T. 3. Red. B. B. Cronhile. Cambridge: Harvard University Press 1950 p. 98.
[627] Cf. Allport. *Personality and Social Encounter* p. 213.
[628] CT p. 67.

mystical body of Christ as the Sacrament of the altar (spirit). By the presence and action of the Holy Spirit in the Church, the bishops, as successors of the Apostles, receive a mission from Christ to transform the human heart and safeguard the faith. Z. Grocholewski writes that the Church is the begetter of vocations that transform a person.[629]

The transforming culture of the Church makes Christians understand that maturity does not depend on the concept of who is right or wrong during formation. The Church considers the maturity of a man who has his constancy produced among the community of the faithful. The truth on which the Church lives has been guided by the goodness of the man, together with reasonable, just opinions on events and people. This feature of the moral influence of the Church and through the Church must lead to the conversion of hearts. This is man's dual purpose—to bring forward the mature faith that is born in the soul and become a true disciple of Christ by a deeper and more orderly knowledge of the person and teachings of Christ.[630]

If G. Allport is right in saying that most of today's societies are characterized by external morality, so that extremity has a rather deconstructive impact on one's personality (which is typical for some of today's postmodern societies). So, this extrinsic form of morality serves only to satisfy one's instincts or selfish, immature interests and has little in common with the Christian integral morality. Meanwhile, the role of the Church in moral self-formation is to pay more attention to an internalized, mature attitude that plays a creative role in Christian life and promotes a mature relationship with God and other people. There is a clear need for updated moral standards in terms of internalized adult behaviors that meet not only egocentric wants but also the noble motives of an authentic life in God.[631] Following Christ, a man commits himself to the fullness of humanity because he "recognizes in Him the authentic pattern of life." The Church's teaching of self-formation internalizes morality and constructs warmer, more affectionate contact with other people, while at the same time, it sensitizes

---

[629] Cf. Z. Grocholewski. *Guidelines for the Use of Psychology in the Admission and Formation of Candidates for the Priesthood.* Watykan (6.11.2008). "Church is begetter and formator of vocations." Cf. PDV p. 35.

[630] CT p. 19.

[631] The term "egocentricity" is used not in the pejorative but in a descriptive sense to refer to the inability of an immature person to adopt another person's point of view. Such an inability to accept someone's vision (without losing one's self) refers to moral norms and logical correctness, gradually taught by repeated interactions under which the person is obliged to adopt a new view of another person. Cf. Piaget. *The Origins of Intellect Piaget's Theory* p. 63.

the human conscience. [632] The sincere attitudes of a Christian always contribute to the human values of the individual.[633]

The Second Vatican Council, in *Gaudium at spes,* teaches that "man, who is the only creature on earth which God willed for itself, cannot fully find himself except through a sincere gift of himself to others." [634] Christianity, therefore, emphasizes the dynamism of charity formed by *koinonia.* An appropriate pattern of loving is necessary to shape the sense of the sacred. Because the dynamism of love is an essential educational influence in the consciousness of young people when their faith is the least experienced, they see their colleagues in faith. [635] With inner work and sustained love in the community of faith, the pupil, enriched "from the inside," creates a unique gift of self for others and deepens his horizons in terms of extension of self. Regarding personalistic upbringing within the Church, every person accepts values as if they were jewels. That way, the trainee "co-creates, transforms and reproduces them for communication with others."[636]

The Church impacts and educates young people in the mature behavior such as "a sense of security, the ability to restrain and control their own behavior, deepen their association with others in capacity to live together, following the rules of morality exercised in the cultural environment."[637] Allport also notes that without modeled attitudes of the Church of Christ, man, in his life progress, rather chaotically makes mistakes, hence there seems to be a need for a lifelong life of self-formative attitudes.[638] Self-formation, as the Church's pedagogical discipline, strives for authentic and comprehensive development, particularly based on an integral vision of man.

---

[632] "Our understanding of other people is derived from our capacity to imitate (…) the behavior of the person we are trying to understand." Allport. *Personality a Psychological Interpretation* p. 531.

[633] Pope Francis often draws attention to self-control and not speaking ill of others: "Rumors always harms the quality of people, their work and the entire environment. "Cf. *Przemówienie, Kościół wzrasta dzięki atrakcyjności świadectwa"* (Asyż 4.11.2013). OsRomPol 11: 2013 no. 11 p. 14.

[634] KDK p. 24.

[635] Cf. J. Mariański. *Moralność w procesie przemian. Szkice socjologiczne.* Warszawa: Instytut Wydawniczy PAX 1990 p. 6.

[636] J. Majka. *Wychowanie chrześcijańskie – wychowaniem personalistycznym.* IN: Wychowanie personalistyczne p. 157.

[637] Bazylak. *Postawy religijne młodzieży* p. 179–180.

[638] "Without guiding attitudes, the individual is confused and baffled. (…) Attitudes determine for each what he will see and hear, what he will think and what he will do." Cf. Allport. *Personality* p. 806.

The man, created in the likeness of God, who has been redeemed by Jesus Christ, aims to develop his "self" to become a mature son according to the image of Christ. The Church strives, through the process of formation, to transmit the contents of moral support, allowing children and all of the faithful to mature into the fullness of humanity.[639] In the community of life, that task is asked of every Christian. Therefore, the thesis of "becoming" more human is the anthropological basis of self-formation. In the supernatural and natural space, the Church shows that the target of structural becoming is the path to sanctification and salvation. Through the Church, man is exalted in Christ, who is "the Way, the Truth and the Life," and the formed self can more fully follow Christ, *the sequela Christi*.[640] Becoming a man in the community of faith has a spiritual dimension, too; each man is gifted by God in the community by many physical, biological, and spiritual riches. Those undertaking self- becoming particularly feel the need to acquire higher qualities of inner freedom, which includes co-Creation.

In the community of believers, man is the subject of healthy activity and authentic interpersonal dialogue as he experiences the material world and clings to the spiritual transcendent God who internally unites his Christian personality. Every man, younger and older, is responsible for the gift of integral life. When he reaches the stage of maturity, he says that he needs to give his life a different meaning. The community of believers supports the youth in determining the meaning of life and initiating the process of Christian formation. Over time, this takes on the characteristics of self-formation, mainly through various engagements and charity.[641]

As for the community of faith, each person is important, and this means that a *persona Christi* cannot be manipulated by ideology in any way. Similarly, Allport recognizes Churches' autotelic character, stressing that man cannot be treated instrumentally.[642] So, the community has a presupposed belief in the sanctity of every person.

Man, through his faith, notes that his moral and personal development does not end in childhood but allows him to better verify his

---

[639] Cf. *Ogólna instrukcja katechetyczna* DOK (1998), adhortacja Pawła VI: *Evangelii nuntiandi* (1975), oraz *Catechesi tradendae* (1979), KKK1994, i Dyrektorium ogólne o katechizacji (1998).

[640] CT p. 5.

[641] "Catholic Charities had earned a significant voice in the development of American welfare (…). Catholic charities' network of 1,400 social agencies and institutions and more than 200,000 volunteers assisted more than eleven million Americans through emergency service and social service programs." Cf. D. M. Brown. *The Poor Belong to Us: Catholic Charities and American Welfare*. Cambridge: Harvard University Press 1997 p. 197.

[642] "All intermingled agree to form a faith in the sacredness of the human person (…). Our national morale resides in remote corners of our personalities and are not readily available to analysis." Cf. Allport. *The Nature of Democratic Morale*. IN: *Civilian Morale*. Red. G. Watson. Boston: Houghton Mifflin Company 1942 p. 3-4.

previous behavior through the teachings of the community of faith. He subjects himself to the constant transformation of the environment that reconstructs him to the fullness of humanity. Church helps the individual better understand oneself "not just of what someone is, but—what should always have in mind—what might happen in the future."[643] Each person in the community accepts responsibility for their mature attitude, which eventually teaches him to objectify values focused on love, inner strength, and the integration of the whole person.[644] Every well-integrated personality requires a universal dimension of the Church to conduct a meaningful dialogue, and skillful dialogue is the beginning of a community of persons.[645]

The attitude of worshipping God comes from learned virtues of faith, hope, and love. Scripture also inspires Christians to worship God in more than moral action alone. The wisdom of the Word of God builds primary maturity and broadens the horizons of reflection, at the same time improving man's proper skills through free responses to God's call.[646] The community of the Church, in the free response of the faithful selects the most comprehensive way to grow, mature, and bear fruit through moral principles, gifts, and opportunities. The ministerial activities of the young man harmonize with the social environment. Within a slow process of ongoing formation, he moves from a mechanistic treatment of the Sacraments to mature attitudes.[647] Christian liturgical formation in the Church is always transforming; when man lives and internalizes liturgy, he reforms his relationship with God and "changes" the man of the world with better reasoning.[648] With his rational reasons, man participates in the light of God's thought, where he can take responsibility for oneself and be entrusted to the work of sanctification. A relationship with God through worship leads to holiness.

The role of the Church, with respect to liturgical formation, is put forth in apostolic teaching (cf. Mt. 6:11; 2 Cor. 3:18; Acts 21), which indicate the paths to spiritual and moral transformation. In the Scriptures (cf. Rom. 12:2; 2 Cor. 3; Phil. 2:6) a core Greek word *morph* is prefixed by a *meta-* to create verb *metamorphoomai*, which emphasizes "transformation,

---

[643] ChL p. 63.

[644] Cf. J. Nagórny. *Wychowanie do dojrzałej miłości.* IN: *Najważniejsza jest miłość. Księga pamiątkowa u czci księdza Profesora Waleriana Słomki.* Red. M. Chmielewski. Lublin: RW KUL 1999 p. 403–407.

[645] "The deep community of conjugal life and love, established by the Creator and regulated by his laws, is founded on a marriage covenant, or irrevocably personal consent." KDK p. 48.

[646] Cf. Allport. *Waiting for the Lord: 33 Meditations on God and Man.* New York: Macmillian 1928 p. 5.

[647] Cf. Dziekoński. *Formacja chrześcijańska dziecka w rodzinie* p. 452.

[648] Cf. D. B. Forrester. *Moral Formation and Liturgy* p. 379.

transforming, forming." [649] This verb is used only in two other New Testament passages—St. Matthew and St. Mark—in regard to personal transfiguration. St. Paul clearly states that cultic moral transformation is carried out by a cognitive renewal of thinking (logic) and should occur in the life of every Christian, "transformed by the renewing of your mind, that you may discern what is the will of God, what is good, what pleasing and perfect" (Rom. 12:1–2). Paul recognizes this process precisely in Eucharistic worship and prayer. Evil exists in the world in real dimensions and must be overcome during a relationship bond with God. God calls Christians to perfection in a community of love for God and people. St. Paul says: "But we all, with unveiled face beholding the brightness of the Lord as if in a mirror" (2 Corinthians 3:18).

Individual and communal prayers heal and solve internal problems. Starting from early childhood, personal prayer teaches people to accept God as the Truth and the Good, which allows one to make the right choices in daily life. In the ecclesial community, "prayer becomes a human encounter that obliges the individual to live honorably, because of the divine mercy. Mercy and forgiveness are always the positive attributes of a mature personality."[650] Through forgiveness, a man finds his way to maturity. One who prays to God is not exhausted, but in the words and movements of his higher feelings, he brings glory to God. Various methods of ecclesial communal prayer, the Eucharist, individual prayer in the form of *Lectio Divina*, meditation, and the examination of conscience ultimately recognize better ways to find true inner freedom in the pursuit of unification with God. That process of self-formation is often done in an atmosphere of reflective silence, which promotes a bond with loving God. Every prayer, therefore, has the formative character necessary to help a person imitate their loving God.[651] Jesus gave believers the *Lord's Prayer* for spiritual thinking; the gravity of faith in reflective prayer life is an irreplaceable element of a healthy personality.[652]

Worshipping and loving God with prayer is a better way of life, whereas value assets are like flowers acquired for the healthy functioning of the ecclesial community. Man, as I previously emphasized, is the way of the Church. "Christ, who died and was raised up for all, provides man—each and every man—with the light and the strength to measure up to his supreme calling. Therefore, the Church makes every element of human life correspond

---

[649] Cf. H. Hionides. *Greek Dictionary*. Glasgow: Collins Dem 1997² p. 137.

[650] "They refer rather to the quality of regeneration." Cf. L. E. Mayfield. *Their Future Is Now: The Growth and Development of Christian Personality*. New York: The Macmillan Company 1939 p. 322.

[651] Cf. Derdziuk. *Formacyjny wymiar modlitwy uwielbienia*. IN: *Modlitwa uwielbienia*. T. 5. *Homo orans*. Red. J. Misiurek. Lublin: Wydawnictwo KUL 2004 p. 4.

[652] Cf. Pokrywka. *Osoba, uczestnictwo, wspólnota* p. 155–157.

to man's true dignity."[653] The unifying strength of the Church's culture calls for the promotion of love, and Catholicity calls for enriching wealth of personal diversity. Apostolicity summons man to the shared truth received from Christ, whereas goodness is an essential dimension of holiness. Moral formation within the Church is an integral part of communion, through which members of the Church become fully who they already are by the grace of being faithful to God.

Within the Christian community of faith, self-formation means the responsible use of freedom. The dignity of man requires him to act out of consciousness and free choice, motivated internally, not through blind impulse or external pressure. He achieves dignity when he is freed from all bondage passions, through a free choice of good. "Only in freedom can people direct themselves toward goodness."[654] Freedom means the ability to choose between good and evil. Christian freedom stems from the saving memory of Christ. Therefore, formed Christians are involved in communion with God by building a meaningful future.[655]

Sunday is not only the seventh day of the week but is eschatological time—or the first day of creation. Through the Sacrament of the Sunday's Eucharist, the Church remembers not only the past but also foresees future victory over death and the gift of eternal life by God. Jesus calls Christians to the frequent religious practices of moral perfection to form mutual love (cf. Mt. 5:48; 2 Cor. 3:18). Ecclesial formation strengthens the moral life of the individual when it is authentically converted. At the same time, conversion to God contributes to self-transformation. Becoming a holy man gives individual the true freedom: "The Lord is the Spirit, and where the Spirit of the Lord is, there is freedom" (2 Cor. 3:17).

The Church cares for the mature life with God and opens a young man to the common good. The important educational mission is realized through the community's social teaching while maintaining elementary justice and the dignity of every person. In the context of social life, the relationship of freedom and morality—as rightly observed by M. Pokrywka—manifests itself in responsible participation in society. And it does not mean abandonment of rational reflection developed by anthropological sciences.[656] Allport presumes that a person participating in social life discovers his vocation, which contributes to a meaningful life. Self-education moves one toward good self-control.

---

[653] RH p. 14.

[654] *Gaudium at Spes* p. 17.

[655] "Remembering the future, experiencing the eschatological future, encountering the heavenly reality now, and appropriating the past." Cf. Forrester. *Moral Formation and Liturgy* p. 379.

[656] Cf. *Osoba, uczestnictwo, wspólnota* p. 84.

The autoactivate process of the continuous development of the pupil, in a social context and in light of a well-understood truth about himself, stems from a conscious choice to participate. Allport notes that participation and engagement considers the action plan and ennobles human nature to such an extent that it enriches the average person (*gratify the man in the street*).[657] Man chooses to participate in a set of higher goals. John Paul II says that the "teacher is one who is born in a spiritual sense. Religious upbringing and education, in this sense, may be simultaneously considered a genuine apostolate. It is participation, in other words, by truth and love. A living means of communication, (...) not only creates a profound relationship between the educator and the one being educated, but also makes them both sharers in truth and love, that final goal to which everyone is called by God the Father, Son and Holy Spirit."[658]

The basis of true participation is the principle of solidarity that considers the personal dimension of the man with his social character, allowing him to overcome (...) extreme models of society: individualism and collectivism."[659] By the principle of solidarity, Christians already belong to the same community of faith, prayer, and love of the Church and are subject to needed integral formation. For Allport, becoming an integral person happens by *participation.* [660] When there is no in-depth and creative participation in social life, religion, family, professional life, intelligence, and interests, there is no possibility of becoming entirely mature.[661] M. Pokrywka rightly observes that any participation in society must be based on recognizing the fundamental truth that a person is a valued asset, and as such, is the center of social life. The subjectivity of every person is realized through the exercise of rights and fulfillment of all sorts of obligations including ethical obligation.[662] A person moves to higher levels of integral life only through love when he evolves from being focused on himself and his needs to on an enlarged circle of people, affairs, and universal truths. Only then can we talk about the personal extension of self. Genuine emotional participation in the Church and through the Church helps a person exhibit more self-discipline. [663] The sense of actual participation refers to the work, family, leisure, faith, prayer, love, and all aspects of life. The more fully a person is

---

[657] Cf. Allport. *The Psychology of Participation* p. 118.

[658] Cf. LdR *Gratissimam Sane* 16.

[659] Pokrywka. *Osoba, uczestnictwo, wspólnota* p. 166.

[660] Cf. Allport. *Personality and Social Encounter* p. 181–197.

[661] "It seemed that poor morale was more likely to lead to answers indicating feeling miserable, nervous, and grouchy, worrying too much, having one's feelings hurt, all accompanied by a sense of social isolation, inferiority, and unhappiness." Cf. Allport. *Civilian Morale* p. 277.

[662] Cf. *Osoba, uczestnictwo, wspólnota* p. 141.

[663] Cf. Chrobak. *Koncepcja wychowania personalistycznego w nauczaniu Karola Wojtyły – Jana Pawła II* p. 97.

involved in a multitude of honorable ideas, activities, and contacts, the more mature and sane he can be.

It is worth noting that the formative role of the Church takes place in various Catholic associations, movements of formation, youth organizations, youth ministries, and charities. Studies conducted by Michael Gottfried and Jacob Kirksey on Catholic education prove that religious discipline positively influence a child's behavior.[664] These environments, through reflection, music, and sports activity, develop healthy patterns of personal growth and integrative education. K. Czajkowski also sees a tremendous opportunity to educate and form children, in their free time, "who voluntarily adopt social responsibility."[665]

The main components of harmony between values and purposeful education is group solidarity, partnership, and participation in the implementation of the greater good. Of course, the educational impact of these values cannot be overestimated. The engagement of peer groups, as the Church teaches, provides a huge impact on the formation of the person; these youth groups form a framework of activities that encourage learning social behavior in young people's free time.[666] Christian youth associations are intended to positively motivate solidarity among its members. These groups teach tolerance, courage, and responsibility for one's self and others.[667]

Equally important are rich social interactions among youth. Christian culture provides young people support and assistance in achieving better self-control. Entering the world of moral norms means developing motivated conviction and participation in community life. Allport confirms in his findings that a group changes and forms the worldview of its members.[668] Ethical talks and verbalization about life within Christian families provides inner harmony and peace.[669] A sign of that integrative formation creates human bonds. Peers within church associations create a spontaneous forum

---

[664] M. Gottfried and J. Kirksey. Foreword & Executive Summary by A. M. Northern and M. J. Petrilli. *The self-discipline and Catholic Education.* p. 7. 05.31.2018.

[665] *Wychowanie do rekreacji. Warszawa: Wydawnictwa Szkolne i Pedagogiczne* 1979 p. 12.

[666] PH p. 77.

[667] "In the group, the individual is aware of specific tasks that he must carry through, of problems that he must solve, to defend and extend his store of values. His immediate purposes are held clearly in view, with the result that his convictions are channelized into coordinated, skillful, and decisive action." Cf. Allport. *Nature of Democratic Morale* p. 4.

[668] "People band together voluntarily in programs of group dynamics because they dissatisfied with their skill in human relations." Cf. Allport. *Personality and Social Encounter* p. 247.

[669] Cf. Paweł VI. *Orędzie na X Światowy Dzień Pokoju* "Jeśli chcesz pokoju, broń życia" (Watykan, 01.01.1977); Chrobak. *Koncepcja wychowania personalistycznego w nauczaniu Karola Wojtyły – Jana Pawła II* p. 97.

for interconnectedness around the group principles. Allport's study on group participation verbalizes a mature sense of responsibility and sense of duty as a method of growth.[670] He notes that the Church's meaningful preaching helps directs a sense of responsibility for others. The proper formation of personality in the Church emerges from solidarity and friendship in these peer groups. Through friendship, young men satisfy their social need to belong and to participate in good projects. In the Church, an educator or a leader of youth group relates to young people in the spirit of truth, justice, and friendship by the model of Christ.[671] Those responsible for group formation ought to truly know the parish or school in which they work as well the family and peer environment of the juveniles with whom he works. This knowledge broadens his understanding of the group and creates a sense of solidarity with his students. According to A. Derdziuk, adherence to Christ strengthens the virtue of solidarity with every person by humbling the teacher to share in the fate of a child, the fear of an immigrant, or the problems of struggling person.[672] Sensitivity to injustice, learned within the community of faith, becomes a pupil's initial stage for self-formation toward morality. Any group within the Church has a task to provide a positive environment, including a civilization of love within a community of believers.[673] Allport appreciates the Church's social teaching, claiming that it is integrally linked to evolving values and shaping the personality within peer groups. He compares it to scenes of secular and anti-Church approaches. He notices, however, that selective and negative treatment of personal values reduces their integral human development.

Contemporary life has a pluralism that significantly reduces the role of Christian formation, which—according to Allport—adapts secular amorality and ignores important codes of universal ethics. [674] Errant

---

[670] "An Ethical Discrimination Test. This measure was an attempt to tap the boy's qualities of character. His sophistication about ethical issues and his ability to verbalize his moral discriminations were assessed using his comments concerning a series of short stories descriptive of psychological or immoral behavior. A boy's answers to such questions (...) were presumed to test his ability to discriminate evil intentions from wrong outcomes and to compare the relative 'goodness' or 'badness' of the actor's intentions. Other tests read to the boy's sense of justice and responsibility and to show the extent to which he had overcome local group-centeredness. The T-boys achieved a significantly higher score on this test." Cf. Allport. *An Experiment in the Prevention of Delinquency. The Cambridge-Somerville Youth Study.* New York: Columbia University Press 1951 p. 312.

[671] Cf. Allport. *An Experiment in the Prevention of Delinquency: The Cambridge-Somerville Youth Study.* New York: Columbia University Press 1951(co-authors: E. Powers I H. Witmer) p. 103, 149, 164, 320, 321, 494, 505.

[672] *Solidarność jako cnota społeczna.* RTM 4(59): 2012 p. 21.

[673] Cf. PH p. 77.

[674] Cf. Allport. *The Use of Personal Documents in Psychological Science.* New York: Social Science Research Council 1951 p. 79.

postmodern approaches reduce references to the sacred essence of humanity. The multiple aspects of the truth about man—emphasizes M. Pokrywka—leads to confusion in response to the question: Who is a man?[675] How could it be otherwise, when many claiming to be Christians have lost the experience of *Sacramentum trimendum* and mystery? Almost everywhere in the West, postmodern consciousness is steeped into pragmatism and instrumentalism. In the absence of sacred, even the worship, does not fulfill the role sensitizing conscience. The perverse influence of secularism and materialistic ideology in Western culture greatly limits Christianity. Its eschatological experience loses ground and inhibits moral and spiritual power because splits the ties between the liturgical community and the culture of everyday life. Secular ethics based on Kant, Hegel, and Marx take an important mission—which is necessary to build an attitude of openness and faith—away from the community of faith. [676] The secular education and upbringing of young people has materialistic components which do not allow any faithful person to manifest faith publicly. Consequently, mankind suffers from weakened interpersonal bonds of the transformative role of God and at the same time increases human individualization.

Today's neoliberal educators often provide a psychoanalytic model of education, stating that education should take place in a climate free from higher values, Christ, and true images of humanity. Thus, the individual is deprived of essential knowledge and personal development. In the so-called secular world, deliberate anti-Church falsification of classical values can prevent pupils from understanding social norms and higher culture, which can truly fulfil human needs. Simply adapting oneself to the group is insufficient. Often informal peer groups do not allow youth to discover the higher moral models on which the world is dependent.[677] B. Kiereś notes that many of today's educational environments can be described as anti-pedagogical—systems that de facto serve the purpose of deformation, leading to the reduction of any dignified life to the level of an animal consumption,. This, in combination with permissiveness, undermines moral standards and relativism and causes the rejection of objective good and truth. This ultimately leads to self-destruction and the degradation of humanity.[678]

In this context, I want to emphasize that moral formation shapes an intentional life and meaningful life. The Church, as community of faith, truth, and goodness, fulfills the formative task and strives to choose the first best

---

[675] *Człowiek i moralność w postmodernistycznym świecie.* RTM 3(58): 2011 p. 79.

[676] Cf. D. B. Forrester. *Moral Formation and Liturgy.* ER 49: 1997 no. 3 p. 378.

[677] "It has been a time when values have become individualistic a matter of one's own opinion." J. Lowen. *Is Everything Permitted? Reconnecting Psychology and Ethics.* "Free Inquiry" 13: 1993 no. 3 p. 22.

[678] *Wychowanie a wychowanek. Wspomaganie czy kształcenie* p. 82.

option, which "shapes the entire moral life."[679] The role of the Church, in all areas of life, has an educational function, combining the harmony of faith, sacrifice, and service to God through neighborly love.[680] The involvement of the Church is urgent in the face of contemporary challenges and threats to moral laws—threats that question the nature of human life. The Church's dialogue with the world is based on authentic human values: love, truth, freedom, and justice. The role of the Community of faith is enormous because it can reveal the truth about meaningful existence. Its contribution is not limited to verbal communication but brings needed context to self-formation with hope and ethical values that underlie life. A. Krąpiec could not have said it better: the Church is a natural community of formation that helps any human person correctly read signs of the time without replacing or eliminating personal decisions and personal responsibility[681]

---

[679] VS p. 65.

[680] Chrobak. *Koncepcja wychowania personalistycznego w nauczaniu Karola Wojtyły – Jana Pawła II* p. 101.

[681] Cf. A. Krąpiec. *Człowiek i prawo naturalne*. Lublin: RW KUL 1993 p. 244.

CHAPTER 4

The self formation and maturity

Formation toward a mature personality has been influenced by many interrelated factors because maturity affects the physical, moral, social, mental, and emotional spheres. Every person who exceeds their next stage of development should have a set of principles and skills that shapes his life. Therefore, the road to a mature personality is a process of internal self-actualization of potentiality. According to Allport, maturity develops through life according to moral principles and a personal "commitment to the ideals," which are indicators of the mature life. He greatly appreciates the responsible self-formation of a juvenile, considering the relevant principles and moral virtues as the essential to that process. [682] Rules, principles, nurturing, tolerance, and dignity make a teacher truly human. At the same time, in a professional manner, man implements students' principles of voluntarism and freedom.

The pursuit of developing personal maturity is required by everyone who is responsible for their own life, before God and other people. According to Allport, reaching a mature personality requires not only in-group formation of individuals but self-formation, too. Self-formation considers the natural gift of intelligence as an important tool for solving personal problems because it teaches the avoidance of schizophrenia and the creation of two worlds: internal and external. So, mature personality evolves via three main ways of development: on the road of widening interest (development of identity), the drive of detachment, and insight into self-formation.[683] It is by way of the well-developed image of our own Christian identity that we are able to master the responsible emotionality and enthusiasm that contributes to the integrity of human solidarity in the world. At this point, it must be emphasized that interest in the ethical aspects of existence become a source of integrating personality. Self-education toward maturity must rest on each person. Therefore, personal Christian self-formation happens in responsible cooperation with God's grace, involving the incorporation and development of the virtues and gifts received from God.

---

[682] Cf. Allport. *Osobowość i religia* p. 42; Cf. Allport. *Becoming* p. 44.
[683] Cf. Allport. *Osobowość i religia* p. 140.

A. The formation of a mature emotionality

The initial stage of formation toward mature personality is, as I already mentioned, initiated mainly by parents but also teachers, catechists, and pastors. The emotional participation of engaged educators creates a similar mental, moral, philosophical perception. It is the method accepted by the existing social environment that leads youth to the next stage of maturation. According to Allport, the engine of this process is the internal force (i.e., genotype). This way, the self-formatting person actuates his own natural values.[684] Individual self-formation takes root in the motivation of educators who make mature choices that protect them from deformities and frustrations, which can exist in surroundings of nihilism or the culture of death.

An important factor associated with the formation of personality is the emotionality of a pupil overcoming immature emotions in a healthy way. Emotions may be described as feelings that express love, hate, fear, guilt, or punishment. Mature emotions strengthen the affective side of the self and relate to the values of the person. Any grown man, in expressing one's beliefs and feelings, counts on the opinions and feelings of others and should not feel threatened by them.[685] An example of immature emotionality in the heteronomous stage, for instance, is selfish emotionality; one might consider it an act of evil when he causes punishment or disapproval. Another example of emotional immaturity manifests in irresponsible behavior and interest. An immature persons accepts the common rules of conduct, but only when they meet one's feelings and interests. It is evident that without a healthy personality, intentional formation may be difficult or impossible.[686]

Allport appreciates Christian self-formation as a useful tool in following the healthy image and example of Jesus Christ: "Whoever wishes to come after me, let him follow me" (Mt 16, 24). Elsewhere, Jesus says, "Be ye therefore perfect, even as your Father is perfect" (Mt 5, 48). At this point, it must be emphasized that self-formation is a long and demanding process.

---

[684] "When an interest system has once been formed it not only creates a tensional condition (…) leading to overt conduct in some way satisfying to the interest, but it also acts as a silent agent for selecting and directing any behavior related to it esthetic interests." Cf. Allport. *The Nature of Personality* p. 86.

[685] Cf. Płużek. *Psychologia pastoralna* p. 55.

[686] "The concept of intention which I am here opposing to reactivity, expectancy and infantile fixation (…). I argue it is necessary. Term intention signifies those aspects of thought and of motivation that plays a leading, but now neglected, part in the compound, affiliative, moral conduct of men. I believe it precisely the 'private' worlds of desire, aspiration, and conscience that must be studied if we are to succeed in the task of social engineering." Cf. G. W. Allport. *Scientific Models and Human Morals* PSRev 54: 1947 no. 4 p. 185

The expected obligation of self-formation is present in the teaching of the Church and has been for a long time. However, according to A. Derdziuk, the word *self-formation* has appeared in recent pedagogical and theological studies. [687] Theological anthropology conveys a holistic conception of man in which attention is paid to issues of integral self-formation. It is the leading task to adult reactions, which are in line with moral values and social norms. The holistically constructed man is the answer to pragmatic and immature modern human functioning. Terms such as *self-control, self-realization, self-improvement, becoming, and self-knowledge* are associated with *self-formation.*

Self-formation improves man's emotional life and view of the world, according to desired patterns of personality. In a narrower sense, the person is responsible for his own maturity, setting his own tasks and deciphering reliable methods to evaluate them regarding the best decisions. As stated by A. Derdziuk, one's "own responsibility is one key issue of the essential dimensions of maturity." [688] The wider base of self-formation leads to consciously upgrading its realistic similarity to the ideal "model of personality perfection." By identifying discrepancies, a man can use self-criticism to improve and evolve his personality. Mature striving for self-improvement reveals two basic forms. In the lower form, it outweighs man's negative intention to remove perceived major flaws such as impatience or excessive indulgence. However, in a higher form of individual self-reintegration, one must develop a definite purpose that enriches his firm characteristic, which is more important to shaping will, duty, consciousness of obligations, and the ability to make permanent self-control provisions over immature emotionality.[689]

Allport confirms that people who are concerned with self-discovery have an increased need for aesthetic value and can better shape their attitude of deeper self-awareness.[690] Becoming a holistically mature person requires self-formation that facilitates not only biological maturation—which takes a toll on the frontline of one's own mental development—but also in building moral and spiritual components. We hypothesize that it can, therefore, be argued that self-knowledge, self-control, and self-formation are somehow inscribed in human nature in a way that leads to fast maturation. Most importantly, however, is the active desire to integrate one's own experiences for the sake of human development. Taking responsibility for positive thinking promotes healthy images of a man in the process of

---

[687] Cf. *Formacja moralna a formacja sumienia* p. 19.

[688] Ibid p. 26.

[689] Cf. T. Ślipko. *Etos chrześcijański. Zarys etyki ogólnej.* Kraków: WAM 1974 p. 305–325.

[690] G. W. Allport. *The Individual and his Religion.* New York: The Macmillan 1950. p.15.

multidimensional mature becoming.[691] Hence, self-education, as a formative tool, can be achieved through moral awareness and natural human intelligence.

Man, in consciously making self-formation decisions, creates emotional stability, which is free of neurotic behavior and malice. Thus, the integral formation provides responsible emotionality in overcoming the erratic behavior of children. Emotional formation in the family is based on the fact that the child or young man ought not to be threatened with abandonment as a form of punishment for bad behavior. Psychologists and educators perceive this kind of unhealthy relationship as an "anxiety bond," which presents a serious educational obstacle.[692] Thus, in the process of healthy emotionality, justified growth creates a healthy relationship between mother and child. Contrary to the earlier study, the emotional bond is not learned but has been innate in forming a sense of security in life.[693] Supported mother–child and father–child bonds are the first educators in a child's life. Parents provide quality, relational experiences that lead to strong relationships with significant people in the future. In shaping good emotionality, self-formation teaches healthy communication mechanisms rather than using different forms of enslavement such as threatening or blackmailing. There is no doubt that the guided formation of mature emotionality protects a child against anxiety. Most of all, it teaches stable family connections and social ties. Even though fear and threats can lead to obedience from the pupil, it is worth considering whether, at the expense of this negative approach, we actually cause more damage. Surely, this approach leads to neurosis and more deformation of the student.

A better approach is being an authentic witness who forges mature behavior within a young person through skillful handling of clear moral principles. Formators, themselves, ought to have emotional maturity characterized by, among other things, the ability to their control of anger. In this way, the educator is able to establish and maintain warm, direct contact with children that is based on trust. As for the development of these crucial relationships, more is expected in voluntary contacts based on the dignity of the person undertaking formation.[694] Personal relatedness resulting from emotional bonds deepen one's responsibility for another person, contained at least in the words of the fox character in Antoine Saint-Exupéry's *The Little Prince:* "It is only with the heart that one can see rightly; what is essential is

---

[691] Cf. M. Wójcik. *Specyfika ludzkiej płciowości.* IN: *Człowiek. Osoba. Płeć.* Red. M. Wójcik. Łomianki: Fundacja "Pomoc Rodzinie" 1998 p. 116–117.
[692] Cf. Allport. *Pattern and Growth in Personality* p. 508–509.
[693] Cf. Allport. *Becoming* p. 25, 34.
[694] Cf. Jan Paweł II. *Przemówienie "Godność kobiety – małżonki i matki."* OsRomPl. 15: 1994 no. 8 p. 18–19.

invisible to the eye. People have forgotten this truth, but you mustn't forget it. You become responsible forever for what you've tamed." Our maturity may become responsible for what we have tamed.[695]

The Church's Magisterium often calls for the development of emotional maturity, pointing to aspects of spirituality modeled in the example of Mary. In the case of emotional immaturity, man usually "panics," is afraid, and fails to balances his emotionality. This is often experienced through suffering, but with courage, it can lead to the self-acceleration of integral maturity. Maturity is thus characterized by solutions that survive emotional uncertainty. The Congregation for Catholic Education makes it clear that contemporary culture adopts this moral order to "reach affective maturity."[696] Responsible human emotionality is closely connected with social participation and self-formation. It should be noted that the same word, *formation,* connotes the word "relationship:" through interactive involvement in one's community, one's reason can be positively integrated. Interrelation makes one more capable to constructively participate in society. Participation in social life prepares every person emotionally to fulfill important and responsible social roles.[697] Christian activism, however, should not mislead one from the goal of personal salvation.

Brotherhood and community involvement, Allport notes, promote the development of responsible emotionality, too. The absence of sufficiently warm relationships, both in families and with friends, leads to superficial behavior that is often dominant or subordinate. Open and warm relationships are often positive mechanisms of maturity. In contrast, the use of immature mechanisms of suppression, denial, self-justification, losing interest, vengeance, superstition, and devaluation almost always distort healthy behavior or lead a warped overview of reality, which are most often immature. At the same time, interpersonal relationships cannot be deprived of their uniqueness, dignity, and respect for others. There is no place for intrusion because it inhibits reactive attitudes and personal uniqueness. In other words, it is essential to the formation of such skills to adapt an attitude that does not offend anyone's feelings and values. Unhealthy criticism, toxic jealousy, backbiting, gossip, and envy are perverse ways to harm others.[698]

Besides, skillfully developed tolerance is a manifestation of personal freedom but also a task for each person who undertakes formation. Compassion for others is important, too, whereby the highest degree of inner tranquility comes from engaging love and compassion. Empathy shown to others stems from imaginative and healthy feelings toward people (i.e., an

---

[695] A. de Saint-Exupery. *Mały Książę.* Transl. J. Szwykowski. Warszawa: PIW 1997 p. 65.

[696] DIK p. 1.

[697] Cf. H. Muszyński. *Wychowanie moralne w zespole.* Warszawa: PZWS 1964 p. 27.

[698] Cf. S. Witek. *Duszpasterstwo w konfesjonale.* Poznań: Pallottinum 1988 p. 257.

imaginative extension of the self).[699] The mature attitude of a healthy person is expressed in tolerance, without judging human weaknesses. Man understands the rights of others in order not to harm them. A healthy attitude is associated with adaptability that contributes to proper social adjustment.[700]

The positive attitudes of beauty, truth, goodness, and empathy for other human beings is born with a trait of openness. Therefore, integral formation widens interest in other people in the form of an extended self and expresses individuals' genuine need for participation in the spheres of human endeavors, activities, interpersonal relationships, and interests. But a person's life cannot be limited to activities related only to only loved ones' needs and responsibilities.

On the way of achieving mature Christian personalities includes self-acceptance, which gives people a new quality of adult life. In addition, the expanding self requires cordial relations and a significantly realistic attitude—both to himself and to external reality—which includes a variety of skills, tasks, and projects. In a healthy and mature personality, there is little internal conflict and high tolerance to frustration.

Allport states that in the context of the psychology of participation, every person grows through their own efforts, activities, and interests. The opposite of this *anthropology of involvement* presents a man who is rebellious and authoritarian; who often complains, gossips, and slanders; and who achieves low productivity at work.[701] M. Pokrywka, referring to issues of the theology of participation, considers a social commitment as more than one type of action by which man carries out meaningful collaboration with others. It is not only about what a man brings to social life, but above all, what a man is and who he becomes by participating in social life. Therefore, the formed self ought to not only participate but simply be a "person involved."[702]

In addition to self-acceptance, responsible attitudes control immature emotions. Control over negative emotions plays a decisive role in the social upkeep and social functioning of individuals. This control, in a positive sense, redirects emotions to something more constructive. This is

---

[699] Cf. A. Sheehy. *Biographical Dictionary of Psychology*. New York: Taylor & Francis 2002 (co-authors A.J. Chapman, W. A. Conooy) p. 11.

[700] Cf. Allport. *Pattern and Growth in Personality* p. 283–296.

[701] "Facts of this sort prove to us that people have to be active in order to learn, (…) to build voluntary control, to be cured when they are ill, restored when they are faint." p. 123. "When he does not really participate, then come rebellion against authority, complaints, griping, gossip, rumor, scapegoating, and disaffection of all sorts. The job-satisfaction is low." p. 124. "In insisting that participation depends upon ego-involvement. Often, indeed, the ego is clamorous, jealous, possessive and cantankerous." p. 125. Cf. G. Allport. *The psychology of participation*. PsRev. 53: 1945 no. 3, p. 123–125.

[702] Cf. *Osoba, uczestnictwo, wspólnota* p. 78.

different than repressed feelings. A mature person demonstrates fine qualities, traits, and security. The mature person reacts to threats by formulating corresponding convictions that help him cope with stressful situations. For the formed self, frustration is not emotional mutilation, which happens in the case of a neurotic person. It is about healthy challenges in the sense that a person fully perceives the objectively realistic world around him.

Healthy emotionality always expresses itself in the present but also applies to the future. Emotion acts as the psycho-physical unity of one space and time. Emotionality can be briefly described as the "totalities and singularity of persons" that always express itself in the present. Emotions and thoughts are, then, dynamic and fully integrated.[703] The peculiarities of the idea of singularity are that man's attitude needs to be characterized by mild disposition, which can be worked out in social relationships. The advantage of intelligent disposition reduces the reactivity of the individual, especially in times of severe authoritarianis.[704] To intelligently overcome authoritarianism, one must be mindful of the world and have a critical attitude toward the idealized authority of their own group. Thus, mature emotionality engenders enthusiasm that penetrates a person's interior life. At the same time, healthy emotionality in self-formation allows individuals to be more holistically oriented to the environment in which they are rightly embedded.[705]

A unique tool for self-formation is a person's consciousness of transcendence and unconditional truth, which allows a man to gain an understanding of who he is, unlike the rest of creation. Based on Revelation, the man, compared to the physical and biological world, realizes who he is within the rest of establishment: the crown of creation and the most valuable *Cogito ergo sum*. As I discussed earlier, man not only has intellect, will, and responsibility for himself and others but also sensitivity to the truth, goodness, and beauty—or the ability to be self-aware, creative, and transcendent.[706] The superiority of human existence testifies that man has dominion over his sinful nature, including the immature forms of his personality and the ability to conquer an emotional disorder. [707] The morally influenced man, through his discovered values, gets on the road to self-formation and can be guided continually to mature manifestations of his personality in the past, present, and future.

Our search for humane behavior, on the planes of pedagogical and anthropological discourse, leads to a close relationship with the moral

---

[703] R. B. Burns. *The Self Concept in Theory, Measurement, Development and Behavior.* New York: Longman 1979 p. 50.

[704] Cf. G. Allport. *Normative Compatibility In the Light of Social Science.* RelEd 53: 1958 no. 1 p. 62.

[705] Cf. R. Gifford. *Review of "Inventing personality: Gordon Allport and the Science of Selfhood" by Ian A. M. Nicholson. Canadian Psychology/Psychologie Canadienne* 45: 2004 p. 187–188.

[706] Cf. M. Łobocki. *Wychowanie moralne w zarysie.* Kraków: Impuls 2004 p. 153.

[707] Cf. Allport. *The Individual and his Religion* p. 65–66.

discipline and formation of "the new man" in Christ. The conscious entrance of a man, on the path of self-formation, enables him to make fundamental decisions—from the smallest to the heroic. Reading the signs of the time and the purpose of God in human nature, man tends to accept the claim that human existence come from God, an infinite being. God's infinitude is continually expressed in conscious selection on the path of truth, goodness, beauty, and life. Moral maturity allows a rational being to overcome the limitations of material elements, be directed to the infinite world of values, live in holiness (the sacrum), and evolve to the transcendent God. Both elements of human nature, the body and immortal soul, are quintessential parts of the "substantial person, and remain in the mutual relationship of the same nature."[708] Therefore, moral self-formation, among other mechanisms such as skilled reading and dialogue, strengthens self-conscious acts that belong to a higher sphere of life.

According to Allport, the primary tool for influencing moral and ethical reasoning is the talking with the pupil, which aims him toward the process of self-knowledge and mature objectification of his condition as so-called the principle of "strengthening moral courage." The principle plays a great role, whereby a teacher offers a student courage in solving problems based on his strong personality characteristics.[709] Another formative tool for teaching positive self-esteem is setting successful goals for pupils. That might happen in the context of already achieved successes and effects. The long-term dialogue helps them build high self-esteem, especially if those individuals can find a rational assessment for their own lives.

In the formation of a mature personality, critical skills make a man's social contacts stronger, which is characterized by calmness and stabilization of the internal tensions. Students are more responsive to the criticism and correction. Usually, persons with high moral self-esteem are more optimistic about life. Normally, pupils who are more optimistic, take greater responsibility for their evolution than pessimists do, who overestimate their failures.[710] In both cases, Allport considers that self-formation impacts positive self-assessment.

According to the intentional concept of formation, analyzed processes of learning and becoming, based on the inspired patterns of saints, allow the formed man to acquire similar moral behaviors and provide other beneficial consequences. Even old inspirational patterns stimulate reflection today in terms of taking similar moral steps to follow natural laws, which are imprints in the person who is seeking self-improvement. This type of

---

[708] Z. Marek. *Podstawy wychowania moralnego* p. 19.

[709] Cf. Allport. *Becoming* p. 23.

[710] Cf. G. W. Allport. *The Nature of Personality*. Cambridge: Addison Wesley 1950 p. 22.

insightful imitation lasts a lifetime as a fundamental choice.[711] The self-improving person does something meaningful and significant, imitating his Creator.[712]

Authentic conformity to the model of maturity sanctifies the person. Anyone who conforms to the pattern of maturity has seen, in the person of Jesus, personal likeness to the Creator. [713] By taking responsible actions, men develop positive feelings, intellect, and will, and they consciously transform themselves according to the model of perfection in God. Helpful in this are the Sacraments. Baptism places men and women "within the new and eternal covenant, in the spousal covenant of Christ with the Church."[714] This fundamental Sacrament initiates the process of formation (1 Cor. 12:12–13; Gal. 3:27–28). [715] The Eucharist forms the emotional plane, creating a "communion of persons," which leads to redemption, restoring the co-Creating ability that diminished the sin of Adam. Through the Sacraments, Christ communicates his saving power at every stage of life: marriage, professional work, and social life. K. Jezyna writes that "the Sacraments are the places of theophany, the revelation of God and His blessings. (…) Sacraments implement a communion of life, personal communion with God and through God."[716]

Allport argues that identification serves the human community better than imitation does because it creates a new man, resembling the Creator. Imitation has its negative drawbacks, though, in that it adopts some of the prejudices of immature persons.[717] A lexical understood imitation (Lat. *imitatio*) refers to a rather artificial and an immature process. Thus, for purposes of self-formation, a more appropriate term identifies the pattern that imprints on the personal characteristics of the model. The individual character of identification "gives importance to personal norms, commandments, and rules that are realized and implemented. (…). Pattern—in the narrowest sense—means a person is given a 'subjectivity'".[718] It is also about identifying with mature emotions.

---

[711] Cf. Allport. *Personality* p. 155.

[712] Wolicka's statement is so interesting in that it makes a personal likeness associated with the ability of being: "as far as (…) the nature of the metaphysical man is being a person, so to the nature of the person should be "made in the image of God." *Biblijny archetyp człowieka.* [IN]: Jan Paweł II. *Mężczyzną i niewiastą stworzył ich. Chrystus odwołuje się do "początku"* p. 163–164.

[713] John Paul II teaches that "revealed truth about man" as the image and likeness of God "is a consistent basis for all Christian anthropology." Cf. MD p. 6.

[714] FC p. 13.

[715] Cf. Forrester. *Moral Formation and Liturgy* p. 379.

[716] K Jeżyna. *Sakramentalny charakter życia moralnego.* IN: "*Roczniki Teologii Moralnej*" T. 2(57) Lublin: TN KUL 2010 p. 6.

[717] Cf. G. W. Allport. *Personality* p. 156.

[718] T. Zadykowicz. *Sequela Christi et imitatio hominis. Paradygmaty naśladowania we współczesnej refleksji teologicznomoralnej.* Lublin: Wydawnictwo KUL 2011 p. 415.

Responsible emotionality based on love of one's neighbor should be described as a choice that has its purposefulness (*telos*). This selected purpose considers the good of the neighbor and obedience to God. Consistent obedience to God in self-formation enables one to develop humanistic ethics, standing in opposition to all forms of nihilism or authoritarianism.

Outside of the conscious kindness and goodness that one cultivates, we should also pay attention to self-love, which can trigger a selfish attitude. Self-love is flawed because it does not promote pro-social attitudes. It is guided by the question: What will I get out of it, from this relationship? Both internal and external motives of loving exist in mutual association and connections.[719] Motives provide evidence of mature or immature love.[720] Extrinsic love orients itself toward the absorption of one's own traits. In that way, selfish self-love excludes the adoption of altruistic attitudes in loving people as the highest value of creation. Goodness has a quality of loving—an internal feature of man in his world of being charitable—not only in the principle of being a good but above all, for the ability to bestow goodness. Goodness is a feature given freely to every person. In that sense, being a good person is truly a commitment to higher feelings of loving. "Abide in me, and I abide in you (…). I am the vine, you are the branches. Whoever abides in me, and I in him, bears much fruit, because without me you can do nothing" (Jn. 15:1–17). In ethical self-formation, God expects love from a man. That love is not an isolated act, but rather, a duty of being in love—to truly live one's own life well. Love is a personal and mature form of existence and prepares man to react accordingly. Therefore, the self-formation of responsible emotionality causes am individual to mature in the Christian personality.

Any preoccupation with oneself and self-centered love rules out the adoption of the prosocial attitude of loving people—the highest value. The same social virtue of kindness is desired as the intrinsic personal value expressed in brotherly love. God requires every man on Earth to stand for his greatest capacity so he can become co-Creator and not the destroyer of goodness, truth, and beauty.

B. The intellectual self-formation of the individual

---

[719] Cf. G. W. Allport. *The Use of Personal Documents in Psychological Science*. New York: Social Science Research Council 1951 p. 76.

[720] The eccentric (i.e., external) way of morality differs from the intrinsic way and is considered a means of utilitarian ethics, which are useful oneself to ensure his own peace. Example: going to Church, for business reasons, as a show of piety. Regarding eccentric personality, psychology considers it immature. Cf. Allport. *The Person in Psychology* p. 150, 265.

The most important criterion of intellectual maturity, coupled with emotional and mental processes, are the mature intellectual functions of acquired knowledge. As a result of intellectual formation, the person reaches a more consistent expression of ego. From the early stages of development, one's individual mental ability is characterized by his perception and differentiation of objects and phenomena. Gradually, in the educational process, the student develops integrity by concentrating his attention on relevant and less-relevant content. Piaget asserts that with practical thinking, applied logic helps to understand the cause-and-effect relationships of cognitive-sensory recognition. [721] In any intellectual training, a person perceives the characteristics and properties of objects in other similar facilities. Thus, he discovers cause-and-effect relationships.[722]

Intellectual formation involves repetition and organizational experience according to ethical considerations. Thus, the intellectual discovery has habits of proper looking and listening. The ability to listen is achieved in long-term development. Schools help develop memory and assimilate all sorts of general knowledge. The mind, when it is directed through the will of a person, manifests as early as in one's preschool years, when man has a great capacity of remembering, recalling, and playing. School-age memory processes are not yet targeted by thinking and reasoning, but with a time, the process of thinking shapes logical memory, combining individual parts. School formation develops the characteristics of memory such as speed, durability, and capacity. Only in the next period of upbringing do students acquire segregation and classification abilities.

We can divide the developing thought processes of younger schoolchildren into two phases. In the early stage, children from 7 to 9 years are concerned about the perception of things but not the world of ideas and concepts. Their maturing educational orientation is based mainly on action and visual contact with learned things and events. Children often misunderstand various phenomena and have difficulty making sense. When those phenomena are reasonable presented in the story, they link them logically as the cause and effect. In the next stage of puberty, ages 9 to 11, there is significant development of logical thinking that broadens the scope of interests while expanding mental capacity.[723]

The intellect helps in self-objectification and insight into oneself. Intellectual maturity depends on a critical tool of self-objectification, which

---

[721] Cf. *The Psychology of Intelligence*. London: Routledge 1967 p. 123.

[722] Cf. Piaget. *The Moral Judgment of the Child* p. 191.

[723] As a result of intellectual maturation, the formed man discontinues perceiving rules as unchangeable and begins to understand that people have different views. During this period, any formed person evaluates his own actions within the context of the various aspects of the situation. The progressive stages of maturing are, according to Allport, one continuous process of becoming. Cf. *Becoming* p. 35.

arises out of concern for "insight into oneself."[724] The more a child uses self-objectification, the greater his level of self-understanding will be. Knowledge about oneself requires insight into the relationship between what a man thinks of himself and what he is and does. Most educators would agree with Allport's claim that persons who have greater "self-insight" are much richer spiritually, as opposed to people who do not care for self-reflection. Self-objectification and self-knowledge, expressed precisely in humor and joy, are educational tools, too. The self-objective person can laugh at his own follies.[725] This sense of humor comes not from hostility or derision but from personal integration. Intelligent expressions of humor stem from reflection on one's own inherited weaknesses that in comic life situations.[726] Without correctly self-formed moral conscience, man is not always aware of the real motives of his actions, especially those that are prejudicial. Therefore, in dialogue with Allport's theory of becoming, we must agree with his opinion that a rational man, without reference to God, can only partially understand his antisocial and harmful reflexes. It is important to note that the human person, without God, can modify and often distort information imparted by the Creator in natural law. Man can easily denature himself through various cynical defense mechanisms, which are usually signs of intellectual immaturity. Therefore, man needs to shape his growth mechanisms based on altruism, anticipation, asceticism, and humor.

Positive mechanisms based on altruism, anticipation, asceticism, and humor shape moral convictions in the self-reforming person. For example, wise beliefs help one select good.[727] The structure of the self has at least two functions. The first is sensible self-identification, and the second is the interpersonal function that forms social relations. On the one hand, the personal "I" needs to identify with other people; on the other hand, it creates its unique worldview to freely and responsibly respond to the gift of vocation he has received. Moral convictions are authentic when they result from the original dimension of faith and come from a healthy self-image, self-respect, self-discipline, and self-esteem. Moral beliefs, derived from God's voice in the heart of believer, enable relationships with other people who are open to the higher values and tolerance. Those without this sense poorly choose right from wrong and manifest less-mature dispositions that are often characterized by superficial and eccentric extrinsic personalities.

Those who care for internalization of values in self-formation through mind training eliminate shallow elements of eccentricity. Therefore,

---

[724] Cf. Allport. *The Mature Personality* p. 22.
[725] Cf. Allport. *The Individual and His Religion* p. 92–93.
[726] Cf. W. B. Frick. *Personality Theories: Journeys into Self.* New York and London: Teachers College Press 1984 p. 64.
[727] Cf. L. Rasmussen: *Moral community and moral formation.* ER 47: 1995 no. 1 p. 13.

for the sake of a man's maturity, an integrative outlook on life helps him achieve a rational concept of reality based on goodness and truth—a meaningful life's purpose. Such rational conception leads to realization of life's goals as well.[728] In comparison, childish heteronomy is not at all conducive to defined goals. In adolescence, rational goals start to form and integrate a person. However, at that level of weak internalization of moral goodness, they are still poorly defined. Only in adulthood, with the support of rational reasons, do ethical goals become more specified. Therefore, in the intellectual self-formation of young people exists a gap that helps them define moral goals—not so much their earthly life goals, but those of the supernatural influence—in the form of inspiration and imperishable values.[729]

Intellectual formation appears to be valid if it leads to valued action based on acquired truth. In his vocational choice, a man transforms his life with the help of the grace of God, moving in a more profound direction toward a worthy goal and following God's call.[730] A man, in answering the call, intentionally selects wise moral goals and maturely decides about his deeper life. Therefore, Christian morality, by its very nature, has a mature sentiment that deals with the dimension of the moral good. For example, Socrates did not separate truth from rightness, and thus he understood ethics and morality as the largest structures of truth and soul through the activity of real participation.[731] Mature formation communicates the truth by acts of true loving. Therefore, any rejection of the truth initiates offenses against conscience, especially in situations where there has been a violation of the rules of verification. Specifically, knowledge and truth are not mechanical or depersonalized processes but are conditioned by the structure of the whole person, which, among other things, refers to the ethics of truth.[732] Self-learned practical wisdom includes the ability to make a good judgment in the context of a moral choice at an appropriate, reasonable level. Doing good adheres to practical wisdom in its path to mature moral judgment and Christian formation of relevant personality traits.

Just like ethics and moral philosophy has the task of education, self-formation has the causative task of applying directives and ethical obligations. However, casuistic obligation (do this, don't do that) is not apodictic law but allows a self-formed person to increase his virtues. After all, an ethical person

---

[728] Cf. G. W. Allport. *A Psychological Interpretation.* Henoy Holt and Company, New York 1937, p. 220–234.

[729] "But the significance of definite crisis (...) lies in the hunger it arouses, and in the charting of a direction of search for appealing this hunger. Almost always the individual who has once experienced a vividly religious state of mind sees throughout his life to recapture its inspiration." Cf. Allport. *The Individual and His Religion* p. 34.

[730] VS p. 67.

[731] Cf. Bartnik. *Hermeneutyka personalistyczna* p. 266.

[732] Ibid p. 267.

confronts problems reasonably and changes them into a better, healthier reality.[733] In this case, concrete decisions and actions always have a higher personal reference at their core: what a person may become. Christian formation—and more specifically self-formation—is, therefore, a commitment to accountable self-formation of the personality, which is the fruit of experience and expertise, but above all, better personal decisions and actions.[734]

An interesting phenomenon in the secular systems is often opposition to "mature" interpersonal teaching models. Delicately, we accept the thesis that people often express opposition to the principle of greater responsibility because they are searching for unique and individual ways of life. The word "immature" is not always an apt description or explanation. For young adults, "immature" often connotes too-stringent requirements of old-fashioned formation that is devoid of spontaneity. The higher expectation of young people for the mature lifestyle often causes opposition. Therefore, any imposed socialization on the adolescent generates rebellion and strong reactions. Among other identity crises manifested in the form of rebellious intolerance, fear from changing may be the behavioral factor. Too often, suspecting a young person of wrongdoing—when really, he just thinks differently— should not set the red flag for his approach[735] Goal-oriented methods might be solution when crises hit hard. Crisis provoked in the pupil's sphere call for appropriate self-reflection, debate, and the realignment of unrealistic expectations. Thus, educators should always consider teaching young people how to appropriately respond to adversity.

In the face of a challenge, intellectual maturity comes from valuable reading and reflection. Spontaneous and positive poetic reflection is a cognitive tool that helps man reject negative attitudes that deviate from generally accepted moral norms. A student's regular contact with the great works of Christian writers, characterized by the examples of their lives, their spirits, and their sacrificial love, is a necessary inspiration tool in intellectual formation. Likewise, reflection and prayer comprise a self-critical approach to enlarged intellectual curiosity about oneself and the world.[736] Intelligence strengthens self-formation in the way of balanced self-criticism, which allows one to shape the objectives of true pedagogy and integral life. Intellectual

---

[733] Cf. Thompson. *Teach Yourself Ethics* p. 10.

[734] Cf. Witek. *Duszpasterstwo w konfesjonale* p. 102.

[735] "Crisis phenomenon, a blind emotional nationalism intolerant of dissent and fearful of changes to come their campaign results in the creation of a suspicion of everyone who thinks independently and sponsors any change in the status quo (…) it forges an easy weapon for any person or group that would prefer to call names rather than to discuss issues." Cf. Allport. *The Nature of Prejudice* p. 257.

[736] Cf. J. Elliot. *Moral & Values Education.* JME 32: 2003 no. 1 p. 67–76.

formation must be based on the triad of goodness, truth, and beauty in the process of evolving and mature development. Any mental activity focused on reading, meditation, and reflection enlarges one's horizons and individual personality. Reflection evoked by reading teaches logical thinking. One's mindful organization of his internal states of feeling allows for the discovery of new talents and greater abilities to improve them.[737]

Individual reading provides an indispensable tool of human development. The man who reads becomes a rational subject of dialogue, consistent and aware of his place in society. Spiritual reading in ethics is especially helpful toward achieving the desired goal of being smarter and creating new shapes of excellence within the dimension of time. Even wishful desires to enter a higher level of perfection evolves the man on the course to reaching perfection. [738] Therefore, personalistic and intellectual self-formation understandably prioritizes his goals because it effectively leads to personal excellence. However, the formed self needs specific, well planned time for that formation.[739]

The mature personality also needs theological reflection drawn from divine Revelation as handed down in Scripture and tradition. Interiorization helped St. Augustine in the mature integration of his life. After his conversion, he emphasized, in the rules of ascetic life, the need for deepening knowledge, culture, and tradition of the Church Fathers and Scripture. The impact of the intellectual achievements of classicists are also valuable educational keys. Maxims engraved on churches and other buildings, expressing general wisdom and truth, encourage motivation (e.g., *Verba docent, exempla trahunt*, "Words teach much, but examples involve us.") They can inspire the young to choose the good and reject the bad and obey valuable rules of life. Jesus to His disciples, for example: *"Fructibus eorum cognoscetis eos"* ("By their fruits you shall know them); *Bonum ex malo non fit* ("Good is not born out of evil"); Seneca's *Corrumpunt bonos mores colloquia mala* ("Bad conversations corrupt good manners"); and *Discenda est virtus* ("Virtues should be taught"); or St. Paul's *Vince in bono malum* ("Overcome evil with good"); or *Repetitio mater studiorum* ("Repetition is the mother of study").[740]

Although intellectual curiosity allows for proper problem solving, ethical reasoning teaches one to distinguish between more and less important problems in the context of specific situations and to act justly and rule in favor of truth. Contemporary life emotionally challenges every Christian who faces grave dilemmas that require smart decision-making. Higher integration of mind and soul is the more righteous choice a student can make in accord

---

[737] "One aim of education is to make available the wisdom of the past and presence so the youth may be equipped to solve the problems of the future." Cf. G. W. Allport. *The Person in the psychology*. Boston: Beacon Press 1968 p. 154.

[738] Cf. Z. Marek. *Podstawy wychowania moralnego* p. 18.

[739] Cf. VC p. 71.

[740] Cf. F. M. Wheelock. *Wheelock's Latin*. New York: Harper Collins 1995 p. 7.

with his conscience. Often, a person needs spiritual and moral guidance to be insightful. So, part of that formational task has to do with knowledge of clear rules and principles.

Allport describes six criteria for the mature, emotionally healthy adult personality. The mature adult:

1. has a sense of his God-given uniqueness;

2. is no longer dominated by childhood impulses but is functionally autonomous;

3. cultivates education and morality;

4. relates warmly to other people, exhibiting openness and charity;

5. holds a unifying philosophy of life, which directs his personality toward future goals; and

6. views the human person as a spiritual-corporal composite and appreciates the integrity of spiritual-corporal activity.[741]

Intellectual maturity fosters virtue and contributes to vitality. These qualities include: love, wisdom, hope, caring, determination, will, competence, and loyalty. Interrelated, healthy attributes characterize a mature individual and determine the whole structure of the human person in the process of intelligent formation. It refers to the rational realm of the personal and cultivates retained cognition. Intelligence is an individual logical ability that allows one to learn, develop creative skills, and understand the core meaning of his experience.[742] Under the influence of intelligence, an active mind has a faster learning ability for principles, ethics, and social roles. In conjunction with the capacity to memorize, together with intuition and correct judgment, intelligence leads a person to a fuller life and the objective truth about himself. Intelligence provides "raw material from which personality is shaped" and cannot properly function without personality and vice versa.[743]

Emotionality and intelligence are interrelated in that sense that personality, without any of these factors, is unable to manifest a personal self. Although self-formation, with the support of the intellect, is a normative discipline, man mostly tries to gain an adequate understanding of deeper experience. The partial task of self-formation comes from analysis of any

---

[741] Cf. P. Moskal. *Religia i Prawda*. Lublin: Wydawnictwo KUL 2008 p. 125. Allport follows the Aristotelian/Thomistic doctrine that man is not only a soul *("Anima mea non est ego")* but a composite of soul and body. Cf. G. W. Allport. *The Nature of Personality: Selected Papers*. Reading: MA 1950 p. 78.

[742] "Allport and Myrdal personify the insistence that thoughtful, moral, rationalistic social scientists must be the contemporary custodians of such enduring human 'values as justice—and that trained human intelligence is an important weapon in the ongoing struggle against ignorance, superstition, and injustice." Cf. G. W. Allport. *The Nature of Prejudice* p. 10.

[743] Cf. Allport. Personality: *A Psychological Interpretation* p. 53.

ethical situation relevant to the empirical parameters that emphasize the shape of moral judgment. Ethical formation, as a devoted normative discipline, helps man grasp objective truth and find the best strategies to incorporate loving one's neighbor in charity, thus implementing the will of God in the concrete form of human existence. On the other side, mature intellectual formation leads youngsters to fast growth that evolves the direction of their will to ethical standards so they can function reliably and independently.[744]

The intellectual capability allows faster social adaptation, too. Intelligible application—whether linguistic, religious, musical, logical, mathematical, spatial, motoric, or interpersonal—testify to the essential core of the intellectual education so man might gain early maturity in moral judgments. Evidently, when students are less intelligent, they rely more on the results of their actions rather than their intentions. Maturity, therefore, can be achieved through intellectual exercises and stimulation, which cannot be separated from ethical and moral influence elements. This is simply because classical thought clearly defines the triad of goodness, truth, and beauty as being inseparable for any human growth.

Also, social learning contributes to achieving maturity—commonly known as socialization. Even though Allport uses the concept of socialization he relates it to group formation (*formation of in-group*).[745] In his opinion, the process of socialization and basic humanity training takes place in group interactions. According to Allport, this type of socialization speeds up process of maturation without the need of extra special exercises and didactics.[746] In group interactions, we find a sort of social intelligence. Some socialization fulfills man's basic security needs, especially in early development. In later stages, man continues this autonomously. In the 60s, socialization had become a buzzword in the process of formal and informal intellectual education. At that time, socialization also stressed, socio-cultural factors. But R. Arum recalls the words of E. Durkheim, who said that the aim of education is mainly the socialization of the person, where parents and schools are mediators.[747] The concept of socialization carries within its meaning friendly connotations of belonging to the civilized human community. I could speak about cognitive, linguistic, emotional, motivational, and moral socialization, as well as socialization in childhood,

---

[744] Cf. W. Gubała. *Wychowanie moralne młodzieży*. IN: *Teoretyczne założenia katechezy młodzieżowej*. Red. R. Murawski et al. Warszawa: Wyd. Salezjańskie 1989 p. 201.

[745] Cf. Allport. *The Nature of Prejudice* p. 29. Cf. Allport. *Osobowość i religia* p. 33. In the early stages of development, socialization takes on a form of conformism, which, for a person, means two variants of becoming one and relying on the heredity and another in the individual development.

[746] Cf. Allport. *Personality: A Psychological Interpretation* p. 147.

[747] Cf. R. Arum. *Judging School Discipline: The Crisis of Moral Authority*. Cambridge: Harvard University Press. 2003 p 1.

socialization styles, techniques, practices, institutions, environment, education, needs, and even the rehabilitation of outcomes.[748] Allport states that socialization begins with the internalization of social standards. Church involvement helps with spiritual internalization. An important factor in the socialization process is one's self-esteem.[749] This creates their environment. The very process of the socialization and formation of a person assumes the acquisition of human values associated with the course of becoming in social affiliation. A child, similar to an adult, undergoes certain affiliations and is dependent on the environment.[750]

Studies show that children form an important disposition to be accountable through concrete ideas of morality but never through unethical habits and antisocial behavior. In the process of moral socialization standards, they are also dependent on the age of the pupil: older children learn desirable social norms faster by being honest in their cultural impact through self-control and a sense of duty. [751] We can conclude that parental expectations lead gradually to acceptance of the altruistic social code. In adulthood, we often see people who have transformed their selfish impulses into a life for others, but what is much harder is to develop tests and measurements for the maturity of the social, moral judgment and ethnic prejudices. However, the adult egoist might also develop similar traits and socially acceptable masks, characterized by a lack of positive socialization in its attitude or behavior.

Socialization is such an important intellectual process of learning in the community. [752] About 50 percent of human behavior is genetically conditioned. Although most human genes are responsible for shaping personality, behavior results also from culture, beliefs, values, and

---

[748] Cf. W. Berezinka. *Socialization and Education: Essays in Conceptual Criticism.* Transl. James S. Brice Westport: Greenwood Press 1994 p. 15.

[749] "A factor important to the socialization process (…) is the self-image of the individual. The child stops sucking his thumb, and when was asked why, he responded, 'Big boys don't suck their thumb.' In other words, it suddenly came through to him that he was a big boy. (…) The concept of becoming also includes the self-image, maturation, identification, and all forms of cognitive learning." Cf. Evans. *Gordon Allport: The Man and His Ideas* p. 53.

[750] Cf. Allport. *The Mature Personality* p. 20.

[751] Cf. Allport. *Personality: A Psychological Interpretation* p. 253–254.

[752] "Our relentless cultural emphasis on individualism and autonomy has often blinded us to the importance of moral socialization and character. If all goes well, children are socialized or trained by their parents, their religious communities, and their schools to be honest, hardworking, and compassionate people who, when confronted with moral problems, will act honestly and compassionately." Cf. M. Beaty, D. Henoy. *The Schooled Heart: Moral Formation in American Higher Education* p. 33.

experiences. In this respect, it belongs to random, adaptive, and focused self-formation.[753] Positive socialization leads to strengthening the social group to which a person belongs. Those who internalize social norms are less prone to breaking the law and making radical changes. In primary socialization, at the level of the adult–child relationship, the fundamental structure of formation is the family, which takes the greatest responsibility, especially in developing the essential values of pupils and the transmission of healthy habits.[754] The smallest cell of society, despite its many weaknesses, naturally becomes the subject of formation steeped in the special meaning of the Christian self-formation.[755] An important factor of socialization is the sense of security given by the community and the nation, in addition to the family. However, one should bear in mind certain risks; some socialization process may have excessive control of personal freedom like the overarching structure of political influence.

In analyzing the techniques of socialization used in various cultures to raise children, I need to note the positive impact of societal norms relative to parental attitudes and formal teaching methods. Usually, the standard way is to use different forms of praise. Various groups also use threats or offensive jokes. The fundamental question is the following: How does socialization help build a valuable and mature man? In every community, there is an accepted social pattern of personality, which determines how one should behave.[756] For example, there is no doubt that Christian moral norms foster a pro-social attitude.[757]

Typically, pro-social attitudes expressed in usefulness to others are open to the welfare of every human being formed in the process of educative formation and socialization at various stages of ethical development. Social impact, which provides socialization, introduces the young man to a generally

---

[753] Cf. Allport. *Osobowość i religia* p. 54.

[754] "On the adult-to-child level of socialization the primary structures usually are allocated the largest amount of responsibility; specifically the family is the greatest single structure which plays a significant role in the value formation of the subject." Cf. J. Gillespie and G. W. Allport. *Youth's Outlook on the Future* p. 8–10.

[755] Both the person and the family are the subjects of mature formation and internal development. So the purpose of such whole person supported evolving in all dimensions of life whether moral, personal, fraternal, apostolic, cultural, professional, charismatic, or patriotic is to experience union with God. That union stated in the bible comes from natural laws of God, through love. "'Love the Lord your God with all your heart and with all your soul and with all your mind. This is the first and greatest commandment. And the second is like it: 'Love your neighbor as yourself.'" (cf. Mt 22: 37–39).

[756] Cf. J. Górniewicz. *Teoria wychowania—wybrane problemy*. Toruń—Olsztyn: Glob 1996 p. 10.

[757] Moral norms and standards are understood here as the essential elements that make up culture and dictate acceptable conduct in a given cultural setting, required by all people within this circle.

accepted and approved system of values applicable in the community. A social group imposes on a young person pro-social, moral, and acceptable standards and behaviors. It is mainly a group of pro-social conduct, which turns around the world of the universal values of the young.

The Christian culture of socialization that transforms the individual's reconstructed images of self acquaints them with a wider knowledge of faith, allowing trained youth to explore reality. Christian socialization entails the development of intercultural moral ideals of personality at a younger age. Education, therefore, depends on what is typical in each socializing environment, although what constitutes perfection in one culture might not necessarily be best in another. The ideal of ethical internalization begins in adolescence. School age is the most intense level of growth because adolescents look for ideals to follow, especially moral.

Young people must be inspired by Christian culture with the help of the Catholic school. Within its model, there is always morally and socially desirable self-formation. As a social institution, the school teaches in addition to valuable moral lessons, patriotic and social behavior as well. In cooperation with the Church's pastors, it teaches ethical principles and rejects a reductionist view of the human person as an autonomous entity. Therefore, any "Re-education (…) helps rebuild the personality and references to the world of people and values." [758] A young person may acquire valuable socialization in the peer group. Although achieving the fashionable ideal of a small group gives the individual positive self-esteem in the form of various privileges, one's behavior is still incompatible with the culture and still meets with negative sanctions. [759]

We must admit that certain socialization also carries some risks. [760] That first threat is personal servitude when the socialization comes from political structures. Secular socialization proves that the function of raising children is not to be subordinated to the family, but to the state, industry and, the explicitly understood codes of ethics therein. [761]

Media, health, social services, and various agencies have assumed many socializing functions (which are rightly due to the family) in educating a young person under the dictate of secularizing science and technology. Unfortunately, government prevention programs, involving the fight against

---

[758] WW p. 105.

[759] "There are various socializing factors, such as commensalism, compatriotism, sport, community of interest, and nationalization. Obstacles to socialization are Bolshevism and unrest, differences of race, food, manners, and traditions, and a resented imputation of inferiority." Cf. F. H. Allport. *Social Psychology*. PsBu 17: 1920 no. 1 p. 85–94.

[760] Cf. KKK p. 1883.

[761] Lasch. *The Culture of Narcissism* p. 154.

the various pathologies, do not bring success, because it seems that they not concerned with the anthropological truth about man but about power over man.

Stable social patterns always represent the essence of metanoia on the road to mature moral life. The influence of traditional biblical formation, transmitted orally, socialized many communities and people in the past. Human metanoia, in relationship with the loving God, yields goodness in life (cf. Eph. 4:7–16). The book of Genesis refers to the image of personalized love that man received because of God's freely given gifts so that the best humane activity can be conveyed to all people. For this reason, each man has unique, individual blessings with the capacity to be a saint. As T. Zadykowicz indicates, a saint embodies the sacred ideal and thus becomes a model for others.[762] The inspired man knows who he is in communion with the God of love and realizes who he may become. However, there is a necessary step to apply Adam's method of personalization that allows people to visualize their personal imperfections and move toward a healthy social and moral standard.

In most processes of socialization and education, a formator's authority teaches respect for divine and human law. A teacher should be fair, humble, and merciful. M. Pokrywka states, for example, that an educator of justice must consider both the personal and moral formation of an upright conscience concerned with the appropriate legal order, which is one of the essential elements of democratic social order.[763] The right attitude of the teacher ought to be characterized by honesty, a direct focus on higher goals, moral standards, and culture. Despite this, the educator must be like a child among children, a young man among youth. A good teacher knows how to listen to the opinion of the ward and always encourage good. He should be capable of treating people integrally and with the dignity. Other characteristics of a good teacher include truth-telling, forgiveness, free-given time to explain moral principles, and the willingness to defend students if they are unjustly treated.

Intellectual transformation of the individual is quite tedious, and a man often avoids the effort, assuming that is too difficult. But the mature man, who personalizes his weaknesses with an internal desire for peace, always chooses the path of conversion. For most Christians, the only sure way of moral development and development in the divine image is identification with Jesus, who calls us to self-denial and transformation in Him. In a responsible life, there is the disposition that according to the spirit, may "direct self-formed toward God."[764] The real challenge is to not see the transformation as a problem but rather as a gift, which will help one achieve harmonious unity of life with God. Formation, in other words, requires

---

[762] *Sequela Christi et imitatio hominis. Paradygmaty naśladowania we współczesnej refleksji teologicznomoralnej.* Lublin: Wydawnictwo KUL 2011 p. 365.

[763] *Rodzina szkołą cnót społecznych.* RTM 4(59): 2012 p. 159.

[764] RP p. 5, 26.

personal transformation. It is important that one does not give up the effort of good work on oneself and continually perseveres with a good attitude. John Paul II points out that "not only the world but the man himself has been entrusted to his care and responsibility. God left a man in the 'hand of his counsel' (cf. Sir. 15:14), to seek his Creator and freely attain his perfection."[765]

In the process of the ethical socialization and education of the young person, the personalization method allows men to turn away from sin, which ruins his personality development. Discovery and free acceptance of God's love in the community of faith transforms the prodigal son and allows him to adopt friendly attitudes. A person intellectually shapes a positive image of himself by following the mental picture of the loving God. According to Allport, the deforming factor of an individual's positive self-image is often distorted by the immature culture of his parents manifested in their messed up priorities. Active love, although often associated with suffering and struggles, integrally forms a man.[766] The reason integral self-formation is neglected at school, within the family, or in the workplace is a lack of appropriate intellectual training and a careless approach to virtues and motivational exercises. It is often fear of developing to a higher level of life. Reducing holistic self-formation, for many different reasons, always degrades the life of man.

The German Nazi structure of enslavement, for example, was based on images of human destruction. It blocked rational inferences and destroyed the potential of goodness. Bad imagery makes adults often fickler than children in too-easy demoralization. Subject to his whims and using contempt instead of intelligence, man ruins one's life in material existence without God. According to K. Wojtyła, the implementation of good images of thinking and personalistic norms are necessary keys to building interpersonal relationships based on the fundamental essence of society within the family—a community of persons, or *communio personarum*. The application of ethical norms, in sharing good manners to all individuals, comes from the command of loving. The commandment of loving is a personalistic norm because the person differs from any other physical matter in his structure and perfection.[767] Personalistic norms specify that man, as created in the image of God, is meant to be subjective and capable of planned and deliberate action. His capability to decide about himself ought to aim at a higher good and self-evolution.[768]

---

[765] VS p. 39.

[766] Cf. D. Lang. *The Penguin Companion to Classical Oriental and African Literature*. T. 4. Red. M. D. Dudley. New York: McGraw-Hill Book Company 1969 p. 127.

[767] K. Wojtyła. *Miłość i odpowiedzialność*. Lublin: KUL 1982 p. 24.

[768] LE p. 6.

Contemporary intellectual self-development, in the form of graphic communication, teaches essential principles through educational films or computer programs. Current pedagogy has many ways of engaging the pupil in learning moral good, through film and computer technology, but this has not been used to its full capacity. The formative impact of these tools on human behavior is enormous and should be implemented in the way a mother inspires her child. Also, testimonies of the saints from hagiographies show an educative path. We are aware, as Benedict XVI states, that "this is not just about didactic teaching, about perfecting methods of transmitting knowledge, but education in the strict sense of the direct, personal encounter with the man who witnesses authentic faith, hope, and love. And most of all, such values are derived directly from one person to another person. This genuine encounter with another person must be first heard and understood. John Paul II became such a perfect model for meeting with a man."[769]

Ethical self-formation, as an intellectual exercise, should result from a large educational experience, knowledge, and natural ability. It aims to change disordered emotions and thought into more harmonious, responsible ways to improve quality of life (both individual and collective) in society. The difficulty arises from the present hedonistic and narcissistic culture in which people cannot form altruistic behavior and self-giving sacrifice. Moral self-formation is necessary for moral order, which in its diversity, contributes to a positive and qualitative transformation of the present death culture.[770] The intellectually mature man does not have the right ideals for himself but lives great values and shows his noble attitudes. Besides, he does not acquire them in a purely private and subjective way. Therefore, mature personality manifests itself in more than just reductive urges and drives.[771] The mature personality comes from the aspirations that attract human person from outside: first, in the ability to express feelings, thoughts, and needs; second, in self-restraint, when needed; third, in the capacity to negotiate needs; fourth, in interpersonal dialogue: fifth, in trusting others; sixth, in discovering the truth about oneself through appropriate behavior and constructive thinking; seventh, in receiving exaggerated criticism without guilt, rejection, or hatred; eighth, in the intellectual ability to control negative feelings and overcome impulse; ninth, the capacity for sensory perception as a child when it is safe, but also as an adult in emergency situations; tenth, in learning from

---

[769] Benedict XVI. *Przesłanie Benedykta XVI do polskich biskupów. "Pedagogika Katolicka"* 1: 2007 no. 1a.

[770] "The purpose of moral education is to change people for the better and, in so doing, to improve the quality of life in society, so that, individually and collectively, we are to become better people than we might otherwise be." Cf. Hunter. *The Death of Character* p. 220.

[771] Cf. G. W. Allport. *Basic Principles in Improving Human Relations*. Red. W Bieglow. IN: Cultural Groups and Human Relations. Oxford U: Bur 1951 p. 8–12.

the experiences of others; and finally, eleventh, desiring to better oneself without coercion.

F. Bednarski stresses the importance of acquiring Christian values in the self-formation of young people. He draws attention to the objectives and social welfare ideals of the self-educative adolescent's character and goodwill. He notes that Boy Scout programs engage young men to control their weaknesses and cultivate positive emotions.[772] The formation of a healthy personality requires clear communication wherein positive and honest behavior leads a child to educative consistency. [773] A youth's transition from resistance to cooperation usually takes time. A juvenile expects peace, patience, and reasonable consequences from educators and parents so he may achieve good results. Directives should always be expressed in a few simple cultural words and with a gentle tone that communicates stability. On the contrary, when a parent uses a severe voice and expresses nervousness, he is often met with resistance and negative results. Children pick up on their teachers' frustrations or hesitations. Besides, nonverbal contact is essential, too, to draw attention to the importance of expressed directives (i.e., forgiving communication). It is always important to compliment the student's positive reactions; this is a critical motivational technique for encouraging a child to do what is right and good. For example, a young child who puts his toys away can be told, appreciatively, "I am proud of you. How nice your room looks now."

Parents or educators should use learned directives and appreciate a child's positive achievements by a means of verbal and nonverbal communication, thereby helping the child develop right conduct confidently and quickly. Scrutinizing their defects and errors leaves children with adverse reactions and can lead to neurotic behavior.[774] An experienced teacher does not apply hurtful, threatening slogans or excessive requirements beyond accepted and age-appropriate educational norms. Substantive lessons teach a pupil to avoid bad behavior. For example, a preschooler who uses force against a weaker peer should gain appropriate experience in the art of

---

[772] Cf. *Wychowanie młodzieży dorastającej*. Warszawa: NAVO 2000 p. 167.

[773] Allport notes that honesty and lying do not constitute one's character traits but are child's reactions resulting from educational pressures. "Honesty or dishonesty is not a unified character trait in children, but a series of specific responses to specific situations." Cf. G. W. Allport. *The Nature of Personality:* Selected Papers. Reading: MA 1950 p. 24.

[774] "Individuals who have partly regressed or never risen above infantile level (...) are chiefly in neurotic or infantile personalities that they hold sway. Normal people are not prisoners of the past." Cf. G. W. Allport. *The Nature of Personality: Selected Papers*, reading. MA 1950 p. 166. Allport points out that the neurotic personality may shape the erratic behavior of the student.

apologizing. The teacher should teach the student how to apologize and should touch the injured child at the site of his injury.

The teacher says, "Jack, apologize to Tommy for unintentionally hitting him." This methodology proves that one should talk less and do better.[775] For an older child who behaves inappropriately, a more appropriate form of education is to take away his privileges until he has made reparations: cleaning up the mess he made, repairing what he broke, or doing something good in a spirit of contrition. Good communication and explanation is needed, especially when the child does not control his behavior and cries. The educator should always communicate lessons with the child without any shouting or threats because the growing child needs love and attention. If children express rebellious and aggressive interactions, they require specialized counseling.[776] When a child understands well that there is no value in bad behavior, he begins his integral development. Any success in educational and formative work calls for the precise enhancement of values and skillful communication. Social values are more efficiently carried out in a more mature process of socialization and social education.[777] There is no doubt that intellectual formation should be based on in-depth reflection rooted in God's revelation. Personal religiosity allows the individual to find a more adequate way to form an integral personality.

C. The spiritual aspects of the self-formed personality

G. Allport, A. Maslow, and many other contemporary scholars agree that the integrating religious and spiritual influence reaches deep into the structure of the human personality. The spiritual person is mainly focused on good, reasonable goals that are not only temporary but eternal. Therefore, the formed self is motivated by the desire to achieve these goals. A man who holds strong aspirations and motives shapes others with his unifying philosophy of life. His leading motivations engage him toward long term goal achievement. Therefore, proper concern about good motives is a necessary condition for the full self-realization of human existence. Allport claims that high values and motivations are essential elements in the elaboration of a unifying philosophy of life and overcoming personal crises. In the face of a

---

[775] Cf. G. Edwards. *Use of negative consequences in parent training*. New York: ADHD 1953 p. 13–14.

[776] Cf. T. Seeman. "Health Psychology: What is an unhealthy environment and how does it get under the skin?" *Annual Review of Psychology*. 48: 1997 no. 2 p. 411

[777] "Cultural tradition, social norms, what the child is taught and how he is taught it, the parental model, semantic confusion, ignorance of group differences, the principle of category formation, and many other factors play a part. Most important of all is the way the individual weaves all these influences, including his unconscious conflicts and his psychodynamic reactions, into a whole style of life." Cf. Allport. *The Nature of Prejudice* p. 392.

crises, A. Derdziuk states, it is necessary to interiorize and accept a hierarchy of values, according to which a self-formed individual can adopt more effective self-defense measures and embodying principles.[778]

In the case of a rather neurotic personality, where valuation is not sufficiently high to unite all aspects of life, a healthy personality has a noticeably deeper sense of purposeful directedness in life. He or she has a worldview and philosophy of life that promotes self-worth. Therefore, the formed self devotes all of his energy to his primary purpose in life.

A mature personality manifests a self-achieving person who devotes his energy and thoughts to valuable ideas, and affairs, even beyond his safety or status quo. C. Rogers puts it bluntly: to form meaningful fullness in life, one must have a sense of dignity and value.[779] Essential in that process is also a deep faith.[780] Such thinking represents humanists Allport, A. Maslow, C. Rogers, E. Erikson, C. Jung, and D. Batson, among others, as well as the School of Lublin personalists, M. Krąpiec, Cz. Bartnik, Z. Chlewiński, A. Biela, and others. They note the need for the presence of the sacred in the culture of man. If we intentionally minimize the sacred in our human life, one's state of mind contributes to reductionism and a gradual process of making people unhappy. Reductionism always detracts from the essence of humanity, what we live for. Reductionism in the state of human profane, is the state of deliberate exclusion from the circle of *humanum*.[781]

Religious groups transmit the gift of faith as "the theological virtue by which people believe in God because God is truth itself."[782] And faith becomes a fundamental attitude of ascetic personality. Hence, Allport, as a man of deep faith, determines that man's faith is a universal phenomenon. Faith, for him, is a practical hypothesis of the *sēnsū strictō* existence of the non-material world. The message of faith strengthens and broadens man's relationship with the world and it's Creator.[783] The shaping of moral personality in the context of faith can help one discern a specific vocation based on personal predispositions. This predisposition of belief not only allows a man to make his life more reasonable but leads to a richer inner life. For faith forms a person, his inner life as a self-conscious being.

Therefore, religious formation contributes to the inclusive concept of life around the essential characteristics of humanity. Spiritual formation,

---

[778] *Formacja moralna* p. 20.

[779] "A formator has to have fundamental belief in the worth, dignity and significance of each individual." Cf. C. Rogers and R. Beckers. *A Basic Orientation for Counseling.* PaPs 1: 1950 no. 1 p. 26.

[780] Cf. C. Rogers. *On Becoming a Person.* Boston: Houghton Mifflin p. 8.

[781] M. Rusecki i in. *Z zagadnień światopoglądu chrześcijańskiego.* Lublin: TN KUL 1989 p. 63–67.

[782] KKK p. 1,814.

[783] Cf. Allport. *Osobowość i religia* p. 222–223.

through its principle of the example and service, makes the world a better and more tolerant place, going against man's lower needs and impulses. Self-becoming, when subjected to higher ideals, harmony, and moral norms, makes anyone more responsible. Thus, personal self-formation, interacting with the norms, values, and actual good moral content, becomes transparent. However, values, skills, and ascetic qualities must first be strengthened by the formed self so that he can pass them on to others. Forming a man requires the necessary internalization of faith and virtues. The religious formation of the juvenile not only gives him insight into others but also an opportunities to learn Christian realism from his perception of self and others.[784] Forming a better man requires the necessary internalization work. Deepened faith, as a formative tool, integrates a person in such a way that it gives him optimism for the future, and promotes a culture of life of individual energy.[785]

The believer sees faith as supporting one's reasoning so that individual morale becomes an important personalistic argument rather than a hedonistic one. The moral formation of the hedonist, at each stage, takes time and is difficult because hedonism is derived from the doctrine that the pursuit of pleasure and material goods is the primary goal of human life. The pursuit of materialistic pleasure always has a reductionist view of the person.[786] On the opposite site, the rich transmission of faith can often counter the deformation of the hedonist.[787]

Most young people know they need to integrate faith into their maturing personalities to find fulfillment on the road to the meaningful life. Unfortunately, the negative media's image (which is often anti-religious) drowns out that interior need. The contemporary culture of postmodern relativism removes moral codes, faith, and other precious values stemming from good, traditional philosophy. Current liberal tendencies do not want to recognize the absolute truths that reinforce confidence. The younger generation has no aspirations to come to deeper faith due to official propaganda and hence do not see the strengths of religiosity. Thus, believers must see faith as a fundamental option, the choice of saving the man, in

---

[784] Cf. G. W. Allport. *Personal Religious Orientation and Prejudice.* JPSP 5: 1967 no. 4 p. 434.

[785] Cf. G. W. Allport. *Personality: Psychological Interpretation.* New York: Holt and Company 1937 p. 226.

[786] According to Bp. J. Wróbel in hedonism, the body is not perceived objectively, but as the source and place of sensations that man reaches by manipulation. *Antropologia ludzkiej płciowości: powołanie do życia w komunii prawdy i miłości.* IN: *Ocalić obraz człowieka. Antropologiczne podstawy moralności.* Red. P. Morciniec. Opole: RW WT Uniwersytetu Opolskiego 2003 p. 89.

[787] See. B. Häring. *Free and Faithful in Christ: Moral Theology for Priest and Laity.* T. 2. Middlegreen, Slough: St. Paul Publications 1979 p. 467. "The beginning, the subject and the goal of all social institutions is and must be the human person, who for its part and by its very nature, stands completely in need of social life."

which God the Person plays the most essential role.[788] Religious maturity then plays an important role in shaping the moral personality.

The formation of a religious and spiritual sphere requires time, commitment, and especially patience translated into dialogue.[789] In reading, playing, and spending time with children, one remembers to choose quality time over beautiful attractions. Youth will not remember that he had a fantastic toy, but he will remember when his dad showed it to him. He will remember how to deal with moral issues and fix relationships. His mother's lullabies might signify more than teaching emotional bonds at bedtime. The experience of goodness and truth requires training so that self-formative, lifelong learning becomes invaluable to a person.

To this point, we know that religious and spiritual formation stems from normative ethics. Uniqueness and human dignity demand that the human person is "the principle, subject, and purpose of all social relations."[790] John Paul II reaffirms the need to internalize one's life through spiritual self-formation realizing that it would be insufficient to grow only in the flesh. What is needed, above all, is spiritual growth. Men achieve this capacity simply by practicing the skills that God filled within them to gain genuine and confident maturity, corresponding to the dignity of Christians.[791] The clear task of religious and spiritual self-formation is the implementation of essential life principles. This poses an important and challenging task for theological anthropology, both from a scientific and pastoral point of view. Always, however, religious and spiritual formation should support moral norms. In his *Letter to Families*, John Paul II states that the moral structure of the person enables man to grow in his call "to live in truth and love."[792]

The lack of a permanent formation for authentic love presents a serious problem in modern times. Z. Płużek notes that "for a mature person, life is more than just getting food, drink, feeling safe and dealing with the opposite sex; it is something more than what can be directly or indirectly referred to as 'libido reduction.' As long as a man does not gain interest in a world existing outside him, yet being a part of him, life will be more like an animal's life than a human's."[793] Similarly, M. Pokrywka notes that the role of self-formation in communal life is natural participation in society, which supports a recognition of the fundamental truth that every person is valuable

---

[788] Por J. Nagórny. *Posłannictwo chrześcijan w świecie.* Lublin: RW KUL 1998 p. 78–80.

[789] Cf. Benedict XVI. Orędzie na Światowy Dzień Pokoju "Wolność religijna drogą do pokoju" (Watykan, 1.01.2011). OsRomPol. 32: 2011 no. 1 p. 4–11.

[790] KDK p. 25.

[791] Cf. See *Speaches, "Szkoła i parafia – dwa warsztaty pracy"* (Watykan, 05.03.1980). IN: *Dziecko w nauczaniu Jana Pawła II. Antologia wypowiedzi.* Red. C. Drążek, J. Kawecki. Kraków 1985 p. 121–123.

[792] LdR p. 16.

[793] *Psychologia pastoralna* p. 52.

and, as such, cannot be reduced only to material things.[794] With participation comes committed educational work and healthy efforts to do good. Allport says clearly that a person dies without compassionate involvement and participation.[795] Active self-formation becomes important in the unification of Christ's humanity when significant participation is executed through self-disciplined work.

It is God, through the free example of Jesus, who truly motivates man to respect natural laws both in his individual and social life. From this anthropological perspective, man discovers himself as a creature whose goal is union with God and realizes his likeness to God, resulting in co-Creation. The way to union with God is the humanity of Christ, whose selfless example challenges us to preserve moral principles in the lives of individuals and society. For Allport, the lives of the saints are particularly important because they illustrate the path of the testimony of faith as an integrating formation key.[796] In the community of believers, there was never a shortage of people whose lives edified others. In their attitudes and deeds, a believer recognizes what is valuable and worthy of imitating.[797]

The saints show us that holiness is realizable. In this case, to change human behavior, we must have a positive impact on the entire community. There is no single healing remedy or medicine to eliminate immaturity and any unethical actions, including those features of human discrimination.[798] The transmission of faith would not make sense if it broke communal solidarity. Mature, religious self-formation makes sense when it practically corresponds to the fundamental questions which pervade human life: Who am I? Where have I come from, and where am I going? The common source of these issues is a deeper need to rediscover the kind of human existence

---

[794] *Osoba, uczestnictwo, wspólnota* p. 141.

[795] "If the body muscles are tense, the brain reacts much more quickly and intensely, but if they are relaxed, it may respond weakly or not at all." Cf. Allport. *The Psychology of Participation* p. 121. Cf. Allport. *The Nature of Personality* p. 147.

[796] Personality analysis of St. Augustine's based on his *Confessions* indicates the personal integrity of the saint. Allport, using the coherent method of personality testing, confirms the intrinsic character of the saint, expressed in the consistency and coherence of Augustine's words with his actions. So, here is the "principle of truth" viewed in the correspondence of words with his deeds. Using Allport's unique intrinsic-extrinsic distinction, we may conclude with certainty that Augustine's personality is "originally internalized" and well self-formed. B. Spilka. *Traits and Allport: Ideography in a Nomothetic Mold? International Journal for the Psychology of Religion.* 4: 1994 no. 4 p. 235–237.

[797] Cf. T. Zadykowicz. *Sequela Christi et imitatio hominis. Paradygmaty naśladowania we współczesnej refleksji teologiczno moralnej.* Lublin: Wydawnictwo KUL 2011 p. 369.

[798] Cf. G. W. Allport. *Techniques.* IN: *Forms and Techniques of Altruistic and Spiritual Growth.* Red. P. A. Sorokin. Boston: Beacon Press 1954 p. 253.

that man feels from the very beginning in his heart. The answer to these questions depends on which direction the formed person takes.[799]

The natural inclination of the religious personality is its natural subjectivity. The subjectivity of the participating individual is the pursuit of the common good (e.g., in the spirit of a responsible and patriotic attitude). Natural participation provides the self-formative person with the best results of mature reflection. For the Christian, it means the unique and lived Revelation where, within the community of the Church, God's revelation furnishes a constructive means for the development of individuals—a *communio personorum* that leads them to a deeper understanding of the social laws the Creator inscribed in the spiritual and moral norms of man.[800] Such moral consistency is a fundamental and unquestionable universal value. Of course, this involves the moral principle of the objective truth, whose primary element is well-understood by all concerned in the process of growing. What self-growing and self-formation should be is the self-actualization through a sincere gift of self, accepted by both students and educators.[801]

Ethical self-formation is based in community activity because it expresses co-educative participation, ranging from families, schools, parishes, peer group mass media, etc. So, this cultural and educational environment should fruitfully interact for the benefit of the better integration of the young and the future of the world. Lack of needed cooperation in these environments leads to incompatible intentions, contradictions, and high damages, making ethical formation less efficient and undermining the positive efforts of the group devoted to co-educating.

Christian self-formation, in its transmission of faith, has a significant role in enhancing individuals who enter the path of conversion. From the time of the early Church, Christian tradition has called for Christian initiation; it is no coincidence that the beginning of this path is the grace of Baptism so that the neophyte, within the community, embarks on formation, as Christian theology understands it.[802] The path of religious formation is divided into three stages: purification, enlightenment, and unification. Although active evolution requires the significant, continuous efforts of others despite minor and individual setbacks, it has an essential motivating role in human

---

[799] FR p. 1.

[800] KDK p. 23.

[801] Cf. KDK p. 24.

[802] "The ultimate purpose and the mission of the Church is *aedificatio continua Ecclesiae* toward the end of salvation." Cf. Ecclesiae Catholica. *Abyśmy nie ustali w drodze: list biskupów polskich do prezbiterów Kościoła w Polsce o stałej formacji kapłańskiej.* Poznań: Księgarnia św. Wojciecha 2007 p. 2.

development.[803] Mature religious formation has an attitude of conviction and trust in achieving noble goals that require courage and friendship with God.

Many positive effects in moral formation bring interpersonal friendship. One is a unique method of resolving personal disputes and excessive personal ambition. Friendships are more conducive to effective moral action, lifting relationships out of the realm of abstract ideas. A felt sense of friendship between student and teacher (without compromising professionalism) leads to responsible action. It promotes co-responsibility for the welfare of a higher good: better education, not only ideological but real, what is at the stake of every Christian community. Every mature relationship developed within even the smallest community is carried out in association with others, never in isolation from the prayer group and the community of faith, and it retains a mature sense of responsibility and opportunity to positively influence others.

A mutual sense of connectedness based on friendship triggers the virtue of self-giving, sacrifice, and care for a better tomorrow for all. The concept of virtue *arete* is constantly belittled and ignored in secular society.[804] These acquired virtues are a function of mature personality. Thus, the consideration of *arete* in self-formation is an important and authoritative instrument in the perspective of the psychology of virtues. Nevertheless, contemporary research on personality traits confirms, in five- and six-factor models, the importance of those factors in relation to moral virtues. Today, social studies state that moral virtues contain terms corresponding to social virtues such as compliance, diligence, honesty, and modesty, all of which should be understood as moral virtues, especially the integrity trait. Integrity is the sixth factor of a healthy personality, emphasizing credibility, lack of greed, and lack of guile. Most studies confirm that integrity, authenticity, and honesty create the fundamental power of human interaction in moral formation. The majority of society highly esteems personal virtue and morality.[805] Hence, spiritual formation, based on the values of virtues and friendship, engage with interpersonal communication. Therefore, all educators must support clean, noble, and selfless human intentions.[806] With

---

[803] "In a general way, we know what mental health requires. It requires that we learn to grow muscles where our injuries were. In the words of the Eighty-fourth Psalm, that man is blessed (Psalm 84:6) who, going through the value of misery, uses it for a well (...). It requires both the poetic and prophetic metaphors of religion and the precise, hard grammar of science." Cf. Allport. *The Person in Psychology* p. 142.

[804] "The aspect of personality that engenders stability and dependability, that is responsible for sustained effort in the face of obstacles." Cf. Allport. *Personality: A Psychological Interpretation.* New York: H. Holt and Company 1937 p. 51.

[805] Cf. Mu Shou-uan. *The relationship between virtues and personality traits of Chinese college students.* "Social Behavior and Personality: an international journal." 39: 2011 no. 10 p. 1,379.

[806] KPK p. 1,029.

virtue (as the attitude of lasting value), friendship is born in nature and cannot function. Mature faith formation stimulates interpersonal skills and friendship, conjuncts the self-course for conversion. John Paul II emphasizes that for each of the faithful, self-formation should serve as a guiding and unifying role of being a good Christian and acting like a Christian.[807]

To correctly answer the question—what role does religious and spiritual maturity serve in individual life?—it should be noted that healthy motivation, in the process of self-development, sees formation as an art and a skill developed from the virtues and principles of moral guidance. Moral formation is, therefore, the art of an anthropology of becoming, which for Aristotle, meant productive activity. This skill consists of knowing the rules of life, which, according to Aristotle, should be acts of "production consistent with accurate reasoning"[808] Moral formation is, therefore, the art of shaping a more mature life with the ability to evaluate well. In the words of Sarah Banks, formation plays a shape-playing role, translating into a student's acquired skills and qualitatively moral decisions.[809]

Interviewed students from different countries (Finland, Great Britain, and France), who were subjected to difficult moral questions, affirmed that moral teaching should give them the courage to act in accordance with the virtue of duty. That examination showed the cognitive impact on their integrative development and that science ought to engage in more serious thinking about the formation of moral impulses beyond reasoning and logic. Man, from the moment of conception, is brought up heavily influenced by family and the whole human-embedded environment in which he grows. Thus, the self-development of religious personality depends not only on the external environment and internal factors but also on the activity of the self-growing person.[810]

Being the facilitator of an external environment, the educator needs to strive for religious and spiritual maturity as well. Because integral education requires that they're interested in shaping moral character, they must stabilize the internal models and emerging emotions of young people as their priority. [811] Those intelligent emotions communicate discovery of the

---

[807] PDV p. 45.

[808] Arystoteles. *Etyka Nikomachejska* IN: Arystoteles. *Dzieła wszystkie*. T. 5. Transl. D. Groma. Warszawa 2000 p. 196.

[809] "Implications for teaching include the need to develop skills and qualities in students that enable them to recognize the ethical dimensions of difficult situations and to develop the courage to act on their decisions." Cf. *The Ethical Practitioner in Formation: Issues of Courage, Competence and Commitment. "Social Work Education"* 24: 2005 no. 7 p. 737.

[810] Cf. Allport. *Osobowość i religia* p. 78.

[811] R. Zigle. *The Formation and Transformation of Moral Impulse.* ME 28: 1999 no. 4 p. 445–457.

objective truth and serve students with normative understandings of the law. The revealed law of God in nature ought to fascinate the young in terms of recognizing the truth about himself, in practicing the commandments of love, and critically monitoring his own progress to become a more compassionate person. At the same time, the trainee becomes more educated and responsive to his call.[812]

Thus, the mature standards of Christian religious background are an imperative and integrative core of personality development. Mature religiosity and spirituality give purposeful meaning to human life and create an integrated system of human values, particularly through appropriate motivation and behavior. Healthy religious and spiritual experience involves a person seeking God and the principles of life on a deeper level. What follows from that claim comes the proposal that in the knowledge of God the individual is accompanied by the dimension of love. It is unconditional love manifested from the Supreme Being of a dynamic structure. The enconter with unconditional love of God motivates a juvenile's self to improve a relationship with other people, and all of God's Creation. Then the individual's "personality becomes the internal and dynamic organization, that determines its unique adaptation to the environment."[813] The uniqueness of this adjustment makes the formed person more open to the transcendent dimension, allowing him to permanently acquire the consistency of religious beliefs and an integrative life. Also, personal involvement in faith community services and peer groups reinforces the development toward inner life and holiness. Man's evolution manifests itself, among other things, in significant changes of perception.

Religious maturity, in the life of a believer, should be the most-praised value. Intrinsic commitment to a reflective life of prayer and external orientation toward people with positive attitudes toward the commands of God's law creates the essential core of an integrated Christian. That integrity of religious and spiritual life makes for a mature personality, which is characterized by consistency in his emotional, intellectual, and volitional spheres. Similarly, concrete external structure of a man focused on God, people and spiritual ideas integrates one as well.

On the path of Christian formation, the aim is to connect one's personal story with the transcendent God, who constantly teaches in Revelation how to live and realize central values. Getting to know and accept oneself as a child of God is not a goal in itself. It is more about finding God's plan and rediscovering integrative maturity: to live better and to realize the value of Christ's message. The task of self-formation in the anthropology of becoming is carried out in a ministry that requires an attitude of humility in meeting Christ.[814] Mature self-formation is an integral part of becoming more

---

[812] KKK p. 1879.

[813] Allport. *Personality: A Psychological Interpretation* p. 45.

[814] Cf. PDV p. 43.

like the co-Creator. In fact, besides self-formation in the religious-spiritual, intellectual, doctrinal-catechetical, personal, human and professional spheres, there is the need for a comprehensive formation in the spirit of the New Evangelization, where it comes to formation for authentic love, to be spiritually alive. A Christian neglected in the postmodern world nevertheless determines a mature evolving in the lifelong goal of integrated personality. Self-formation, in other words, allows sooner growth toward adult life. It targets attitudes in discovering the true values of goodness and beauty that man can permanently acquire, and thus become the loving personality of integral emotionality.[815]

---

[815] Cf. J. Nagórny. *Sumienie, źródło wolności czy zniewolenia?* IN: "Człowiek sumienia." Red. J. Guzowski. Olsztyn 1997 p. 41–70.

CONCLUSION

Christian moral formation determines a much more mature human development, so man achieves the ideal of an integrated personality. Christian moral formation, in other words, enables the student to become a mature person. [816] Orienting one's actions and moral attitudes toward discovered values such as goodness and beauty enables one to become a moral personality, emotionally mature in the Christian spirit, in which he discovers his vocation to good—a call to love. Above all, the fullness of Christian formation stems from emotional maturity, sustainability, responsibility, honesty, noble motivations, and many other factors. The mature model of human perfection is Christ himself, who revealed the fullness of being a man in his attitude toward others. The road of self-formation, to which God calls man, involves conversion, growth, and maturation, bringing forth the fruit to which Christ always calls.

In this theological-humanistic perspective, I have undertaken mature personality teaching of G.W. Allport as the interpretive lenses for self-formation. Analyzing the teachings of the American personalist can help many individuals understand that Christian self-formation is necessary for the development of the integral personality. Of crucial importance for this research was the sensitization of people to moral issues in this era of rapidly progressing scientific and technological development. [817] A sound moral evaluation of modern science and technology is needed, in the light of God's revelation and the Church's tradition.

First, my research focused on the conditions for self-formation in the light of humanistic impact through the interpretative lenses. According to Allport, human attitudes that make a man good result from his conscious perception and implementation of life's ethical norms and obligations, which are consistent with the ideas described in the ethics of E. Kant.[818] Leading personalists developed the position that humans cannot squander the tremendous educational achievements of the Christian tradition coming from the Bible. The works of other communities of faith in no way distort that vision but broaden personal horizons in the relationship with God in Jesus Christ, who is often ignored and neglected by reductionist concepts in anthropology. The evaluative approach of a religious value system is still valid

---

[816] Cf. PDV p. 43b.
[817] Cf. Allport. *The Individual and His Religion* p. 70.
[818] Cf. A. F. Kleinberger. *Moral & Values Education*. JME 11: 1982 no. 3 p. 147–158.

because it forms a healthy personality especially in a community of believers who help all those experiencing doubts and crises of identity.

All educational activities—to be able to achieve its goal—must be based on the full truth about man in a relationship with a loving God. From the truth about man and God, we derive the moral implications of human action. Man can discover God's goodness, friendship, and the truth about himself. [819] Therefore, not only the Christian media in the form of interpersonal communication, images, and thoughts but the underlying environment, too, teaches personal dialogue between people, nations, and cultures that eliminates many reductionist visions of man. Thanks to the "fuller spiritual culture," a healthy, formed man becomes a social educator not only for the sake of today but also future generations.[820]

Family, school, and the community of faith are all necessary environments for self-formation. Personalistic pedagogy emphasizes the need to return to the primary and developmental tasks of the family. The family is the fundamental community of persons who care for one another. From the family, all members learn the principles of respect, mutual responsibility, and love on which depend the wellbeing of a humane society. For the family to fulfill its objective educative and formative roles, it must function as an evangelizing community that is subject to continuous evangelization. Good upbringing in the family, examples of sacrifice, intellectual exercises in school, and a strong community of faith shapes, in young people, traits such as a sense of duty, a responsibility for oneself and others, love for all people, kindness, shared values, and cheerful attitudes toward life or sympathy. The self-formed personality is, therefore, the sum of the positive moral qualities that value the person.[821] Thus, a person who forms must be consistently mature in his conduct with a pupil in the world of moral thinking and acting, which shows him that values are non-negotiable in life. All educators have an ancillary role in self-formation—and not just as witnesses. The more we are formed, the more we are aware of the necessity of continuing and deepening our self-reflection. Effective formation depends, in part, on well-planned structures, but first and foremost, it depends on people engaging youth. The attitude and actions of the educator

---

[819] Cf. A. Derdziuk. *Formacja do modlitwy*. HD 62: 1993 no. 4 (230) p. 24–34.

[820] "One thing is certain: Pluton and Aristotelian strands of thoughts are found in all western theory, past and present." Cf. G. Allport. *The Nature of Prejudice* p. 6. For the integral formation speaks 50-year practice of personality psychology focused on positive experience and exposure to the values and virtues of classical philosophy of Plato and Aristotle.

[821] "Attitude toward child training. Forming a strong impression that our student populations firmly accept the moral standards prevailing in civilized countries. The virtues of honesty, truth-telling, reliability, decency, and integrity are acclaimed." Cf. Allport. *An Experiment in the Prevention of Delinquency* p. 9.

must be geared toward high values, which in turn can be transmitted to students. Formators, who try to make the pupil's path successful, ought to create a healthy environment for necessary growth and earn authority of youth.[822]

Deepened and internalized morality not only has a creative role in the formation of moral personality, but it is associated with a commitment to God and the fulfillment of moral principles. Faith and morals are not used to satisfy one's own needs but result from the central motive of happiness: giving oneself to God and neighbor. The multiple consequences of integration are always positive and bring fruit to the individual and society. Therefore, on the social level, the expression of personal freedom is associated with tolerance, lack of biases, compassion, empathy, and sensitivity to the needs of others. An awareness of one's own gained liberty results from human subjectivity and a responsible life.[823] This availability allows the youth's path to be marked by kindness, encouragement, and warning signs in case of potential challenges. Freedom of co-Creation in Christian self-formation is never associated with an attitude of domination.[824] We should keep in mind, however, that freedom, to be true, cannot be detached from the truth.[825] Internalized morality manifests itself in warmer contacts with other people and is determined by Allport's extension of personality (i.e., an extension of self). It is simply a healthy personality trait. Thus, the moral attitude integrates internally and makes the person capable of expressing intimate feelings of compassion, especially in the face of suffering. Moral formation enriches the personality in a sense that it helps man move from the exterior behavior to a more profound moral attitude and maturity, according to the golden rule of conduct: "So in everything, do to others what you would have them do to you, for this sums up the Law and the Prophets" (Mt. 7:12). Therefore, in today's post-modern world, there is a great social need for altruistic, ascetic, and moral personalities to orient family and society toward higher values.

The becoming of mature character demands that man enters the path of self-acquired formation through the environment of parental love.

---

[822] Cf. T. Pettigrew. *Gordon Willard Allport* p. 424.

[823] Human subjectivity, for the anthropology of becoming, comes in an active relationship of the educator to the subject of formation to have a positive influence in the process of education. According to the Latin adagio *"operari sequitur esse"* (in a defense of subjective engagement), every activity constitutes its essence. Therefore, I claim that a human person has the positive reason or co-reason of ethical influence—at the same time is a relevant subject of the moral activity. That's why any concentration on high-integral aims makes the self-formed personality more mature.

[824] Cf. Jesionek. *Wychowanie moralne* p. 11.

[825] Cf. J. Nagórny. *Sumienie, źródło wolności czy zniewolenia* IN: *Człowiek sumienia*. Red. J. Guzowski. Olsztyn: 1997 p. 41–70; DWCH 1.

Christian self-formation is, therefore, a continuous educational process on the path of integral becoming, resulting from the *ordo amoris* as people who know the human person is and who that person may become in a relationship with an infinitely loving Christ. According to A. Derdziuk, the role of self-formation, or modeling of the mind and heart, is the evolving discovery of the treasure we already have—even when we do not use it well.[826] The desirability of Christian formation comes from multiple spheres of human cognition and above all, from the awareness of being implanted in the life of Christ, who shapes duty, mature harmony, and a meaningful life. Personal maturity is, therefore, the essence of personality that allows healthy functioning. Not without reason, Christian self-formation is the way for mature character evolvement.[827] Thus, it expresses a continuous process of becoming a person *in persona Christi*. Christian faith fulfills the call to holiness and perfection.

The above analysis of the influence of Christian formation shows that intellectual, emotional, and voluntary maturity is more than one's acquired cognitive element as his whole personality in moral action. I clearly distance myself from reductive approaches to psychoanalytic theories, adopting a personalistic model of self-formation. I desire to conclude that consequent self-formation of a young person is neither socialization nor individualization but active personalization that makes the human being whole. Such becoming integrates the person in every respectful way of taking from and giving to others mature care and love.[828] It should be noted, then, that the personalistic dimension of faith and morality clearly influences integral personal formation. A more mature change—it has to be emphasized once again—is possible only on the basis of the integral truth about man.[829] Further studies are therefore required in the anthropology of becoming truly human.

---

[826] A. Derdziuk. *W odpowiedzi na dar miłosierdzia*. Lublin: Red. Gaudium 2010 p. 64.

[827] "Ingredients of morale have to do respectively with the preparation of the individual, with his participation, and with the solidarity of the group." Cf. Allport. *Nature of Democratic Morale* p. 4–5.

[828] State socialization can carry a danger in general formation brought on by the fact that overall, the blatant influence of the state, different cultures, or any structures of power have been significantly threatening individual initiative and human freedom. Cf. Allport. *Osobowość i religia* p. 33.

[829] "Prejudiced people, evidently, have little concern with the truth as a value. The failure of this value to stand higher for tolerant people is no doubt because, important though it is, aesthetic, social, and religious values are still more decisive in the formation of tolerance." Cf. Allport. *The Nature of Prejudice* p. 440.

INDEX OF ABBREVIATIONS

ChL -John Paul II. Apostolic Exhortation *Christifideles laici* (30.12.1998).

CT -John Paul II. Apostolic Exhortation *Catechesi tradendae* (16.10.1979).

CV - Benedict XVI. Encyclical *Caritas in veritate* (1.06.2009).

CA -John Paul II. Encyclical *Centesimus annus* (1.05.1991).

CCC - The Catechism of the Catholic Church. Poznań 1994.

CHL -John Paul II. Apostolic Exhortation *Christifideles laici* (30.12.1988).

CT -John Paul II. Apostolic Exhortation *Catechesi tradendae* (16.10.1979).

CV - Benedict XVI. Encyclical *Caritas in Veritate* (1.06.2009).

DFK -Vatican II. The Decree on Priestly Training *Optatam totius* (28.10.1965).

DIM -Pius XI. Encyclical *Divini Illius Magistri* (31. 12.1929).

DinM -John Paul II. Encyclical *Dives in misericordia* (30.11.1980).

DOK -Congregation for the Clergy. *General Catechetical Directory* (15.08.1997).

DP -Congregation for the Doctrine of the Faith, on certain bioethical questions *Dignitas personae* (8.09.2008).

DAA -Vatican II. Decree on Apostolate of the Laity Apostolicam actuositatem (18.11.1965).

DWCH -Vatican II. Declaration on Education Gravissimum educationis (28.10.1965).

DWR - Vatican II. Declaration on Freedom *Dignitatis humanae* (7.12.1965).

EdE -John Paul II. Encyclical *Ecclesia de Eucharistia* (17.04.2003).

EG -Francis. Apostolic Exhoration *Evangelii gaudium* (24.11.2013).

EN -Paul VI. Apostolic Exhortation *Evangelii nuntiandi* (08.12.1975).

EV -John Paul II. Encyclical *Evangelium vitae* (25.03.1995).

FC -John Paul II. Apostolic Exhortation *Familiaris consortio* (22.11.1981).

FR -John Paul II. Encyclical *Fides et ratio* (14.09.1998).

HV -Paul VI. Encyclical *Humanae vitae* (25.07.1968).

KDK -Vatican II. Pastoral Constitution *Gaudium et spes* (7.12.1965).

KPK - The Code of Canon Law (23.01.1983). Poznań 1984.

KSS -Pius XII. Apostolic Constitution *Sedes Sapientiae* (31.05.1956).

KO -Vatican II. Dogmatic Constitution *Dei Verbum* (10.11.1965).

LC - Congregation for the Doctrine of the Faith, Instruction *Libertatis Conscientia* (22.03.1986).

LE -John Paul II. Encyclical *Laborem exercens* (14.09.1981).

LG -Paul VI. Vatican II, Dogmatic Constitution on the Church *Lumen Gentium* (21.11.1964).

LdM -John Paul II. Apostolic Letter to Youth *Parati semper* (31.03.1985).

LdR -John Paul II. Letter to Families *Gratissimam sane* (02.02.1994).

MD -John Paul II. Apostolic Letter, *Mulieris dignitatem* (15.08.1988).

MiN -John Paul II. Man and Women He Created Them: *A Theology of the Body* Vatican City: Libreria Editrice Vaticana, 1986.

MS -Paul VI, Instruction on Mixed Marriages. *Matrimonii Sacramentum* (18.03.1966).

PDV -John Paul II. Apostolic Exhortation on formation *Pastores Dabo vobis* (25.03.1992).

PH -Congregatio pro-Doctrina Fidei. Declaration concerning Sexual Ethics *Persona Humana* (29.12.1975).

PP - Paul VI. Encyclical on the development of people *Populorum Progressio* (27.03.1967).

ReP - John Paul II. Exhortation *Reconciliatio et paenitentia* (2.12.1984)

RFIS -Congregation for the Clergy *Ratio fundamentalis institutionis sacerdotibus* (6.01.1970).

RH -John Paul II. Encyclical. *Redemptor hominis* (4.03.1979).

RPtH -Congregation for Catholic Education. Instruction concerning the *criteria for Discernment with regard to Persons with Homosexual Tendencies* (4.11.2005).

SC -Benedict XVI. Apostolic Exhortation *Sacramentum Caritatis* (22.02.2007).

SRS -John Paul II. Encyclical *Sollicitudo Rei socialis* (30.12.1987).

SS -Benedict XVI. Encyclical *Spe Salvi* (30.11.2007).

TMA -John Paul II. Apostolic Letter. *Tertio millennio adveniente* (10.11.1994).

VC -John Paul II. Apostolic Exhortation *Vita consecrata* (25.03.1996).

VS -John Paul II. Encyclical. *Veritatis splendor* (6.08.1993).

WdS -„Congregation for Catholic Education." Wskazania dotyczące studiów i nauczania doktryny społecznej Kościoła w ramach formacji kapłańskiej (30.12.1988).

WW -Congregation for Catholic Education Educational Guidance in Human Love (1.11.1983

ABBREVIATIONS

AJPs -„American Journal of Psychology." Austin (Tx.) since 1887-

AJPs -„American Journal of Psychology."Austin (Tx.) since 1887-

AK -„Ateneum Kapłańskie". Włocławek since 1909-

AmPs -„American Psychologist." Washington since 1946-

BJP -„British Journal of Psychology." London since 1904-

ChSM -„Christian Science Monitor".Boston since 1808-

ComP -„Communio" Przegląd Teologiczny. Poznań since 1981-

Cur -„Currenda." (Since 1909„Currendeae Consistorii Tarnoviensis;" to 1922 „Currendae Consistorii Episcopalis Tarnoviensis," and 1939 „Currendae Curiae Diocesane Tarnovieniensis") Tarnów 1851-

ED -„Edukacja Dorosłych." Warszawa since 1993-

ER -„The Ecumenical Review" Before „Christendom". Chicago   since 1935-, Geneve 1948/49-

ENM -Jan Paweł II. Encyklopedia nauczania moralnego. Red J. Nagórny, K. Jeżyna. Radom: Polskie Wyd. Encyklopedyczne 2005.

ETH -„Ethos." Lublin, Instytut Jana Pawła II KUL since 1988-

Gilson-Böhner-E. Gilson, P. Böhner Die Geschichte der christlichen Philosophe von ihren Anfängen bis Nikolaus von Cuez, Padderborn 1953 (Historia filozofii chrześcijańskiej. Tłum. S. Zalewski. Instytut Wydawniczy Pax. Warszawa 1987).

HD -„Homo Dei." Przegląd ascetyczno-duszpasterski. Tuchów1932-39. Wrocław 1940-56. Warszawa 1957-

IJPR -„Journal of the Psychology of Religion."Philadelphia since 1991-

JBP -„Journal of Black Psychology."Thousand Oaks, CA since 1970-

JASP -„Journal of Abnormal and Social Psychology" (since 1975 „Journal of Abnormal Psychology"). Cambridge 1906-

JCCP -„Journal of Consulting and Clinical Psychology "(since 1969 „Journal of Consulting Psychology "). Washington since 1937-

JHP -„Journal of Psychology" Thousand Oaks, CA since 1961-

JSI -„Journal of Social Issues. Worchester since 1945-

JSP -„Journal of Social Psychology." Provincetown (Mass.) since 1930-

JME - „Journal of Moral Education." London since1971 –

JP -„Journal of Psychology." Provincetown (Mass.) since 1935/36-

JPe -„Journal of Personality." Hoboken, NJ since 1932-

JPSP -„Journal of Personal and Social Psychology." Wash. since 1965-

LJM -„Lancet Journal of Medicine." London, since 1823-

OsRom -„L'Osservtore Romano." Citta Vaticano since 1980-

OŚDP -Paul VI, John Paul II. Orędzia Red. K. Cywińska, T. Konopka, M. Radwan. Rzym-Lublin: RW KUL 1987.

PCh -„Pedagogia Christiana." Toruń UMK since 1997-

PaPs -„Pastoral Psychology." New York since 1950-

PEF -„Powszechna Encyklopedia Filozofii." Lub. Szkoła Filozoficzna. Red. Nauk. A. Maryniarczyk. Lublin 2000-

PsB - „Psychological Bulletin" Columbus (Ohio) 1904-40

PSRev -„Psychological Review." Washington od1894-

PST - The Old Testament. Red. S. Łach. Poznań 1961-

POQ - „Public Opinion Quarterly." Oxford since 1937-

RelEd -„Religious Education." The official Journal of the Religious Education Association. Chicago 1906/07-

RT -„Roczniki Teologiczne." Lublin since 1953 T N KUL

SG -„Studia Gnesnensia," Gniezno since 1975-

S. Th. -Sancti Thomas Aquinas. Summa Theologica 1939 (Suma Teologiczna I-III, T. I- XXXIV London 1962-86).

STV -Studia Theologica Varsaviensia. Warszawa 1963-

WDr -„W drodze". Miesięcznik , Poznań 1973-

ZNKUL -„Zeszyty Naukowe KUL," Lublin od 1958-

Biblical abbreviations and quotes come from the King James online Bible

BIBLIOGRAPHY

I. SOURCES

Adamski F.: *Rodzina między sakrum a profanum*. Poznań: Pallottinum 1987.

Adamski F.: *Poza kryzysem tożsamości*. Red. F. Adamski IN: W kierunku pedagogiki personalistycznej. Kraków: WNPA 1993

Adler M. J.: *The Time of Our Lives: The Ethics of Common Sense*. New York: Fordham University Press 1996.

Allport. W. G.: *Waiting for the Lord: 33 meditations on God and man*. New York: Macmillan 1928.

Allport. W. G.: *The study of personality by the intuitive method: An experiment in teaching from The Locomotive God*. JASP 24:1929 no 1 p. 14–27.

Allport. W. G.: *Studies in Expressive Movement*. New York: Macmillan Co. 1933 [Coauthor P. E. Vermon].

Allport. W. G.: *Personality: A Psychological Interpretation*. New York: H. Holt and Company 1937.

Allport. W. G.: *The Functional Autonomy of Motives*. AJPs 50:1937 nr 1/4, p. 141–156.

Allport. W. G.: *Presidential address*. Forty-seventh Annual Meeting of the American Psychological Association. PsBu 37:1940 nr 1 p. 1–28.

Allport. W. G.: *The Psychologist's Frame of Reference*. Boston: Harvard University 1940.

Allport. W. G.: *Motivation in personality: Reply to Mr. Bertocci*. PsRev 47:1940 no 6 p. 533–554.

Morale: American style. ChSM 26.04: 1941. No 1–2 p. 13-18.

Allport. W. G.: *Psychological service for civilian morale*. JCCP 5:1941 no 5 p. 235-239.

Allport. W. G.: *Defense seminars for morale study and morale building*. JSP15: 1942 no 2 p. 221-420.

Allport. W. G.: *The Ego in Contemporary Psychology*. PSRev 50:1943 no 5 p. 451–478.

Allport. W. G.: *Restoring morale in occupied territory*. POQ 7:1943 no 4 p. 606-617.

Allport. W. G.: *The Psychology of Participation*. PSRev 53:1945 no 3 p. 117–132.

Allport. W. G.: *A Secondary Principle of Learning*. PSRev 53: 1946 no 6 p. 335–347.

Allport. W. G.: *The Psychology of Rumor*. New York: Henry Holt 1947 [Coauthor L. Postman].

Allport. W. G.: *Scientific models and human morals*. PSRev 54:1947 no 4 p. 182–192.

Allport. W. G.: *The Nature of Personality*: Selected Papers. Reading: MA 1950.

Allport. W. G.: *How shall we evaluate teaching?* IN: *A Handbook for College Teachers*. Red. B. B. Cronkhile. Cambridge: MA 1950³ p. 82-98.

Allport. W. G.: *The Individual and His Religion, A Psychological Interpretation*. New York: The Macmillian Comp 1950.

Allport. W. G.: *The Role of Expectation.* IN: *Tension that Cause Wars.* Red. H. Cantril. Urbana: University of Illinois Press 1950 p. 70- 92.

Allport. W. G.: *The Use of Personal Documents in Psychological Science.* New York: Social Science Research Council 1951 p. 19-210.

Allport. W. G.: *An Experiment in the Prevention of Delinquency: The Cambridge-Somerville Youth Study.* New York: Columbia University Press 1951 [Coauthor: E. Powers, H. Witmer].

Allport. W. G.: *Basic principles in improving human relations.* Red. KW Bieglow IN: *Cultural Groups and Human Relations.* Oxford UK: Bur 1951 p. 8–28.

Allport. W. G.: *The mature personality.* PaPs 3:1952 no 4 p. 19–24.

Allport. W. G.: Forms and *Techniques of Altruistic and Spiritual Growth.* Red. P. A. Sorokin. Boston: Beacon Press 1954 p. 230-258.

Allport. W. G.: Motivation *in Personality: Reply to Mr. Bertocci.* IN: *The Study of Personality*: A Book of Readings. Red. H. Brand. Boston: John Wiley & Sons 1954 p. 83–99.

Allport. W. G.: *The Nature of Prejudice.* Cambridge: Addison Wesley 1955.

Allport. W. G.: *Normative Compatibility in the Light of Social Science.* Rel Ed 53: 1958 no 1 p 62-68.

Allport. W. G.: *The Nature of Prejudice.* Garden City NY: Anchor Books 1958.

Allport. W. G.: *Personality and Social Encounter.* Boston: Beacon Press1960.

Allport. W. G.: *Pattern and Growth in Personality.* Boston: Beacon 1961.

Allport. W. G.: *Youth's outlook on the future; a cross-national study.* New York: Garden City 1955 [co-author: J. Gillespie].

Allport. W. G.: *Personal religious orientation and prejudice.* JPSP 5: 1967 no 4 p. 432–443.

Allport. W. G.: *The Person in Psychology: Selected Essays.* Boston: Beacon Press 1968.

Allport. W. G.: *The religious context of prejudice.* IN: Personality and religion: the role of religion in personality development. Red. A. Sadler. New York 1970 p. 73–88.

Allport. W. G.: *Personality and Religion.* New York: Harper Forum Book 1970.

Allport. W. G.: *Becoming: Basic Considerations for a Psychology of Personality.* New Haven: Yale University Press 1983.

Allport. W. G.: *Osobowość i religia.* Tłum. H. Bartoszewicz, A. Bartkiewicz, I. Wyrzykowska. Warszawa: Pax 1988.

Allport F. H.:"Personality — *the Social Man".* Boston: Houghton Mifflin Company1924 p. 99-125.

Arends R. I.: *Uczymy się się nauczać.* Warszawa: Pax 1994.

ARYSTOTELES. *Etyka Nikomachejska.* IN: *ARYSTOTELES. Dzieła wszystkie.* T. 5. Tłum. D. Gromka. Wyd. Naukowe PWN. Warszawa 2000 p. 8–300.

Ashley B. M.: *Żyć prawdą w miłości. Biblijne wprowadzenie do teologii moralnej.* Trans. M Wójcik. Poznań: W drodze 2008.

Anderson J. H.: *The Role of Storytelling and Personal Narrative in Cognitive, Moral, and Oral Language Development.* Olimpia, WA: The Evergreen State College 2007.

Babik M.: *Rodzice, niezastąpieni wychowawcy – w poszukiwaniu optymalnego środowiska wychowawczego* IN: *Pedagogika wiary.* Red. A. Hajduk, J. Mółka. Kraków: WAM 2007.

Bagrowicz J.: *Edukacja religijna współczesnej młodzieży.* Toruń: Wydawnictwo: UMK 2000.

Bajda J.: *Sumienie i osoba a autorytet Magisterium.* IN: Jan Paweł II. *Veritatis splendor.* Tekst i komentarze. Red. A. Szostek Lublin: TN KUL1995 p. 197-205.

Banks S.: *The Ethical Practitioner in Formation: Issues of Courage, Competence and Commitment.* „Social Work Education". 24: 2005 no 7 p. 737–753.

Bartnik Cz. S.: *Personalizm teologiczny według Kardynała Karola Wojtyły.* ZN KUL. 1979 no 1–3 p. 52–53.

Bartnik Cz. S.: *Hermeneutyka personalistyczna.* Lublin: Polihymnia 1994.

Bartnik Cz. S.: *Historia i myśl.* Lublin: Pracownia Poligraficzna PKLO 1995.

Bazylak J.: Postawy religijne młodzieży i ich związki z wybranymi elementami osobowości. Warszawa: ATK 1984.

Beaty M.: *The Schooled Heart: Moral Formation in American Higher* Education. Waco TX: Baylor University Press 2007 [Co-author D. Henry].

Bednarski F.: *Wychowanie młodzieży dorastającej.* Warszawa: Oficyna Wydawnicza 2000.

Bischof J.: *Interpreting Personalities Theories.* New York: Harper & Row 1970.

Blosser. P.: *Scheler's Critique of Kant's Ethics.* Athens Ohio: Ohio University Press1995.

Bołoz W.: *Eklezjalne aspekty moralności chrześcijańskiej.* Kraków: Wydawnictwo ITKM 1992.

Boros L.: *Okresy życia.* Warszawa: Pax 1980.

Bonhoeffer D.: *Ethics.* New York: Macmillian.1955.

Bowman J. S.: *The Cambridge Dictionary of American Biography.* Cambridge: University Press1995.

Bramorski J.: *Wyzwalająca moc pokuty chrześcijańskiej.* Pelplin: Bernardinum 2004.

Braun-Gałkowska M.: *Psychologiczna analiza systemów rodziny.* Lublin: TN KUL 1992.

Braun-Gałkowska M.: *Środowisko wychowawcze: dom, szkoła, grupa rówieśnicza, parafia.* IN:J. Krucina. *Katecheza w szkole.* Wrocław: Kuria Metropolitalna Wrocławika 1992 p.54-62.

Brown D.: The Poor Belong to Us: Catholic Charities and American Welfare. Cambridge: Harvard University Press 1997.

Brezinka W.: *Socialization and Education: Essays in Conceptual Criticism*, Transl. J. S. Brice. Westport: Greenwood Press 1994.

Buttiglione R.: *Etyka w kryzysie*. Tłum. K. Borowczyk. Lublin: TN KUL. Instytut Jana Pawła II 1994.

Burns R. B.: *The Self Concept in Theory, Measurement, Development and Behavior*. New York: Hillsdale 1975.

Cencini A. Manenti A.: *Psychologia a formacja*. Kraków: WAM 2002.

Chlewiński Z.: *Dojrzałość, osobowość, sumienie, religijność*. Poznań: Wyd. „W drodze"1991.

Chlewiński Z.: *Search for Maturity: Personality, Conscience, Religion*. New York: Peter Lang Publishing 1998.

Chrobak S.: *Koncepcja Wychowania Personalistycznego w nauczaniu Karola Wojtyły –* Jana Pawła II. Warszawa: Wydawnictwo Salezjańskie 1999

Clapton M.: *Social Change and Urban Growth in England and the USA*. New York: Berg. 2003.

Conroy W.: *G. W. Allport.* — IN: *Biographical dictionary of psychology*. Red. N. Sheehy, A. J. Chapman. New York, NY: 1997 p. 9-11.

Craik K.: *50 Years of Personality Psychology*. New York: Plenum Press1993.

Curran C.: *Catholic Moral Theology in the United States: A History*. Washington DC: Georgetown University Press 2008.

Czajkowski K. *Wychowanie do rekreacji*. Warszawa: Wydawnictwa Szkolne i Pedagogiczne 1979.

Dąbrowski K.: *Dezintegracja pozytywna*. Warszawa: Państwowy Instytut Wydawniczy 1979.

Damon W. The Youth Charter: towards the Formation of Adolescent Moral Identity. JME 26: 1997 no 2 p. 117–130.

Derdziuk A.: *Formacja do modlitwy*. HD 63: 1993 nr 4 p. 24–34.

Derdziuk A.: *Formacyjny wymiar modlitwy uwielbienia*. IN: *Modlitwa uwielbienia*. T 5. *Homo orans*. Red. J. Misiurek. Lublin: Wyd. KUL 2004 p. 279-288.

Derdziuk A.: *Formacja formatorów*. „Życie Konsekrowane" 13: 2005 no 1 (51) p. 91.

Derdziuk A.: *Formacja moralna a formacja sumienia* IN: *Formacja moralna, formacja sumienia*. Red. J. Nagórny, T. Zadykowicz. Lublin: Wydawnictwo KUL 2006 p. 13–33.

Derdziuk A.: Wychowawcza rola rodziny w rozpoznawaniu powołania. IN: *Wychowanie w rodzinie chrześcijańskiej. Przesłanie moralne Kościoła*. Red. K. Jeżyna, T. Zadykowicz. Lublin 2008 p. 153-166.

Derdziuk A.: *Moralny wymiar przyrzeczeń pierwszokomunijnych IN: O wielkich postanowieniach małego dziecka. Profilaktyczne aspekty formajci rodziców i dzieci do I Komunii Świętej*. Red. P. Kulbacki. Warszawa 2009 p. 21-54.

Derdziuk A.: *W odpowiedzi na dar miłosierdzia*. Lublin: Wydawnictwo Gaudium 2010.

Derdziuk A.: *W odpowiedzi na dar młodości*. Lublin: Wydawnictwo Gaudium 2010.

Derdziuk A.: *Spowiedź kobiet*. Lublin: Gaudium 2010.

Derdziuk A.: *Teologia moralna w służbie wiary Kościoła*. Lublin: Wyd. KUL 2010.

Derdziuk A: *Solidarność jako cnota społeczna*. „Roczniki Teologii Moralnej" T. 4(59) Lublin: TN KUL JP II 2012 p. 19-21.

Dłubacz W.: *Pedagogika katolicka? Uwagi filozofa*. „Pedagogika Katolicka" 1: 2007 no 1 p. 52–54.

Dovido J. F.: *On the nature of prejudice: Fifty years after Allport*. New York: Psychology Press 2006.

Dyrek K.: *Powołanie, rozeznanie i rozwój aspekt psychologiczny*. Kraków: Wydawnictwo M 1993.

Dziekoński S.: *Formacja chrześcijańska dziecka w rodzinie w nauczaniu Kościoła od Leona Wielkiego do Jana Pawła II*. Warszawa: Wydawnictwo UKSW 2006.

Dziekoński S.: *Wychowanie w nauczaniu Kościoła*.Warszawa: Wydawnictwo UKSW 2000.

Dziewiecki M.: *Kształtowanie postaw*. Radom: „Ave" 1997.

Dziewiecki M.: Cielesność, płciowość, seksualność. Kielce: Wydawnictwo „Jedność" 2000.

Dziewiecki M.: Osoba i wychowanie. Pedagogika personalistyczna w praktyce. Kraków: wyd. Rubikon 2003.

Dziewiecki M.: *Kochać i wymagać*. Kraków: Edycje św. Pawła 2006.

Elliot J.: *Moral & Values Education*. JME 32: 2003 no 1 p. 67–76.

Erikson E. H.: *Childhood and Society*. New York: Norton & Company 1963.

Evans R I.: *Gordon Allport: The Man and His Ideas*. New York E. P. Dutton 1970.

Feist J.: *Theories of Personality*. Chicago: Holt 1990.

Flannery A.: *Decreeon The Training of Priests IN: Vatican Council II: The Conciliar and Post Conciliar Documents,* Optatum Totius nr 16. Dublin. 1981 p.719.

Flower J.: *Stages of faith*. San Francisco: Harper 1995.

Forrester B.: *Moral Formation and Liturgy*. ER 49:1997 no 3 p. 375–379.

Freud S.: *Moses and Monotheism*. Tłum. K. Jones. New York: Vintage Books 1967.

Frick W. B.: *Personality Theories: Journey Into Self*. New York and London: Teachers College Press 1984.

Fuchs J.: *Human Values and Christian Morality*. London: Gill & Macmilla 1970.

Fuller A. R.: *Psychology and Religion*. London: Routledge 1994.

Gaines S.: *Two social psychologies of prejudice: Gordon W. Allport, W. E. B. Du Bois, and the legacy of Booker T*. JBP 20: 1994 no 1 p. 8-28.

Gaillard G.: The Routledge *Dictionary of Anthropologists*. New York Routledge 2003.

Galarowicz J.: *Spór o człowieka a personalizm Karola Wojtyły* IN: *Servo Veritatis*, Materiały Międzynarodowej Konferencji dla uczczenia 25-lecia pontyfikatu Jego Świątobliwości Jana Pawła II, Uniwersytet Jagielloński 9-11 października 2003 r. Red. S. Koperek, S. Szczur Kraków:Wyd. Nauk. PAT 2003 p. 389–404.

Gała A.: *Uwarunkowania wychowawcze* dojrzałości moralnej. Lublin: Oficyna Wydawnicza „Lew" 1992.

Gerkin Ch.: *An Introduction to Pastoral Care.* Nashville TN: Abingdon Press, 1997.

Gifford R.: Inventing Personality: Gordon Allport and the Science of Selfhood. Canadian Psychology 45 2004 no 3 p. 187-188.

Gilligan C.: *In a Different Voice: Psychological Theory and Women's Development* Cambridge: Harvard Press1993.

Gilson E.: *Historia filozofii chrześcijańskiej.* Tłum. S. Zalewski. Warszawa: Instytut Wydawniczy Pax 1987.

Gocko J., Sadowski R..: *Wychowanie w służbie praw człowieka.* Warszawa. Towarzystwo Naukowe Franciszka Salezego 2008.[1]

Goldberg M.: *An Interview with Carol Gilligan.* Restoring Lost Voices. „Phi Delta Kappan" 81: 2000 no 9 p. 701-704.

Graham D.: *Moral learning and development* New York: Wiley 1972.

Granat W.: *Personalizm chrześcijański. Teologia osoby ludzkiej.* Poznań: Księgarnia św. Wojciecha 1985.

Gubała W.: Wychowanie moralne młodzieży IN: Teoretyczne założenia katechezy młodzieżowej. Red. R. Murawski. Warszawa 1989 p. 201–211.

Gula R.: *Making Disciples: A Handbook of Christian Moral Formation,* „Theological Studies". 60: 1999 no 2 p. 394.

Gurycka A.: *Struktura i dynamika procesu wychowawczego. Analiza psychologiczna* Warszawa:PWN 1979.

Haring B.: *Free and Faithful in Christ: Moral Theology for Priest and Laity.* T 2: The Truth Will Set You Free. Slough: St. Paul Publications Middle green 1979.

Harris T.: *W zgodzie z sobą i z tobą.* Warszawa: PAX 1979.

Hionides H.: *Greek Dictionary.* Glasgow:Harper Collins 1997.[2]

Hjelle L.: *Personality Theories.* New York: McGraw-Hill Book Company 1992.

Izdebska J.: *Mass media i multimedia – dominująca przestrzeń życia dziecka* IN: *Pedagogika społeczna.* T. 2. Red. E. Murynowicz-Hetka. Poznań: Wydawnictwo Naukowe PWN 2007 p. 518-533.

Jeżyna K.: *Formacja religijno-duchowa w Akcji Katolickiej w okresie II Rzeczypospolitej* IN: *Świeccy w akcji.* Red.W. Słomka: Lublin : Wydawnictwo KUL 1996. p. 127–132.

Jeżyna K.: *Moralne przesłanie nowej ewangelizacji.* Lublin: Wyd. KUL 2002.

Jeżyna K.: *Eklezjalny charakter moralności chrześcijańskiej* IN: ENM p. 163–169.

Jeżyna K.: *Wychowanie istotnym przesłaniem nowej ewangelizacji.* IN: Formacja moralna – formacja sumienia. Red. T. Zadykowicz, J. Nagórny. Lublin: Wydawnictwo KUL 2006 p.153-171.

Jeżyna K.: *Sakramentalny charakter życia moralnego.* IN: „Roczniki Teologii Moralnej" T. 2(57) Lublin: TN KUL JP II 2010 p. 5-13.

Just A.: *Osobotwórcza funkcja religi.* „Studia Theologica Varsaviensia" 13: 1975 no 1 p. 157-182.

Kahoe R.: *The Development of Intrinsic and Extrinsic Religious Orientations.* „Journal for the Scientific Study of Religion" 24: 1985 no 4 p. 408–412.

Kamiński T.: *Parafia wobec problemów społecznych,* „Chrześcijanin w Świecie" 2:1997 no 1 p. 96-111.

Katz D. *Floyd H. Allport (1890-1978).* "American Psychologist" 34:1979 no 4 (351–353).

Katz D.: *Portraits of Pioneers in Psychology.* APA 1998 no 111. p. 120–142.

Kazdin A.: *Encyclopedia of Psychology.* Oxford: University Press 2000[1] p. 223.

Kegan R.: *In Over Our Heads: The Mental Demands of Modern Life.* Cambridge: Harvard University Press 1994.

Kegan R.: *The Evolving Self.* Cambridge: Harvard University Press 1982.

Kiereś B.: *Wychowanie a wychowanek. Wspomaganie czy kształcenie* IN: *Wychować charakter.* Red. A. Piątkowska i K. Stępień Lublin: „Gaudium" KUL 2005 p. 92-133.

Kleinberger A.: *Philosophy of Education.* JME 11:1982 no 3 p. 147–158.

Kohlberg L.: *Education, Moral Development and Faith.* JME 4: 1974 no 1 p. 5–16.

Kohlberg L.: The Claim to Moral Adequacy of a Highest Stage of Moral Judgment.JPh70:1973 no 18 p. 630–646.

Kohlberg L.: *The Child as Moral Philosopher.* „Psychology Today" 2: 1968 no 4 p. 25–30.

Kowalewski M.: *Mały słownik teologiczny.* Poznań-Warszawa-Lublin: Księgarnia św. Wojciecha 1960.

Kraińska-Rogala I.: *Rodzina wspólnotą miłość.* Kraków: WAM 1999.

Krąpiec M. A.: *Świętość spełnieniem osoby.* IN: M. A. Krąpiec. *Człowiek – kultura – uniwersytet.* Lublin: TN KUL 1982 [Co-author Z. J. Zdybicka] p.59-74.

Krąpiec M. A.:*Odzyskać świat realny.* Lublin: TN KUL 1993.

Krąpiec M. A.: *Człowiek i prawo naturalne.* Lublin: Redakcja Wydawnictw Katolickiego Uniwersytetu Lubelskiego 1993.

Krąpiec M. A.: *Ludzka wolność i jej granice.* Lublin:Polskie Tow. Tomasza z Akwinu 2004.

Kukołowicz T.: *Budzenie zmysłu religijnego u dzieci w wychowaniu religijnym.* „Pedagogika Katolicka" nr 1. Lublin: KUL 2007 p. 55-56.

Kunowski S.: *Podstawy współczesnej pedagogiki.* Warszawa: Wydawnictwo Salezjańskie 1993.

Kwiatkowski.: *Formacja sumienia w kontekście sakramentu pokuty* IN: *Formacja Moralna - Formacja sumienia.* Red. T. Zadykowicz, J. Nagórny. Lublin: Wydawnictwo KUL 2006 p. 35–56.

Lang. D.: *The Penguin Companion to Classical Oriental and African Literature.* T 4.Red. M. D. Dudley. New York: McGraw-Hill Book Company 1969.

Lasch C.: *The Culture of Narcissism: American Life in an Age of Diminishing Expectations.* New York: W. W. Norton 1991.

Lindzey G.: *Gordon W. Allport.* IN: *A history of psychology in autobiography.* Red. C. A. Murchison. Worcester: Prentice Hall 1966[5] p. 1–25.

Łobocki M.: *Wychowanie moralne w zarysie.* Kraków: Impuls 2002.

Łobocki M.: *Altruizm a wychowanie.* Lublin: UMCS 1998.

Maddi R.: *Personality Theories: A Comperative Analysis.* New Jersey: Pacific Grove: Brooks/Cole Publishing Company 1989.

Majdański K.: *Zadania rodziny chrześcijańskiej: tworzenie wspólnoty osób i służba życiu. Refleksje nad pierwszymi dwoma rozdziałami III części Adhortacji Apostolskiej Jana Pawła II* „Familiaris consortio". AK 76: 1984 T 102 z. 449. p. 5-20.

Majka J.: *Etyka społeczna i polityczna.* Warszawa: Wyd. OdiSS 1993.

Majka J.: *Metodologia nauk teologicznych* Wrocław: Wydaw. Wrocławskiej Księgarni Archidiecezjalnej1981.

Majka J.: *Wychowanie chrześcijańskie – wychowaniem personalistycznym* IN: *Wychowanie personalistyczne.* Red. F. Adamski. Kraków: WAM 2005 p. 156–168.

Marek Z.: *Podstawy wychowania moralnego.* Kraków: Wydawnictwo WAM 2005.

Mariański J.:*Moralność w procesie przemian.* Warszawa 1991.

Mastalski J.: *Zarys teorii wychowania.* Kraków: PAT 2002.

Manuel P, C.: *The Catholic Church and the Nation-State: Comparative Perspectives.* Washington: Georgetown University Press. 2006.

Meeks W.: *The Origins of Christian Morality.* New Haven-London: Yale University Press 1993.

Mierzwiński B.: *Mężczyzna istota nieznana.* Warszawa: Oficyna Wydawniczo – Poligraficzna „Adam" 1999.

Migut B.: *Antropologia teologiczna w odpowiedzi na współczesne wyzwania wychowawcze* IN: *Kościół – naród – rodzina. Nauczanie Jana Pawła II w praktyce duszpasterskiej.* Red. B. Moguta, D. Capała. Lublin: Wyd KUL 2004 p. 187-204.

Mitek E. *Sympatyzowanie młodzieży z osobami zażywającymi narkotyki.* „Legnickie Studia Teologiczno-Historyczne" *PERSPECTIVA.* 3: 2004 no 2 p. 160-177.

Mitek E. *Dom rodzinny środowiskiem młodego pokolenia,* „Wrocławski Przegląd Teologiczny" 3: 2005 no 1 p. 95-117.

Mojek S.: *Formacja moralna* IN: ENM p. 205–209.

Mojek S.: *Formacja do czynnej miłości miłosiernej bliźniego w duszpsterstwie parafialnym.* RT 49: 2002 z. 3 p. 115-133.

Moskal P.: *Religia i Prawda.* Lublin: Wydawnictwo KUL 2008.

Mroczkowski I.: *Odpowiedzialność świeckich za odnowę Kościoła w Polsce.*IN: *Ewangelizacja w tajemnicy i misji Kościoła. Program duszpasterski na rok 1994/1995.* Katowice: Red. Wydział Duszpasterstwa Kurii Metropolitalnej1994 p. 281.

Mu, Shou-kuan.: *The relationship between virtues and personality traits of Chinese college students.* „Social Behavior and Personality: an international journal." 39: 2011 no 10 p. 1379-1386.

Muszyński H.: *Wychowanie moralne w zespole.* Warszawa: PZWS 1964.

Nagórny J.: „Opcja fundamentalna w praktyce życia chrześcijańskiego" IN: *Veritatis splendor. Przesłanie moralne Kościoła.* Materiały z sympozjum KUL 6-7 grudnia 1993 r. Red. B. Jurczyk. Lublin: RW KUL 1994 p.75-98.

Nagórny J.: *Formacja chrześcijańskiego sumienia małżonków w perspektywie sakramentu pokuty i pojednania* IN: Małżeństwo – przymierze miłość. Red. J. Misurek i W. Słomka. [Homo meditans t. 15] Lublin: RW KUL 1995 p. 101–127.

Nagórny J.: *Posłannictwo chrześcijan w świecie.* Lublin: Wydawnictwo KUL 1998.

Nagórny J.: *Wychowanie do dojrzałej miłości IN: Najważniejsza jest miłość. Księga pamiątkowa ku czci Księdza Profesora Waleriana Słomki.* Red. M. Chmielewski. Lublin: RW KUL 1999 p. 389–415.

Nagórny J.: *Istota odpowiedzialnego rodzicielstwa. Refleksja teologa moralisty w 25. rocznicę ogłoszenia encykliki* „Humae vitae". IN: Odpowiedzialni za życie i miłość. Materiały z sesji naukowej zorganizowanej przez Duszpasterstwo Rodzin Diecezji Bielsko-Żywieckiej. Red. E. Burzyk. Bielsko-Biała: Wydaw. Wydz. Duszp. Kurii 1996 p. 43–44.

Nagórny J.: *Sumienie, źródło wolności czy zniewolenia?* IN: *Człowiek sumienia.* Red. J. Guzowski. Olsztyn 1997.

Nagórny J.: *Wychowanie do wolności w świetle nauczania Prymasa Wyszyńskiego* IN: *Formacja moralna – formacja sumienia.* Red. J. Nagórny, T. Zadykowicz. Lublin: Wydawnictwo KUL 2006. p.105-127.

Nagórny J.: *Formacja moralna – formacja sumienia.* Red. J. Nagórny, T. Zadykowicz. Lublin: Wydawnictwo KUL 2006 p. 5-12.

Narvaez D.: *Teaching Moral Character: Two Alternatives for Teacher Education,* „The Teacher Educator" 43: 2008 no 2 p. 156–172.

Nicholas M.: *The Lost Art of Listening.* New York: The Guilford Press 1995.

Nicholson I.: *To correlate psychology and social ethics: Gordon Allport and the first course in American personality psychology.* JPe 65: 1997 no 1 p. 733–742.

Nowak M.: *Podstawy pedagogiki otwartej.* Lublin: RW KUL1999.

Nowosad S.: *Prawda człowieka –prawda jego działania.* IN: *Antropologia teologiczno moralna. Koncepcje – kontrowersje – inspiracje.* Red. I. Mroczkowski, J. Sobkowiak. Warszawa 2008.

O'Connell T.: *Making Disciples: A Handbook of Christian Moral Formation.* New York: Crossroad 1998.

Olbrycht K.: *Dylematy współczesnego wychowania.* „Znak" 43: 1991 no 9 (436) p. 41–44.

Opozda D.: *Charakter i specyfika wychowawczej funkcji rodziny* IN: *Wychowanie w rodzinie chrześcijańskiej. Przesłanie moralne* Kościoła. Red. K. Jeżyna, T. Zadykowicz. Lublin: Wydawnictwo KUL p. 36-37.

Pettigrew T.: *Gordon Willard Allport: A Tribute.* JSI 55: 1999 no 3 p. 415-427.

Piaget J.: *The Moral Judgment of the Child.* London: Routledge & Kegan Paul 1932.

Piaget J.: *The Language and Thought of the Child.* New York: Hardcourt and Brace Corp. 1932.

Piaget J.: Play, *Dreams and Imitation in Childhood.* New York: Norton 1964.

Piaget J.: *The Moral Judgment of the Child.* London: Free Press 1965.

Piaget J.: *The origins of Intellect Piaget's Theory.* San Francisco: W. Freeman 1969.

Piaget J. *The Child's Conception of the World.* Cambridge: Harvard University Press 1987.

Pilich M. *Ustawa o systemie oświaty.* Komentarz. Warszawa: ABC 2012⁴.

Płużek Z .: *Psychologia pastoralna.* Kraków: Instytut Teologiczny Księży Misjonarzy 1991.

Pogonowski I.: *Poland: An Illustrated History.* New York: Hippocrene 2000.

Pokrywka M.: *Osoba, uczestnictwo, wspólnota. Refleksje nad nauczaniem społecznym Jana Pawła II.* Lublin: RW KUL 2000.

Pokrywka M.: *Wezwanie do formacji sumienia w świetle nauczania Jana Pawła II.* RT 48: 2001 z. 3 p. 53–68.

Pokrywka M.: *Rola sakramentu pokuty w formacji sumienia.* RT 50: 2003 z. 3 p. 55-68.

Pokrywka M.: *Stosunki pozamałżeńskie, dar czy przywłaszczenie?* IN: *Płciowość ludzka w kontekście miłości. Przesłanie moralne Kościoła.* Red. J. Nagórny, M. Pokrywka. Lublin: Wydawnictwo KUL 2005 p. 165-191.

Pokrywka M.: *Posłannictwo uniwersytetu w integralnej formacji człowieka* IN: *Formacja moralna – formacja sumienia.* Red. J. Nagórny, T. Zadykowicz. Lublin: Wydawnictwo KUL 2006 p. 171-191.

Pokrywka M.: *Rola wstydu w obronie godności osoby ludzkiej.* RT 55:2008 z. 3. p. 139-152.

Pokrywka M.: *Antropologiczne podstawy moralności małżeństwa i rodziny.* Lublin: Wydawnictwo KUL 2010.

Pokrywka M.: *Człowiek i moralność w postmodernistycznym świecie.* RTM 3(58):2011 p. 79-93.

Poznańska M.: *Tożsamość jako element kultury pedagogicznej współczesnego wychowawcy.* ED 2: 1995 no 1 p. 64–65.

Prężyna W. *Funkcja postawy religijnej w osobowości człowieka.* Lublin: RW KUL 1981.

Przybyło W.: „Formacja osoby powołanej jako istotny proces rozwoju psychiczno-duchowego człowieka." *PERSPECTIVA. Legnickie Studia Teologiczno-Historyczne.* 7: 2008 no 1 p. 158- 175.

Pincus F.: *Race and Ethnic Conflict: Contending Views on Prejudice, Discrimination, and Ethno violence.* Red. H. J. Ehrlich. Boulder CO: Westview Press 1999.

Rasmussen L.: *Moral community and moral formation.* ER 47:1995 no 1 p. 12-39.

Rogers C.: *A Basic Orientation for Counseling.* PaPs 1: 1950 no 1 p. 26-34.

Rogers C.: *Toward a Science of the Person.* JHP 3: 1963 no 1 p. 72–92.

Rogers C.: *On Becoming a Person.* Boston: Houghton Mifflin Co 1961.

Rusecki M. *Z zagadnień światopoglądu chrześcijańskiego.* Lublin: Towarzystwo Naukowe Katolickiego Uniwersytetu Lubelskiego 1989.

Rzepa W.: *Nawrócenie jako droga chrześcijańskiej formacji* IN: *Formacja moralna – formacja sumienia* Lublin: Wydawnictwo KUL 2006 p. 211-223.

Sheehy A.: *Biographical Dictionary of Psychology.* New York: Conroy Publisher New York 2002.

Sheehy N. *Fifty Key Thinkers in Psychology*. London: Routledge 2004.

Skinner. B. F.: *G. W. Allport*. IN: *A History of Psychology in Autobiography*. Red E. Boring and G. Lindzey. New York: Appleton-Centry-Crofts 1967[5] p.1-25.

Spilka B.: *Traits and Allport: Idiography in a Nomothetic Mold?* „International Journal for the Psychology of Religion".4: 1994 no 4 p. 235–237.

Sondej M. *Rozwój społeczny młodzieży*. IN: *Teoretyczne założenia katechezy młodzieżowej*. Red. R. Murawski. Warszawa: Wyd. Salezjańskie 1989 p. 38-48.

Spranger E.: *Types of Man: The Psychology and Ethics of Personality*. Halle (Saale): M. Niemeyer 1928.

Stanibula, K.: *The role of faith in the moral personality development*. Lublin Licenciat: KUL library: 2010.

Stanibula, K.: *Formacja ku dojrzałości integralnej*. Lublin: Gaudium 2016.

Suska M.: *Tożsamość a system wartości i postawy współczesnej młodzieży* IN: *Tożsamość osobowa a tożsamości społeczne. Wyzwania dla edukacji XXI wieku*. Red. T. Bajkowski. Trans. K. Sawicki. Białystok: Humana 2001 p. 38-44

Szostek A.: *Wokół godności, prawdy i miłości*. Lublin: RW KUL 1995.

Thomas Aquinas: Contemporary Philosophical Perspectives. Red. B. Davies. New York: Oxford University Press 2002.

Thompson M.: *Teach Yourself Ethics*. Blacklick OH: The McGraw Comp 2006.

Tkocz E.: *Chrześcijańska formacja młodzieży w świetle orędzi Jana Pawła II na Światowe Dni Młodzieży*. Katowice: Księgarnia św. Jacka 2005.

Tracey D.: *The Foundations of Practical Theology*. IN: *Practical theology*. Red. D. Browning. San Franciso: Harper & Row Publishers 1983 p. 61-82.

Tyrała P.: *Bliżej uniwersalnych wartości i realnego życia*. Toruń: Wydaw. A. Marszałek 2001.

Uchnast Z. *Psychologiczne aspekty dojrzałości religijnej*. Częstochowa: Częstochowskie Studia Teologiczne III 1975.

Urbański S.: *Duchowość wychowania w nauczaniu Jana Pawła II*. IN: Jan Paweł II – Mistrz duchowy. Red. M. Chmielewski Homo Meditans.Lublin: TN KUL 2006 p. 127-138.

Walesa Cz.: *Rozwój religijności dziecka*. Lublin: Wydawnictwo KUL 2005.

Watson G. *The nature of democratic morale*. IN: *Civilian Morale*. Red. G. Watson. Boston: Houghton Mifflin Company 1942 p. 3-19.

Wanat S.: *Sumienie* IN: ENM p. 511–517.

Wheelock F: *Wheelock's Latin*. New York: Harper 1995.

Wilson J.: *Personality in the Social Process*. Hillsdale: Lawrence ErlbaumAssociates 1985.

Wielgus S.: *Pedagogia i formacja młodzieży*. „Pedagogika Katolicka" 1: 2007 no 1 p. 11–22.

Winter D.: *Allport's life and Allport's Psychology*. JPe 65 :1997 no 3 p. 723–731.

Witek S. *Duszpasterstwo w konfesionale*. Poznań: Pallottinum 1988.

Wójcik M.: *Specyfika ludzkiej płciowości* IN: *Człowiek. Osoba. Płeć*. Red. M. Wójcik Łomianki: Fundacja „Pomoc Rodzinie". 1998 p. 111-117.

Wojtyła K.:*Rodzina jako communio personarum*. AK 66:1974 T. 83 z 3 p. 347-361.

Wojtyła K.: *Miłość i odpowiedzialność*. T 4. Lublin: Wydawnictwo KUL: 1986.
Wojtyła K. *Osoba: podmiot i wspólnota*. IN: Tenże. *Osoba i czyn oraz inne studia antropologiczne*. Lublin: Instytut Jana Pawła II KUL 2000 p. 371-414.
Woźniak. H.: *Floyd Henry Allport and the Social Psychology* London: Routledge/ Thoemmes Press 1994.
Wróbel J.: *Antropologia ludzkiej płciowości: powołanie do życia w komunii prawdy i miłości*. IN: *Ocalić obraz człowieka. Antropologiczne podstawy moralności*. Red. Ks. P. Morciniec. Opole: Redakcja Wydziału Teologicznego Uniwersytetu Opolskiego 2003 p.87-101.
Zadykowicz T.: *Formacyjna rola mediów* IN: *Formacja moralna – formacja sumienia* Red. J. Nagórny, T. Zadykowicz. Lublin: Wyd. KUL 2006 p. 193–210.
Zadykowicz T.: *Sequela Christi et imitation hominis. Paradygmat naśladowania we współczesnej refleksji teologicznomoralnej*. Źródła i perspektywy. Lublin: Wydawnictwo KUL 2011.
Zając M.: *O wielkich przygotowaniach małego dziecka* IN: *O wielkich przygotowaniach małego dziecka do I Komunii św*. Warszawa: Parpamedia 2009 p. 11-21
Zigler R.: *The Formation and Transformation of Moral Impulse*. JME 28: 1999 no 4 p. 445–457.
Zadroga A.: *Wpływ postmodernizmu na postawy religijne* IN: *Formacja moralna – formacja sumienia*. Red. J. Nagórny T. Zadykowicz. Lublin: Wydawnictwo KUL 2006 p. 245–256.
Zadroga A.: *Współczesne ujęcie etyki pracy w Polsce. Próba oceny z perspektywy teologii moralnej*. Lublin: Wydawnictwo KUL 2009.

2. OTHER SOURCES
Catholic Church - Documents

Vatican II. Dogmatic Constitution *Lumen gentium*. IN: Sobór Watykański II. *Konstytucje, Dekrety, Deklaracje*. Tekst polski – nowe tłumaczenie Poznań: Pallottinum 2002 p. 104-166.
Vatican II. Dogmatic Constitution *Dei Verbum*. IN: Sobór Watykański II. *Konstytucje, Dekrety, Deklaracje* p. 350-363.
Vatican II. Dogmatic Constitution *Gaudium et* spes IN: Sobór Watykański II. *Konstytucje, Dekrety, Deklaracje* p. 526–606.
Vatican II. Dekret o formacji kapłańskiej *Optatam totius* IN: Sobór Watykański II. *Konstytucje, Dekrety, Deklaracje* p. 288-301.
Vatican II. Dekret o środkach społecznego przekazu *Intermirifica*. IN: Sobór Watykański II. *Konstytucje, Dekrety, Deklaracje* p. 87-95.
Vatican II. Deklaracja o wychowaniu chrześcijańskim *Gravissimum educationis*. IN: Sobór Watykański II. *Konstytucje, Dekrety, Deklaracje* p. 314–324.
Vatican II Dekret o Apostolstwie Świeckich *Apostolicam actuositatem*. IN: Sobór Watykański II. *Konstytucje, Dekrety, Deklaracje* p. 377-401.
Vatican II. Deklaracja o wolności religijnej *Dignitatis humane*. IN: Sobór Watykański II. *Konstytucje, Dekrety, Deklaracje* p. 410-421.

Pius XI. Encyclical *Divini illius magistri.* Vatican (31.12.1929).

Pius XII. Apostolic Constitution *Sedes Sapientiae.* Vatican (31.05.1956).

Paul VI. Encyclical *Humanae vitae.* Vatican (25.07.1968).

Paul VI. Instruction *Matrimonii Sacramentum.* Vatican (18.03.1966).

Paul VI. Apostolic Adhortation *Evangelii nuntiandi.* Vatican (8.12.1975).

Paul VI. Orędzie na III Światowy Dzień Pokoju *Samowychowanie do pokoju poprzez pojednanie* IN: Paul VI, Jan Paweł II. *Orędzia papieskie na Światowy Dzień Pokoju.* Red. K. Cywińska, T. Konopka, M. Radwan. Rzym-Lublin: RW KUL 1987 p. 45-46.

Paul VI. Orędzie na X Światowy Dzień Pokoju. *Jeśli chcesz pokoju, broń życia.* Watykan. (01.01.1977).

John Paul II

Encyclical *Redemptor hominis.* Vatican (4.03.1979).

Encyclical *Dives in misericordia.* Vatican (30.11.1980).

Encyclical *Laborem exercens.* Vatican (14.09.1981).

Encyclical *Redemptoris Mater.* Vatican (07.06.1987).

Encyclical *Sollicitudo rei socialis.* Vatican (30.12.1987).

Encyclical *Centesimus annus.* Vatican (1.05.1991).

Encyclical *Veritatis splendor.* Vatican (6.08.1993).

Encyclical *Evangelium vitae.* Vatican (25.03.1995).

Encyclical *Fides et ratio.* Vatican (14.09.1998).

Encyclical *Ecclesia de Eucharystia.* Vatican (17.04.2003).

Apostolic Adhortation *Catechesi tradendae.* Vatican (16.10.1979).

Apostolic Adhortation *Familiaris consortio.* Vatican (22.11.1981).

Adhortation *Reconciliatio et paenitentia.* Vatican (2.12.1984).

Apostolic Adhortation *Christifideles laici.* Vatican (30.12.1998).

Apostolic Adhortation *Pastores dabo vobis.* Vatican (25.03.1992).

Apostolic Adhortation *Vita Consecrata.* Vatican (25.03.1996).

Letter to the Young *Parati semper.* Vatican (31.03.1985).

Apostolic Letter *Mulieris dignitatem.* Vatican (15.10.1988).

Letter to the Families *Gratissimam sane.* Vatican (2.02.1994).

Apostolic Letter *Tertio millennio adventate.* Vatican (10.11.1994).

Orędzie na XIII Światowy Dzień Środków Społecznego Przekazu „Środki społecznego przekazu w służbie ochrony i rozwoju dziecka w rodzinie i w społeczeństwie". Watykan (23.05.1979). IN: Orędzia Papieskie na światowe dni komunikacji społecznej 1967-2002. Red. M. Lis. Częstochowa: Edycje św. Pawła p. 83-89.

Orędzie Na XIV Światowy Dzień Pokoju. „Chcesz Służyć Sprawie Pokoju. Szanuj Wolność!" Vatican (8.12.1980).

Orędzie na XXXIV Światowy Dzień Pokoju. „Dialog między kulturami drogą do cywilizacji miłości i pokoju". Vatican (8.12.2000). IN: International Journal of Humanities and Peace.17: 2001 no 1 p. 4.

Wolność, współdziałanie, uniwersalność, służba człowiekowi – warunkami prawdziwego rozwoju kultury. Madryt (3.11.1982). IN: *Wiara i kultura. Dokumenty, przemówienia, homilie.* Red. M. Radwański. Fundacja Jana Pawła II. Polski Instytut Kultury Chrześcijańskiej. Rzym– Lublin1988 p. 162–163.

Przemówienie. *Jesteście tymi, którzy maja kształtować ludzi wolnych. Do nauczycieli i wychowawców.* Vatican (04.03.1983). OsRomPol. 4:1983 nr 3 p. 27.

Przemówienie. *Szkoła i parafia – dwa „warsztaty" pracy.* Watykan (5.03.1980). IN: *Dziecko w nauczaniu Jana Pawła II. Antologia wypowiedzi.* Red. C. Drążek, J. Kawecki. Kraków: WAM 1985 p. 121–123.

Audiencja dla uczestników kongresu bioetyki (Rzym 17.02.1996). IN: *Uniwersytety w nauczaniu Jana Pawła II.* Red. Warszawa 1999 p. 198–204.

Mężczyzną i niewiastą stworzył ich. Chrystus odwołuje się do „początku". O Jana Pawła II teologii ciała. Red. T. Styczeń. Lublin: RW KUL 1981.

Mężczyzną i niewiastą stworzył ich. Odkupienie ciała a sakramentalność małżeństwa. LEV. Watykan 1986.

Przekroczyć próg nadziei. Lublin: RW KUL 1994.

Benedict XVI. Encyclical *Spe salvi.* Vatican (30.11.2007).

Benedict XVI. Encyclical *Deus caritas est.* Vatican (25.12.2005).

Benedict XVI. Apostolic Adhortation *Sacramentum Caritatis.* Vatican (13.03.2007).

Benedict XVI. *Przesłanie Benedykta XVI do polskich biskupów podczas wizyty ad limina Apostolorum* (Watykan (28.11.2005) IN: „Pedagogika Katolicka" nr 1a. Lublin 2007.

Benedict XVI. Przemówienie podczas spotkania z duchowieństwem w archikatedrze św. Jana. OsRomPol 25:2006 no 6-7 p.15.

Francis. Apostolic Adhortation *Ewangelii gaudium.* Vatican (24.11.2013).

Francis. Przemówienie do księży, „Kościół wzrasta dzięki atrakcyjności świadectwa" (Asyż 4.11.2013). OsRomPol 11:2013 no 11 p. 14.

Kongregacja ds. Duchowieństwa. *Dyrektorium ogólne o katechizacji.* Poznań 1998.

Kongregacja ds. Wychowania Katolickiego. Instrukcja dotycząca kryteriów rozeznawania powołania (...) w kontekście przyjmowania ich do seminariów i dopuszczania do święceń. Vatican 4.11.2005. IN: OsRomPol 5: 2006 p.54.

Kongregacja Nauki Wiary. Instrukcja *Dignitas personae.* LEV Vatican (12.12.2008).

Kodeks Prawa Kanonicznego. (23.01.1983). Poznań 1984.

Katechizm Kościoła Katolickiego. Poznań 1994.

Grocholewski Z.: *Guidelines for the Use of Psychology in the Admission and Formation of Candidates for the Priesthood.* Vatican June 29 2008.

ABSTRACT

Polish

Ponowoczesne czasy pogłębiają fragmentaryzację i dychotomia wartości, które dekonstruują klasyczne wzorce moralności, powodując tym samym trudności w oddziaływaniu wychowawczo formacyjnym na współczesnego człowieka. W duchu chrześcijańskim konieczne jest odpowiednie działanie poprzez samo-formację moralną, aby nastąpiła transformacja cywilizacyjna i kulturowa.

Im bardziej szlachetną motywację człowiek podejmuje, tym piękniejsza staje się jego osobowość, która przejawia się w jego dojrzałym działaniu moralnym. Samo-formacja jest bardziej sztuką aniżeli jakąkolwiek techniką budowania zdrowego wartościowania wychowanka, która wymaga również pomocy organizacji wychowawczo-formacyjnych, takich jak szkoła, Kościół czy zdrowe grupy rówieśnicze. W szerszym rozumieniu chrześcijańska dojrzałość człowieka zauważalna jest w kształtowaniu wartościowych cech interpersonalnych, pomiędzyludzkich i pomiędzykulturowych, ważnych dla człowieczeństwa. Chodzi tu o przyswajanie wyższych cech w byciu lepszym dla drugiego człowieka. W wąskim znaczeniu samo-formacja integralna sprowadza się do szczególnej przestrzeni wzrostu, np. fizycznego, uczuciowego czy też etycznego. Stawanie się dojrzałym w sensie psychiczno-duchowym jest procesem integralnie związanym ze kształceniem sfery intelektualnej, uczuciowej, społecznej i moralnej człowieka. Proces integralnej dojrzałości zawiera wysiłek innych: rodziców, wychowawców, czy pracę osobistą.

Wewnętrzna samo-formacja w oparciu o wiarę i moralność daje motywację, która staje się procesem całożyciowym człowieka. Istnieje więc wielkie zapotrzebowanie społeczne na altruistyczne, ascetyczne i moralne osobowości, które formowałyby rodziny i społeczeństwa i pociągałaby je ku wartościom wyższym. Z pewnością zasady dojrzałej osobowości konstytuują cechy ludzkie, takie jak związek z kulturą chrześcijańską, w której człowiek wyrósł, osobista tożsamość, realizm personalistyczny, pogłębione i szczere kontakty międzyosobowe, inteligentnie wyrażana emocjonalność, zdolność do obiektywizmu, humor i wewnętrzny wgląd w siebie. Personalizacja czyli stawanie się zintegrowaną osobą pod każdym względem umiejętną w przyjmowaniu jak i obdarowaniu osób drugich troską i miłością stanowi istotę formacji ku dojrzałości integralnej.

French Heidi Scheffler

Le postmodernisme exacerbe la fragmentation des valeurs qui déconstruit les schémas classiques de l'éducation, rendant ainsi plus difficile la réalisation d'une éducation intégrale et l'auto-formation de l'homme moderne. Les personnes confrontées à un dilemme éthique à plusieurs niveaux et à une déformation matérialiste ont besoin d'une réponse morale appropriée pour changer leurs modes de penser et d'être. L'auto-formation de la sphère interne est un moyen important pour opérer une telle intégration comme l'a postulé Gordon W. Allport. En revanche, il est presque impossible de la façonner chez des personnes instruites, honnêtes et « entière » ou abouties, personnes qui ont la capacité de discerner, de manière autonome, entre le bien et le mal. L'auto-formation est possible à condition d'avoir reçu une formation éthique solide et bien planifiée, fondée sur des principes moraux, des règles et des normes éthiques qui façonnent la vie de l'individu.

Plus la motivation d'une personne est noble, plus noble est sa personnalité chrétienne. Si la personne a été déformée et nourrie par des stéréotypes, il est presque impossible que sa foi en Dieu grandisse et intègre sa personnalité. Puisque la foi religieuse est un mélange inséparable de pensée, de sentiment et de sens, elle peut grandement influencer l'auto-formation à l'intérieur du foyer chrétien, de l'école et de l'église avec la grâce de Dieu. Devenir plus mature est un processus de vie intégralement lié à la croissance morale, intellectuelle et émotionnelle de l'homme auto-formé. Par conséquent, la socialisation éthique implique l'effort des autres, en particulier des parents et des éducateurs. La voie de l'auto-formation mature comprend aussi la conversion et les efforts de l'individu pour accéder à un mode de vie qui fait sens. Les personnalités altruistes, ascétiques et éthiques sont très recherchées par la société. Il appert que les traits majeurs de la personnalité mature sont des relations interpersonnelles sincères, des émotions articulées, l'humour et l'intuition. L'intégration de principes, de valeurs et de vertus essentiels aide la personne à construire une individualité entière, dans tous les aspects d'une vie saine. En somme, l'auto-formation socioculturelle est un processus continuel de développement de la personnalité éthique associée et en accord avec la conscience de l'homme appelé par Dieu à produire des actions et des comportements responsables.

German Heidi Scheffler

Die Postmoderne verschärft die Fragmentierung von Werten, die die klassischen Bildungsmuster dekonstruieren und dadurch viele Herausforderungen in der integralen Bildung und Selbstbildung des modernen Menschen verursachen. Menschen, die mit mehrstufigen ethischen Dilemmata und materialistischer Verzerrung konfrontiert sind, benötigen ein angemessenes moralisches Vorgehen, um ihre gegenwärtige narzisstische Denk- und Lebensweise zu ändern. Die Selbstbildung der inneren Sphäre ist ein wichtiger Weg zu einer solchen Integration, die von Gordon W. Allport postuliert wird, damit wir wahrhaftig menschlich werden. Es ist fast unmöglich, dies in gebildeten, ehrlichen und integralen Menschen zu formen, die die Fähigkeit haben, Gut und Böse zu erkennen. Jedoch ist die Selbstbildung durch eine solide, gut geplante ethische Bildung möglich, die auf moralischen Prinzipien, Regeln und ethischen Standards beruht, die das Leben des Individuums prägen werden.

Je edler die Motivation eines Menschen ist, desto schöner wird seine christliche Persönlichkeit. Wenn die Person verformt und mit Stereotypen gefüttert wurde, ist es fast unmöglich zu erwarten, dass der Glaube an Gott wächst und die Persönlichkeit einbindet. Im Gegenteil, da der religiöse Glaube eine untrennbare Mischung aus Denken, Fühlen und Bedeutung ist, kann er die Selbstbildung im Umfeld des christlichen Hauses, der Schule und der Kirche mit der Gnade Gottes stark beeinflussen. Immer reifer zu werden, ist ein lebenslanger Prozess, der ganzheitlich mit dem moralischen, intellektuellen und emotionalen Wachstum des gebildeten Mensches zusammenhängt. Diese ethische Sozialisation benötigt die Anstrengung anderer, vor allem von Eltern und Erziehern. Der Weg zur mündigen Selbstbildung umfasst auch die Neugestaltung und die Bemühungen des Individuums, ein sinnvolles Leben zu führen. Es gibt eine große, öffentliche Nachfrage nach gut gebildeten, altruistischen, asketischen und ethischen Persönlichkeiten. Sicherlich beinhalten die Hauptmerkmale der reifen Persönlichkeit die aufrichtigen zwischenmenschlichen Beziehungen, die intelligent ausgedrückte Emotionalität, den Humor und die innere Einsicht. Die Personalisierung von wesentlichen Prinzipien, Werten und Tugenden hilft dem Individuum dabei, eine integrierte Person in jedem Aspekt eines gesunden Lebens zu werden. Zusammenfassend ist die soziokulturelle Selbstbildung der fortlaufende Prozess der ethischen Persönlichkeitsentwicklung, im Einklang mit dem von Gott geforderten Gewissen des Menschen für verantwortungsvolles Handeln und Verhalten.

Russian

Постмодернизм осложняет модели классического образования, тем самым вызывая много проблем в образовании и самостоятельном формировании современного человека. Люди сталкиваются с многими этическими проблемами и деформацией
материалистических взглядов. Это требует изменения действующего образа мышления и реальной жизни. Самостоятельное формирование такой личности описал Gordon W. Olport. Постмодернизм не может воздействовать на образованного и честного человека, который распознаёт разницу между добром и злом. Таким образом, формирование взглядов человека возможно только на основе твёрдых моральных принципов, правил и этических норм, сформированных жизнью человека. Человека делает лучше благородная цель, особенно если это христианская личность. Если же мысли человека были деформированы плохими стереотипами, то почти невозможно ожидать от него веру в Бога. Так как религиозная вера имеет неразрывную связь с мышлением и чувствами, то на это влияет дом, школа и церковь. Они дают человеку почувствовать благодать от Бога. Человек становится более зрелым. Это постоянный процесс нравственного, интеллектуального и эмоционального роста человека. В

этом особенно важны усилия родителей и педагогов. Велика роль и отдельных лиц, формирующих личность. Принципиальной чертой зрелой личности является искренность межличностных отношений, эмоциональность, юмор, внутреннее понимание. Персонализация основных принципов добродетели, должны помочь индивидууму в становлении человека в каждом аспекте здорового образа жизни. Таким образом, социально-культурное формирование является развитием этической личности. Его совесть и есть направляемые Богом ответственные действия в поведении человека.

Spanish Clara Sullivan

El postmodernismo agrava la fragmentación de los valores que de construyen los patrones clásicos de la educación, causando así gran dificultad en la formación integral y la formación del hombre moderno. Personas que enfrentan dilema ético multinivel y deformación materialista, requieren acción moral apropiada para cambiar su actual forma narcisista de pensar y de ser. La formación autodidacta de la esfera interna es una forma importante de tal integración postulada por Gordon W. Allport. Es casi imposible formar en un laboratorio gente educada, honesta e integral que tenga la capacidad de reconocer el bien y el mal. Por lo tanto, la formación autodidacta es posible a través de una formación ética sólida, bien planificada, basada en principios morales, reglas y normas éticas que forman la vida del individuo.

Mientras mas noble sea la motivación de una persona, más bella se convierte su personalidad cristiana. Si la persona fue deformada y alimentada por los estereotipos, es casi imposible esperar que su fe en Dios crezca e integre su personalidad. Puesto que la fe religiosa tiene una mezcla inseparable de pensar, sentir y significar, puede influir mucho en la formación autodidacta en los círculos del hogar cristiano, la escuela y la iglesia, con la gracia de Dios. Madurar es un proceso de toda la vida íntegramente relacionado con el crecimiento moral, intelectual y emocional del hombre formado. Por lo tanto, la socialización ética implica el esfuerzo de los demás, especialmente los padres y educadores. El camino a la formación madura autodidacta también incluye conversión y los esfuerzos del individuo para darle sentido a la vida. Por lo tanto hay una gran demanda pública de personalidades altruistas, ascéticas y éticas bien formadas. Seguramente el principio líder de los rasgos de una personalidad madura, constituye relaciones interpersonales sinceras, inteligentemente emocionales, humor y visión interior. La personalización de principios esenciales, los valores y virtudes, ayudan al individuo a ser una persona íntegra en cada aspecto de una vida sana. Por lo tanto, la formación autodidacta socio-cultural es el proceso continuo de desarrollo de la personalidad ética en línea con la conciencia de un hombre llamado por Dios, para producir comportamientos y acciones responsables.

ABOUT THE AUTHOR

Krzysztof Stanibula was born in 1966 as the youngest son of Janina and Czesław. After finishing at T. Kosciuszko Primary School, he attended Lubycza Technical High School, where he obtained diplomas in technical engineering, and passed the entrance examinations to the Catholic University of John Paul II in Lublin, Poland. Having completed a Bachelor of Philosophy degree in 1990, he passed an English as a Second Language program and entered an American seminary in Michigan. When he finished the program for pastoral theology studies in 1995, Stanibula was awarded a Master of Divinity (M.Div.) degree, and he became a presbyter in the Fall River Diocese. Stanibula, now known as Chris, continued studying counseling at Weston School of Theology in Cambridge, Massachusetts, and obtained a Master of Theology degree (Th.M.). He studied at the Catholic University of Lublin between 1986 and 1990 and from 2008 to 2012, mainly concentrating on philosophy and theology of the person. In 2010, Stanibula successfully presented a Religion & Ethical Theology thesis (S.T.L) and doctoral dissertation on Christian formation and human development, which earned him a Philosophy Doctorate (Ph.D.) in 2016. Most of his professional works have been related to the pastoral and hospital ministry in New Bedford, Attleboro, Fall River, and Cape Cod hospitals in Massachusetts. Stanibula also administered St. Anne's Shrine in Fall River. Lately he has been serving St. Pius X community and at the faculty of John Paul II High School on Cape Cod, Massachusetts. In free time he likes reading books, inspirational stories especially related to the human transformation where things are so close to real life, and enjoys walking in the forests.

Besides two books, his writings include articles on spirituality and philosophy: the "Franciscan spirituality essays. The charisma, and life of Maximilian Kolbe in the light of Franciscan personology. The role of faith in ethical developments. The theological anthropology of the person for meaningful life, Reflections on the ministerial work in the selected hospitals" published at https://**krzysstanibula.wordpress.com**